Companies are wonderful magnifying glasses of the trends shaping our society. As the first place where adult individuals "make society" and as an integral part of our territories, from international megalopolises to local provinces, they are the natural vessel for the technological, sociological, and economic transformations at play. Our doubts, anxieties, challenges, passions, and paradoxes run through them: to observe companies changing is to observe the world around us, in all its complexity. Trying to understand what is happening is trying to move from spectator to actor of these transformations, as an employee, manager, or company director, of course, but also as a citizen, as a human being. This book is essentially about our world's transformations: thorough and comprehensive, it is an essential read for the curious and courageous who wish to grasp the intrinsic complexity of today's buzzwords. As Michel Serres said: "We are experiencing a bankruptcy of thought that prevents us from understanding and qualifying the transitions of the world that is ours". For it is not a question of collectively discharging ourselves from this complexity onto omniscient and omnipotent leaders, but rather that each and every one of us realizes the extent of the responsibility that falls upon us, in times of global transformation. This book has the ambition to pave the way to do so. Enjoy your reading!

Emmanuelle Duez, Founder, The Boson Project

The Digital Transformation of "traditional companies" is a journey. It's full of opportunities, but also has potential pitfalls. This book is full of practical tips that you can use to unlock the Digital Transformation of your company. As an ex-Chief Digital Officer, I would have loved to have this book handy to accelerate the journey of my company. This book is a must read for anyone engaging in this type of transformation.

Eric Chaniot General Manager Microsoft Cross Industry Solutions; Digital Advisory Board of GSK Consumer Healthcare Business.

The Lean Approach to Digital Transformation is a must read for business and IT executives seeking to take advantage of the accelerating digital transformation underway. Caseau expertly lays out a practical roadmap to build the capabilities needed to implement customer-centric digital services using an open information system backbone and Lean software factories.

Paul Daugherty, Group Chief Executive, Technology and CTO, Accenture.

Yves Caseau has written a remarkable book. It provides a coherent view of modern business computing with unusual clarity and innovation, focusing on modern "lean" approaches to product creation and simultaneous corporate change. This is highly recommended reading - not just for the people who are leading the charge toward a truly effective 2020s organization, but also for those who interact with customers, design products, and build deeply technical software). Most importantly, the top executives need to understand how to balance software investments, experiments, and new products. Caseau introduces key new ideas, especially the exponential information system that stabilizes a rapidly improving organization and technology base. This excellent book arises from a brilliant research mind with two decades of corporate leadership and the author of a string of valuable books. The transformation it espouses allows a company to build up technical capabilities while making and selling products, and to absorb modern AI techniques as well as the best of classic engineering.

Stuart Feldman, Chief Scientist, Schmidt Futures

Reading Yves Caseau's excellent book for the second time, I am fascinated by two contradictory observations: on one hand, this book is packed with thousands of interesting ideas which all require serious thinking to be fully appreciated; on the other one, the 8 summary pages offer a very easy way to grasp the coherence and usefulness of these ideas. Harnessing the power of Information Technology is a challenge for any company. This book provides a powerful guide to the solutions to this challenge, and weaves explicitly marketing concepts of customer focus with the most modern prescriptions for distributed AI architectures.

Pierre Haren, CEO of Causality Link

Yves is not only a proven leader for digital transformation, but also a dedicated student of the subject. In his book, he combines real world experience with academic rigor and research. The result is a powerful playbook for IT leaders around the world.

Jedidiah Yueh, Bestselling Author of ***Disrupt or Die*** *and Delphix Founder and CEO*

The Lean Approach to Digital Transformation

From Customer to Code and from Code to Customer

Yves Caseau

A PRODUCTIVITY PRESS BOOK

Originally published in France as:
L'approche Lean pour la transformation digitale By Yves CASEAU

First published 2022
by Routledge
605 Third Avenue, New York, NY 10158

and by Routledge
2 Park Square, Milton Park, Abingdon, Oxon, OX14 4RN

Routledge is an imprint of the Taylor & Francis Group, an informal business

Library of Congress Cataloging-in-Publication Data
A catalog record for this title has been requested

ISBN: 978-1-032-22502-9 (hbk)
ISBN: 978-1-032-22501-2 (pbk)
ISBN: 978-1-003-27281-6 (ebk)

DOI: 10.4324/9781003272816

Typeset in ITC Garamond Std
by Apex CoVantage, LLC

To Beatrice,
my wife,
lifelong mind sparring-partner,
and lifetime antifragile companion

Contents

Foreword .... **xiii**

Acknowledgments .... **xvii**

Introduction .... **xix**

0.1 Digital Transformation xix

0.2 From Customer to Code and from Code to Customer xxi

0.3 Three Capabilities for Success xxiii

0.4 Intended Book Audience xxv

0.5 Plan xxvi

0.5.1 Part I: Digital Transformation xxvi

0.5.2 Part II: The Exponential Information System xxviii

0.5.3 Part III: Software Platforms and Service Factories xxix

PART I DIGITAL TRANSFORMATION: CUSTOMER ORIENTATION AND HOMEOSTASIS

1 Why a Digital Transformation? **3**

1.1 "Markets Are Conversations" 4

1.1.1 The Economy of Attention 4

1.1.2 Conversations and Content Strategy 5

1.1.3 Each Customer Is Unique 6

1.1.4 The Economy of Intention 7

1.2 "The Customer Is the Architect of His Experience" 8

1.2.1 Customer Experience as the Focus of the Digital Strategy 8

1.2.2 Co-Construction with Users 10

1.2.3 Products, Services, and Ecosystems 11

1.2.4 The Obsession with the Customer's Time 13

1.3 Reinventing Products in a Digital World 14
1.3.1 Digital Products and Digital Production 14
1.3.2 Continuous Product Discovery 16
1.3.3 Knowledge Engineering 17
1.3.4 The Role of Objects in the Materialization of Services 19
1.4 Producing in a Digital World 21
1.4.1 The Ambition of Digital Manufacturing 21
1.4.2 Artificial Intelligence as a Complexity Absorber 23
1.4.3 Augmented Humans and Augmented Environment 25
1.4.4 Optimize with Digital Twins 26
Summary 28

2 Homeostasis: Continuous Adaptation to Change 29
2.1 Digital Homeostasis 29
2.1.1 Change Comes from the Customer 29
2.1.2 Accelerating Change, from Uses to Technologies 30
2.1.3 The Multitude Is an Opportunity 31
2.1.4 The "Letting Go" of Digital Transformation 33
2.2 Anticipation and Agility 34
2.2.1 Situational Potential and Anticipation 34
2.2.2 Short Time and Long Time 36
2.2.3 Cultivating Innovation 37
2.2.4 Customer Orientation as a Compass 38
2.3 Scalable Organizations Adapted to Continuous Change 40
2.3.1 Exponential Organizations 40
2.3.2 Networks of Autonomous Teams 41
2.3.3 Enterprise 3.0 43
2.3.4 Continuous Learning 45
2.4 Culture Change and Change Management 47
2.4.1 Which Change for a Digital Transformation? 47
2.4.2 Resistance to Change 48
2.4.3 Motivation and Commitment 49
2.4.4 A Culture without Borders 51
Summary 53

3 Lean Startup: Lean Principles Applied to Co-Creation 55
3.1 Innovation in the Digital World 56
3.1.1 Innovation Is about Execution 56
3.1.2 Innovation Requires Iteration 57
3.1.3 The Business Model Is an Outcome, Not a Prerequisite 58
3.1.4 The Playing Field Is Determined by the Skills 60

3.2 Lean Startup: Formalizing the Knowledge Creation Process..........61
3.2.1 A Machine for Validating Insights..........61
3.2.2 Three Steps: Design, Pretotype, and Grow..........63
3.2.3 Running Lean: Keeping the Promise..........65
3.2.4 Nail It, Then Scale It..........66
3.3 Design Thinking and Minimum Viable Product..........68
3.3.1 Design, Observation, Anthropology..........68
3.3.2 Design Thinking..........69
3.3.3 Minimum Viable Product..........72
3.3.4 User Experience Design..........73
3.4 Growth Hacking..........75
3.4.1 AARRR Metrics and Data-Driven Steering..........75
3.4.2 Product Market Fit: Finding Traction..........77
3.4.3 To Create a Community of Regular Users..........78
3.4.4 The CFLL Learning Loop..........80
Summary..........82

PART II EXPONENTIAL INFORMATION SYSTEMS

4 The Information System as a Foundation for Digital Transformation..........85
4.1 Exponential Information Systems..........86
4.1.1 Which IT for an Exponential Organization?..........86
4.1.2 Outside to Inside Steering..........87
4.1.3 An Information System Open to the Continuous Flow of Technologies..........88
4.1.4 An Antifragile Information System..........89
4.2 Information Systems and Perpetual Change..........91
4.2.1 Multimodal Architecture..........91
4.2.2 The System as an Executable Specification..........94
4.2.3 Reactive Systems..........96
4.2.4 Rules, Reflexes, and Automation..........97
4.3 Managing Complexity and Technical Debt..........99
4.3.1 Information System Complexity and Inertia..........99
4.3.2 Minimize the Size of the Information System..........100
4.3.3 Manage Your Technical Debt..........102
4.4 Resilience and Quality of Service..........104
4.4.1 Site Reliability Engineering..........104
4.4.2 Automation and Monitoring..........105
4.4.3 SRE Practices..........107
Summary..........109

5 Artificial Intelligence and Machine Learning 111
5.1 Taking Advantage of Exponential Technologies 111
5.1.1 The Toolbox and Opportunities 111
5.1.2 The Deep Learning Revolution 114
5.1.3 Hybridization and Meta-Heuristics 116
5.1.4 Reinventing Processes and Products with Artificial Intelligence 119
5.2 Conditions of Implementation 121
5.2.1 The Data Engineering Process 121
5.2.2 Build a Circular Learning Flow 123
5.2.3 Data Lab Culture 126
5.3 Impact on the Information System 128
5.3.1 Data Architecture 128
5.3.2 Data Infrastructure 130
5.3.3 An Information System Designed for Experimentation 133
Summary 135

6 Governance, Architecture, and Situational Potential 137
6.1 Lean and Agile Governance 138
6.1.1 Agile Software Development 138
6.1.2 Adding Lean Roots to Agile Practice 139
6.1.3 The Systemic Conditions of Lean and Agile 142
6.1.4 Governance that Favors the Lean and Agile Approach...... 143
6.2 Which Architecture in an Uncertain World? 145
6.2.1 The Role of the Architect in an Agile Team 145
6.2.2 Architecture and Gardening 147
6.2.3 Continuous Learning of Systems Engineering 149
6.3 Sustainable Information Systems 151
6.3.1 Sustainable Development of the Information System 151
6.3.2 Managing Complexity in a Sustainable Way 153
6.3.3 Controlling the Age of Systems through Flows 155
Summary 158

PART III SOFTWARE PLATFORMS AND SERVICE FACTORIES

7 DevOps and Software Factories 161
7.1 Automate the Software Process 162
7.1.1 Automate for More Quality and Efficiency 162
7.1.2 Continuous Integration 163
7.1.3 Continuous Deployment 165
7.1.4 Automate the Tests 167

7.2 DevOps....169
7.2.1 A Cross-Functional Team to Implement CICD....169
7.2.2 Infrastructure as Code....171
7.2.3 Results of the Early Adopters....172
7.3 Lean Software Factory....174
7.3.1 The Metaphor of the Lean Software Factory....174
7.3.2 The Twelve Principles of Lean Software Factory....176
7.3.3 A Lean Factory for Learning....178
7.3.4 Software Craftmanship....180
7.3.5 From Customer to Code and from Code to Customer....183
Summary....185

8 Putting Platforms at the Service of Digital Transformation....187
8.1 The Platform Approach....187
8.1.1 Which Platforms for the Digital Domain?....187
8.1.2 The Network Effect of Platforms....189
8.1.3 Platform and Communities....191
8.2 The Power of Platforms....192
8.2.1 Innovation Platforms....192
8.2.2 Transaction Platforms....194
8.2.3 Platforms and Artificial Intelligence....196
8.3 Building Stable Platforms to Deliver Changing Services....197
8.3.1 The "Product Platform" Approach in the Digital Context..197
8.3.2 Platforms, Architecture, and Emergence....199
8.3.3 Platforms and Software Factories....201
Summary....203

Conclusion....205
1. The Necessary Success of Digital Transformation....205
2. The Main Things to Remember....208
3. The Necessary Change in Our Companies' Culture....210

Bibliography....213

Index....219

Foreword

Software is the new electricity: it is in everything. Just as with electricity in its time, we struggle with how to use it, what to do with it, and what to think of its implications. Thirty years ago, when I first started visiting plants, I still saw "village processes"—same process machines placed in neat rows as it would have been when they were powered by a central rotating axle. These machines were electricity powered, but people hadn't figured out yet they could be placed anywhere and arranged in the production sequence to create full-flow cells. The pioneers who saw that used the full potential of electricity (the process' speed is not dictated by the energy source) to redesign their machines so that they would fit in continuous flow, radically improve quality, productivity, and flexibility, and so create lasting competitive advantage for their business. The opportunity lay not in replacing mechanical power with electrical power but in grasping what the latter enabled you to do differently.

I feel we're seeing the same now with software. Digital systems are disrupting every aspect of our lives, both at work and at home, but we still struggle with what, exactly, digital does and how to best use it. Even though code is in everything, from your calendar on your smartphone to your TV or your refrigerator, business people still don't make the effort to truly understand "IT," and coders shy away from business issues. Our mental models are driven by the problems we habitually solve and so recognize, and the solutions we usually rely on and that first come to mind. Consequently, our mental models about what is interesting and what is not, what warrants a mental effort and what does not, evolve very slowly. Having an IT director today is like having an electricity director in the 1930s. To succeed today, you want to be the person who fully sees the integration potential of software and business. Blessed with an open mind and curiosity, driven by a spirit of adventure and experimentation, absolutely committed to learning and effectiveness, you can realize the full promise of the digital transformation.

That person is Yves. I have been privileged to discuss these matters with him over the years, both in practical cases (how do you make a better TV box?) and in theory (how can we design better information systems?). Yves has always been rigorous in his scientific thinking, try–fail–analyze–try again and a dedicated hands-on experimenter. He has delved deeply into lean as a learning system, a structured method to figure out what experiments to try: greater customer satisfaction (more value, less cost); faster, more frequent delivery; quicker response to quality issues; deeper involvement of teams and engagement of people in improvement; continuous growing and nurturing of mutual trust between leaders and their teams. This alchemy of a passion for tech and disciplined lean thinking has led him to discover three profound insights about where to look for digital breakthrough.

First, encourage closer conversations with customers about what they want the tech for—and what they don't want. As with any new technology, we don't exactly know what we will actually go for in the end. Clearly, we're looking for services at the tip of a finger—one-touch help. Equally clearly, we want to retain ownership of our digital identities and are driven crazy by endless notifications and solicitations. Vendors, on the other hand, struggle with improving user experience (it's hard), want to hijack all your personal data (it's worth something), and are constantly competing for your attention (ping—you've got a new message). Everyone understands these basics—but what does it mean in practice? Case by case? Where do you find the efficiency boundaries? The only way is to experiment, present services to customers, listen hard to their feedback and observe how they use it, and co-construct new services with them, often accepting to change your mind about what you thought they'd want—in lean startup terms, "pivoting."

Second, as new technologies and applications appear every day, the complexity of your IT systems increases exponentially, and so do transaction costs within your organization and with your customers and providers. To handle this well, you need to design your information system as a strong backbone to all applications. This means learning about its architecture and understanding its "tight/loose" properties: where do you want it to be open; where do you need to keep it proprietary? Getting this right requires a systemic approach to the information system: understanding its modularity and functional interactions and investing in ever stronger APIs at each interface. This involves a radical worldview shift: rather than looking first at what a module or tech does, you learn to start by focusing on the API with the rest of the system—aiming thus to create a stable architecture that allows for easy integration of new technologies and exponential growth. The system is revealed by its interfaces.

Third, real-life capability is the combination of competence and resources. Competence without resources is ineffectual, and resources without the competences to put them at work are simply wasteful. Yves' lean thinking led him to frame the concept of lean software factory: how to put the team-based organization enabled by software to automate the process of software development, integrate, and deploy continuously. The secret to a successful software factory is to create the feedback loop with product development and customer experimentation. As with the machines of old, this involves growing teams with the twin responsibilities of development and delivery. This revolutionizes the concept of "project" as there is no beginning nor end to a product's development. True innovation lies in the constant improvement of the product to find a better customer/product fit by continuous delivery of features and improvement of performance. In Yves' compelling vision, setting up a lean software factory is an act of love: love for users, love for code, and love of learning to develop code that better serves users.

As a user, as an entrepreneur, or as a manager, we all want to be that person—the person with unique deep insights into today's overwhelming tech and how to make the best of it. How to understand it? How to see its potential? Where to look for opportunities? Yves' tremendous book is a clear blueprint to become that person. Having walked this road himself, he now lays out the path with breakthrough concepts and practical learning so that, as a reader, in following his mental journey, a fresher, deeper vision of how to handle tech will blossom in your mind. Whether new to the topic, or an IT veteran, reading Yves is guaranteed to generate new insights and aha! moments every other page. Don't pass on this opportunity: you owe it to yourself.

Michael Ballé
Co-founder of the French Lean Institute

Acknowledgments

This book is the result of a great many conversations and has been enriched by the ideas of many people. Thus, it is hard to know how to organize these acknowledgments or to do so without making many oversights.

I would first like to thank Frédéric Lé for his invaluable help in translating this book into English. His perseverance and the support of the Open Group have been key factors in successfully developing this new version of the book. I am also very grateful to Michael Ballé for his companionship during my Lean journey and for the great foreword that he kindly proposed. I would also like to thank Emmanuelle Duez for her friendship and for writing the preface of the French edition of this book.

I am particularly pleased to thank my reviewers: Yoram Bosc-Haddad, Frédéric Champion, Jean-Pierre Corniou, Thierry Fraudet, Pierre Haren, Kristell Klosowski, François Laburthe, Aymeric Le Page, Benoit Rottembourg, Bruno Rousselet, and Pierre Schaller. Their attention to this work and the quality of their comments were essential to the success of this project.

Among the dozens of Bouygues Telecom colleagues whom I should mention for contributing to my education on IT systems, I would like to thank my teammates from the "box" adventure: Herminio di Faria, Kristell Klosowski, Frédéric Champion, Della Miret, Pierre Schaller, Eric Masson, Patrick Yengo, and Alain Carbillet, as well as my managers Richard Viel and Olivier Roussat, for offering me this opportunity. I am also grateful to Gilles Blanc for his valuable advice on lean software factories.

In the same way, I would like to thank my colleagues at AXA for years of fascinating exchanges around digital transformation, in particular Frederic Tardy, Dirk Marzluf, Karim Bouchema, Jean-Michel Texier, Kristell Klosowski, Marie Bogataj, Béatrice Rousset, Joanne Pupo, Stéphane Delbecque, Vincent de Ponthaud, Paul-Henri Chabrol, Véronique Weil, Benoit Claverane, and Henri de Castries.

I am grateful to my colleagues at Michelin, with whom I participate daily in the modernization of the information system, in particular Thierry Fraudet, Olivier Jauze, Bruno Batisse, Olivier Selignan, Jean-Paul Bouchon, Jean-Marc Berlandi, Christine Massif, Olivier Manaoui, Laura Xu, Dennis Dunn, Richard Frouin, and Sébastien Lance. I would also like to thank my supervisors Marc Henry and Yves Chapot, for their trust and advice, as well as Eric Chaniot, Michelin's CDO, with whom I worked to implement the digital transformation.

Finally, I would like to thank Michel Morvan and Michel Paillet for their enriching conversations that influenced this book. I also benefited from the support of the Academy of Technology network, in particular Francois Bourdoncle, Gérard Roucairol, Gérard Sabah, Christian Saguez, Erol Gelenbe, Jacques Serris, and Laurent Gouzènes.

The views presented in this book are those of the author and do not necessarily reflect the opinions of Bouygues Telecom, AXA, or Michelin or of the persons mentioned above.

Introduction

0.1 Digital Transformation

In 2019, Jeanne Ross, Cynthia Beath, and Martin Mocker, professors at MIT and the University of Texas, published a remarkable book, *Designed for Digital: How to Architect Your Business for Sustained Success*. The book is the result of a two-year study of companies such as LEGO, Schneider Electric, Audi, and Northwestern Mutual, which have undertaken a major digital transformation. The authors studied companies that are going beyond using digital tools to optimize internal processes but leveraged digital to reinvent their business models and offerings. Three ingredients characterize their digital revolution: abundant data, ubiquitous connectivity, and the explosion of computing and processing capacity. The book identifies foundational capabilities, or *building blocks*, that are needed to achieve such a transformation:

- The first is the ability to gather and develop *shared customer insights* because it is not good enough to simply provide digital offerings; you have to discover customers' problems. In this new world, customers expect the products and services proposed by your company to help them do their jobs.[1]
- In a world of constant technological innovation, digital transformation is not defined by a target state; it is a journey through continuous change. Amazon is showcased as a company that can continuously absorb new digital capabilities as they become available and effective.[2]

[1] https://hbswk.hbs.edu/item/clay-christensen-the-theory-of-jobs-to-be-done

[2] The need to evolve to adapt to a changing environment is a key idea we will address in Chapter 2: *"As technologies, customer demands, and strategic opportunities change, a business must adapt."*

- Companies must rely on an *operational backbone*, which covers both processes and the information system (IS), capable of providing all the necessary flexibility through APIs (application programming interfaces, the IT "plugs," which we cover in the second part) with impeccable quality of service. The IS is an essential foundation for digital transformation.
- This *backbone* enables the development of digital platforms, open to partners and external developers. Digital platforms are built and operated by autonomous cross-functional teams. In a digital world, platforms are a key enabler for agility and innovation. The book uses well-known agile organization models, such as Spotify, to highlight the need for new accountability rules.

The authors explain that digital transformation is a long journey and that, for most companies, we are only at the beginning. Everyone has grasped the rapid transformation of the environment, the need to change to adapt to a VUCA (volatile, uncertain, complex, and ambiguous) world. Digital transformation is, therefore, an expected component of any company's strategy. Digital transformation is framed by the dual risk of *digital disruption*—the risk of not making this transformation quickly and deeply enough.[3] If a company does not build the "capabilities" we have just introduced, it is exposed to the risk of being disintermediated and letting other, more digital and more agile players come between itself and its customers. The book *Designed for Digital* highlights the low impact seen by many companies (when new digital revenues are not living up to expectations and investments) and emphasizes that the leaders in these new service areas are, more often than not, new digital companies. Companies today have understood the many pieces of the digital transformation puzzle: customer orientation, digital culture, agile organization, importance of technologies (e.g., artificial intelligence [AI] or connected objects), importance of ecosystems, and thinking about experience and not product. But they often lack the keys to implementing and executing this digital transformation.

The book you are holding in your hands concurs with the diagnosis and solutions exposed in *Designed for Digital*, but it goes a step further in the implementation of solutions, from the *operational backbone* to *digital platforms* through the capture of *shared customer insights*.

---

[3] On the concept of disruption, the reference book remains *Seeing What's Next: Using the Theories of Innovation to Predict Industry Change*, by Clayton Christensen, Scott Anthony, and Erik Roth.

0.2 From Customer to Code and from Code to Customer

Digital transformation takes time because it requires a profound change in culture. To put it simply, or even to caricature it, we can say that we need to instill "love of the customer" and "love of the code" in a company to succeed in this transformation. The first idea is that in a digital world, solutions to customer problems are most often the result of co-creation. Part of *Designed for Digital* is about building *shared customer insights*, which requires strong curiosity and a genuine interest in customers and their needs. In a way, the need for customer orientation precedes the digital transformation, but the digital world makes customer orientation absolutely necessary and provides the company with new methods and tools to carry out this co-construction. The second dimension concerns the interest that must be shown in digital technology to master and make the most of it. This imperative is amplified in the digital transformation world because solutions are constantly changing. The authors of *Designed for Digital* write, "*Because software can and should change regularly, we think of digital offerings and their key software components as living assets.*" What characterizes software in the digital world is that it changes continuously, and this requires even more attention. Leading companies in the digital world demonstrate special attention and recognition of software know-how, from code creation to systems engineering.

The Figure 0.1 is borrowed from a presentation at the 2015 XEBICON conference, which gives this book its subtitle. It is a double arrow. The arrow that goes from customer to code represents the process of co-creating digital services with the customer, following *lean startup* principles. The arrow from code to customer represents the continuous integration and deployment/delivery (CICD) of software solutions (services, applications, etc.) to customers. The objective of the first arrow is to learn to observe, listen, and collaborate with customers to build solutions to their problems and needs in an iterative way. The objective of the second arrow is to automate and control the software manufacturing process as much as possible to reconcile speed (which allows a high delivery frequency) and high product quality, which is a requirement of the modern world. This organization, which I call a *lean software factory*, can be described as a software micro-factory; the term "factory" suggests automation, methods, and discipline, while the term "micro" indicates a production capacity that is integrated with the team that imagines, designs, and markets the product.

The title of the book refers to the lean approach to digital transformation because these two arrows, *lean startup* and *lean software factory*, are directly inspired by lean as practiced by Toyota. The lean approach is present from the beginning to the end of this book. It gives the framework for customer orientation and the love of work well done, which are the conditions for a successful digital transformation.

This book is built around these two arrows. It will try to explain them in detail in the next chapters and to show the links between the two capabilities. In the continuation of *Designed for Digital*, I believe that a company must become excellent in both dimensions to succeed in its digital transformation: to know how to imagine and design new products and services by listening to its customers and to know how to deliver these products with excellence and agility. What we will see next is that these two arrows reinforce each other: frequent iterations based on feedback and usage data improve the quality of the software product, while the ability to quickly renew high-quality software creates a dialogue with users. The drawing of a customer on his bike reflects the B2C (business-to-consumer) inspiration, as shown by many of the examples that will be provided, which corresponds to my experience at Bouygues Telecom and AXA. On the other hand, *lean startup* concepts were born in the B2B (business-to-business) software world before being generalized to B2C. It is, therefore, important to understand that this book is aimed at the B2B world and the B2C world. Everything that will be said, from the co-construction of services with customers to the organization of software micro-factories, applies perfectly to the case where the customers are themselves other companies.

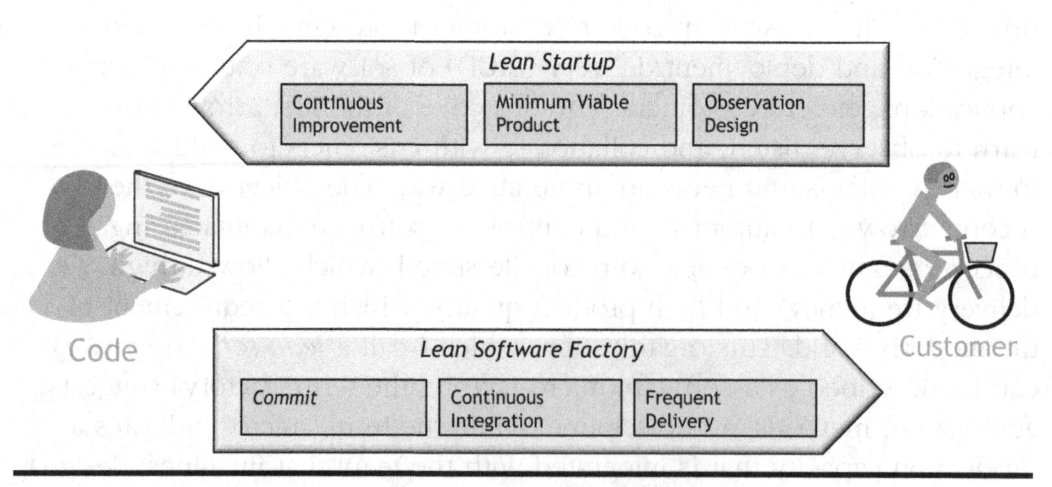

Figure 0.1 From customer to code, from code to customer.

0.3 Three Capabilities for Success

This book is a follow-up to *Designed for Digital* because it explains how to build three of the key capabilities mentioned above to succeed with digital transformation. It focuses on execution since, in the digital realm, it is execution that differentiates companies, which most often have a clear digital strategy.[4] It is easy to write that success is about execution; it may sound like a rhetorical spin. Successful execution depends on multiple factors that are beyond the scope of a book. Nonetheless, it is worthwhile to understand what hinders the execution of a digital transformation strategy. Understanding the three *building blocks* (capabilities) that follow and their interrelationships helps answer questions that we sometimes hear. To illustrate, here are three typical questions—any resemblance to your company's reality would be coincidental—that reading this book should help you solve:

- *"We have the customers, the data, the resources, and the talent, and yet our innovations have less impact on the market than those of startups with fewer resources. We have organized ourselves to foster innovation, but we don't see the impact of our efforts in our results. How can we regain a position of innovation excellence?"*
- *"Our company has been practicing agile for several years, our projects are organized in sprints and follow Scrum practices, yet we still suffer from overruns, lack of flexibility, and poor quality of service. Why are we so far from the digital excellence of the market leaders?"*
- *"Our company understands the strategic importance of artificial intelligence to reinvent our products and processes, but we are struggling to move from proofs of concept to deployment. We're not getting all the value we can get out of our data. How do we develop these digital skills that irrigate the entire company and create indisputable value for our customers?"*

The three parts of this book will, in turn, expose and develop the three capabilities that are essential for a successful digital transformation:

---

[4] The importance of execution is not unique to the digital world; just read *Execution: The Discipline of Getting Things Done*, by Larry Bossidy and Ram Charan. But as we will see in the rest of this book, it is even more true in the complex and unpredictable digital world.

1. To know how to co-create digital services with users, whether they are customers or future customers. This ability combines observation, dialogue, and iterative experimentation. The approach proposed in this book is based on the *lean startup* approach, according to an extended vision that includes *design thinking* and *growth hacking*.
2. To develop an IS that is the backbone of the digital transformation—described as an *operational backbone* in *Designed for Digital*. We have coined the term "exponential IS" to designate an IS that is open (especially on its borders), capable of interfacing and combining with external services, positioned as a player in software ecosystems, and built to handle scalable and dynamic data flows. Exponential ISs are in perpetual change and continuously absorb the best of information processing technology.
3. To build software micro-factories that produce service platforms. This software factory concept covers the integration of agile methods, tooling and CICD practices, a customer-oriented product approach, and a platform approach based on modularity, APIs, and openness. A software micro-factory is a foundation that continuously produces and delivers services that are themselves constantly changing.

These three capabilities are not unique or specific to this book; they are linked to other more well-known concepts or approaches, such as agile methods, *lean* product development, and software production approaches, such as CICD or DevOps. The originality of the book is to propose a common vocabulary and model to all these approaches in order to get more value from digital transformation and to facilitate its implementation. This is what the previous figure sought to express: the three capabilities are interdependent and mutually reinforcing. This book focuses on the "software culture" of a company and how management should evolve to create a *software-friendly* culture. A successful digital transformation does not mean that everyone develops code but that the activity of those who do must be recognized, demystified, and integrated into the company's strategic vision.[5] Innovation in the digital world, because of its volatile and uncertain nature, requires experimentation and continuous learning, which relies on the integration of technical skills as close as possible to the decision-making process.

---

[5] As Aurélie Jean says, "decision-makers need to learn about code to become enlightened leaders . . . we need enlightened decision-makers who are not dazzled by IT."

0.4 Intended Book Audience

This book is primarily aimed at two different populations:

- First, it is written for decision-makers since it seeks to answer their questions and even their frustrations about the execution of their company's digital transformation. It is particularly suited for curious CEOs and technophile CDOs (chief digital officers). Most executives have good intuition and good intentions in the digital domain, but their managerial culture is often counterproductive when confronted with the difficulties of software development. They have understood the digital transformation and the importance of technological waves, they have opened their companies to innovative players such as startups, and they do not understand the slowness of their companies to adapt to these new paradigms. CDOs are often placed in an uncomfortable position, with more responsibilities than resources. They implicitly suffer from an overly ambitious strategic vision—that is, a vision that separates the ambition of digital transformation from the reality of the company's digital capabilities. A digital transformation cannot be separated from the business strategy, nor can it be bought from the outside.
- This book is, of course, written for digital professionals, whether they work in the IT department, in the digital department, or in the service department. These software professionals are in charge of software platforms and are subject to multiple constraints. This book should help them to better communicate with their stakeholders and also to build the capabilities their company will need tomorrow while delivering the value expected today. This book does not pretend to add to the technical skills of professionals who are specialists in their field but to weave a global view reconciling strategy, organization, and architecture, a perspective that may prove useful for a software platform manager.

My goal is to explain the topics in-depth without requiring a prior technical background. However, Chapters 4 and 7, which deal with ISs and software development, may be considered more technical and may be skimmed over by readers whose main interest is business management. This book benefits from my operational experience at Bouygues Telecom, AXA, and Michelin. It combines "lessons from the trenches" that should be of interest to a wide audience of IT professionals, such as architects or project managers, with a rich pedagogical structure augmented with notes and references, which may prove useful to students or curious readers. Finally, even if this is not a book about innovation, it plays an important part in the story, and this book should, for example, through advice on implementing the *lean startup* approach, be of interest to innovation managers, as well as *product managers* and *product owners.*

0.5 Plan

This book is organized into three parts. The first part deals with *digital transformation*—that is, the transformation of the company in the face of the accelerating digital revolution. This part lays the foundations, as it describes the objectives of this transformation: continuous adaptation, innovation, and better intimacy with customers. It deepens the analysis of *Designed for Digital* and enriches it with a complete presentation of the *lean startup* approach to building digital services.

The second part deals with the *IS* and the central role it plays in digital transformation. Software is "eating the world," according to Marc Andreesen; digital transformation affects all the company's activities and businesses beyond the more restricted scope of the IS. IS is the backbone on which new software activities are grafted. It must carry the ambition of openness, agility, and continuous modernization that is necessary for digital transformation.

The third part describes the principles of *software factory* and platform. It is about understanding how to use the best practices of software development, from tooling to automation, from agile methods to *lean* practices, to transform software production. The concept of the software factory also applies, but in a different way, to the heart of the IS and its borders, to produce the "digital platforms" evoked in *Designed for Digital.*

0.5.1 Part I: Digital Transformation

Chapter 1 is titled "Why a Digital Transformation?" The starting point is the radical change in the relationship between the company and its customers in the digital world. In a world of overabundance, the company must build conversations with its customers and develop an intimacy that legitimizes the relevance of the solutions it offers. The digital world is made up of ecosystems and platforms that require more openness and cooperation with partners, letting customers become the architects of their experiences.

Companies should, therefore, approach their digital transformation to better meet their customers' expectations and to better produce the products and services that their customers expect. Digital transformation affects the entire value chain, from R&D and solution design to marketing and operation of these solutions, including the production of hardware and software components. The digital revolution—the ubiquity of connectivity, the abundance of data and the exponential processing power—is invading design and manufacturing, such as through AI applications.

Chapter 2, "Homeostasis: Continuous Adaptation to Change," deals with the profound change in the organization of the company to adapt to the continuous and accelerated change that characterizes the digital world. The company must become an exponential organization (ExO), a network of autonomous and reactive teams, organized around a common goal, capable of absorbing and taking advantage of the continuous flow of technological innovations linked to the digital domain, from connected objects to machine learning (ML). The digital transformation of the company consists in developing, over the long term, the "situational potential"—the digital capabilities—that will enable it to act quickly in the face of an opportunity. Today's digital world is complex and uncertain, and the agility of the response to its opportunities requires a "letting go" of the control. The field of strategy has shifted from the forecasting of actions to the development of capabilities. The first skill of the digital company is its ability to learn from its environment, both technologies and customers, on a continuous basis. The role of managers is changing, as the voice of the customer and the voice of technology become more important, and this change needs to be accompanied.

Chapter 3, "Lean Startup: Lean Principles Applied to Co-Creation," is devoted to the first of the three capabilities, the co-construction of digital solutions with its users. The *lean startup* approach is broken down into three phases. The first, which corresponds to the application of *design thinking*, consists of observing, then formulating and testing hypotheses on the needs, latent or not, of future users. This step, which is the most important, leads to the formulation of a promise to the client, that of meeting a real need. The second step selects, in an iterative way, the different elements of the solution that effectively participate in solving the problem in the form of a minimal product. This minimal viable product, the MVP, is updated frequently and iteratively, according to the explicit and implicit feedback from the customers. The MVP is instrumented to validate, or invalidate, the elements of the solution. The third step, often called *growth hacking*, continues this iterative development to make the experience simpler, more convincing, and viral. The digital product becomes an element of its own marketing and commercialization. The development of virality relies on building a community of enthusiastic users who become ambassadors of this new experience.

0.5.2 Part II: The Exponential Information System

Chapter 4 is titled "The Information System as a Foundation for Digital Transformation." Its theme is the construction of an IS that is capable of frequent renewal and able to leverage the continuous flow of progress in the field of software, such as AI and ML, which will be the subject of the following chapter. There is an obvious parallel with ExOs, and we find similar ideas in the architecture of the exponential IS: the importance of interfaces, openness to the outside world, modularity. The IS is the backbone of the company's management and the development of digital platforms that serve as interfaces with the outside world, whether it be customers or partners. The digital IS must be responsive and agile while guaranteeing the flawless quality of service that customers expect in today's digital world. An IS that is constantly evolving and absorbing new functions must be designed, and above all maintained, to limit its complexity. This chapter discusses design techniques and management methods to limit technical debt, ensure resilience, and optimize the quality of service.

Chapter 5, "Artificial Intelligence and Machine Learning," focuses on AI in the broadest sense, a family of computing methods and techniques that give software significant capabilities, from knowledge processing to the automation of complex tasks. The digital revolution described above—abundant data, ubiquitous connectivity, and dramatically increased computing power—has led to significant advances in these AI techniques, even though they have been around for several decades. Chapter 5 discusses the implementation of these exponential technologies in the enterprise and the success conditions from the host technology systems' point of view, such as the IS. This implementation relies primarily on the enterprise's data architecture and infrastructure. Developing solutions that leverage advances in AI is a continuous learning loop, simultaneously improving data, algorithms, and usage. The role of human operators in the development of this virtuous cycle is fundamental; AI is a skill to be developed, not a magical technology to be acquired.

Chapter 6 focuses on the systemic conditions for building an exponential IS and is titled "Governance, Architecture, and Situational Potential." The first section focuses on the conditions, in terms of culture and organization, for *lean* and agile software development practices to develop harmoniously. The *lean* approach reinforces agile practices to better deal with the complexity and the "living system" dimension of IS. The two keywords of the necessary governance are flexibility and reactivity, especially in decision-making. This approach is also expressed in terms of system architecture, to combine long-term sustainability, performance, and agility of systems. The role of architects is evolving with the implementation of *lean* and agile approaches, but the importance of service-oriented architecture (SOA), modularity, and API reusability is only intensifying in the context of digital transformation. Moreover, a system that constantly evolves through incremental approaches runs the risk of continuously increasing complexity. Governance must be guided by the mastery of complexity to produce sustainable development of the enterprise's digital capabilities.

0.5.3 Part III: Software Platforms and Service Factories

Chapter 7, "DevOps and Software Factories," focuses on the third essential capability for successful digital transformation, the organization of software micro-factories following the DevOps approach. This chapter develops an integrated vision called *lean software factory* by successive steps. The first step is to automate the software product development process to achieve CICD. The second step is to place this CICD process in a product loop organized around cross-functional teams that combine development and operations responsibilities, hence the name DevOps. The DevOps approach is both a collaborative approach (development improves operations automation, and continuous feedback from operations improves development), a technological approach (tools that allow infrastructure to be treated as a scriptable resource increase the scope of automation), and a product approach (unlike an IT project, there is not a beginning or an end but a constant cycle of delivery and improvement). The addition of *lean* practices to the agile approach gets better results through the product approach. The *lean software factory* is a learning factory that develops both the "love of customer" and the "love of code" that we mentioned in the introduction.

The last chapter is titled "Putting Platforms at the Service of Digital Transformation." It provides an in-depth look at the contribution of the platform concept to digital transformation, as highlighted in *Designed for Digital.* The platform is both an extraordinary accelerator of value, thanks to the power of network effects, and a tool for intermediation with an open ecosystem of partners. Knowing how to build digital platforms is, therefore, a necessity if we are to achieve our ambitions of opening up and leveraging the capacities of digital ecosystems. The platform approach can also be applied more locally, as a product platform, to achieve some of the objectives described in Chapter 4: increasing the modularity, reusability, and development of internal user communities. This chapter underlines the adequacy between the construction mode developed in the previous chapter, a software micro-factory, and the operating requirements of a digital platform. The third part is actually in itself an illustration of the principle of this book: the skills and methods of manufacturing determine the speed and quality of execution, which are the indispensable conditions for the success of the strategy, whether it is the whole of the digital transformation or the construction of a digital platform, materialized by the emergence of its ecosystem of partners.

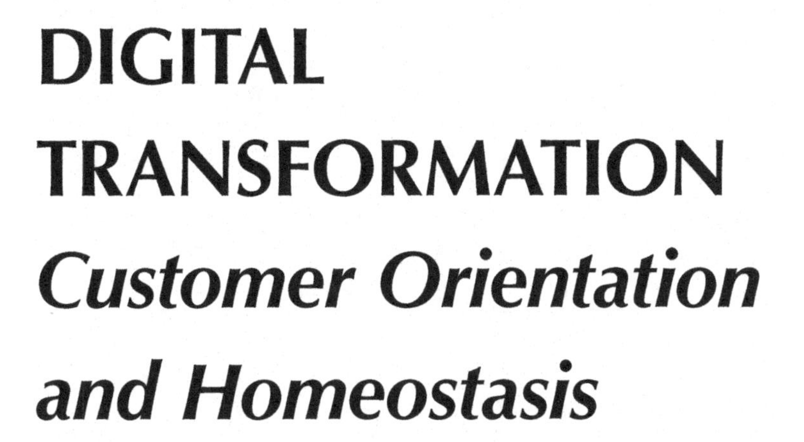

I DIGITAL TRANSFORMATION

Customer Orientation and Homeostasis

Chapter 1: Why a Digital Transformation?

Chapter 2: Homeostasis: Continuous Adaptation to Change

Chapter 3: Lean Startup: Lean Principles Applied to Co-Creation

Chapter 1

Why a Digital Transformation?

The presence of this first chapter in this book is a paradox, as the concept of digital transformation is so common. There are hundreds of books on the subject; the theme of digital transformation has been central to the strategy of all major companies for at least ten years, and some people explain on the Internet or social networks that the era of digital transformation is over and that we have now moved on to something else (AI, the Internet of things [IoT], etc.). However, if we take the time to read through these books or to question these companies, we realize that the subject most often addressed is the "how" (how do we undertake digital transformation?), but the "what" is less clear (what transformation are we talking about?). If we take objective criteria, such as the creation of turnover on digital products and services or the weekly time spent on the company's digital front ends, such as its websites, the digital transformation is only at its beginning. Major digital domains have been conquered by new entrants with different corporate cultures and organizations, leading to talk of "disruption." If you think you are familiar with the subject, you can quickly skip this first chapter. Nevertheless, without being the least bit exhaustive, this chapter is a foundation for the rest of the book because it is essential to understand the stakes of digital transformation in order to then discuss what to do by observing the behaviors of disruptive players who have already successfully taken advantage of this digital transformation.

DOI: 10.4324/9781003272816-2

1.1 "Markets Are Conversations"

1.1.1 The Economy of Attention

The digital world is a world of abundance. I refer you to François Dupuy's books, to my previous book[1] or to the abundant literature that explains that power has changed sides between the producer and the consumer. The 20th century saw the triumph of companies that produced new consumer goods. The 21st century is one of overabundance, and the consumer is spoiled for choice. This observation concerns only a part of the world's population, but it is the one that holds the purchasing power. This situation will not necessarily last for the whole of the 21st century since this overabundance is not sustainable, both in terms of the natural resources it consumes and the production of greenhouse gases that it entails, but it is the situation now. This situation of almost general abundance of supply is due to multiple causes, including globalization and the prodigious progress of logistics. It is even more striking in the world of digital products and services.

As a result, the way to address the customer has changed radically. It is no longer possible for a company to speak at any time to push a message about a new product or service regarding its advantages, its cost, or its conditions of use. Such a message becomes inaudible in the context of permanent information overload. It must, therefore, be rephrased to become the answer to a question the customer is asking, and it must be presented at the right time. This is what we call the transition from *push marketing* to *pull marketing*. The company's communication to the customer is "pulled" by the context and the customer's interest. There is a lot of literature on this subject.[2]

It is thus fundamental to know how to listen and capture the attention of one's clients and future clients. This is what Herbert Simon called "the attention economy" and which has been developed extensively since. In a world where we are bombarded with messages and requests, the challenge for business is to capture our attention. This concept was popularized a few years ago by TF1 CEO Patrick Lelay, who was selling his corporate clients the "available brain time" of TV viewers. In a world of multi-consumption of multimedia content on multiple devices, this attention is even more difficult to capture. The strategy of forcing its passage through "even more

---

[1] Read *The Chemistry of Change*, by François Dupuy. On the attention economy, you should read *The Attention Economy: Understanding the New Currency of Business*, by Thomas Davenport and John Beck.

[2] For French readers, I recommend *Le Marketing Synchronisé*, by Marco Tinelli.

captivating" content has its limits. You have to start by listening to your (future) customers to detect communication opportunities.

1.1.2 Conversations and Content Strategy

The fact that markets become conversations is not a new idea; it is the core of a cult book, *The Cluetrain Manifesto*, dating back to 2000.[3] The concept of conversation precisely captures the need to listen, to understand the context, to respond to the customer's attentions, and to "push" one's own message only incrementally, based on the *clues* given by the customer. The following quote from Randall Rothenberg allows us to appreciate the profound change in the marketing approach: "*Conversations cannot be controlled. They can only be joined.*" There are multiple dimensions to digital transformation, but I think learning to have conversations with customers is the number one issue for most companies. Doc Searls discusses the change in the following way. In the past, the company-customer relationship began with the purchase of a product. Then, thanks to the development of CRM (*customer relationship management*) tools, the company developed a relationship with its customers (loyalty program, after-sales, sale of complementary products and services, etc.). At the end of this process, the company knew its loyal customers and could have conversations with them about their expectations and future purchase intentions. The model of the digital abundance world is reversed. The first step is to gain the customer's attention by participating in conversations. The object of the conversation is the customer, not the company or its products. A series of conversations over time builds a relationship with the customer, gaining their trust and respect. This relationship with the customer creates a two-way flow of information, which can be described as the development of intimacy with the customer (better understanding her context and her intention). This intimacy then allows the company to sell its products and services and, therefore, to obtain transactions.

You can't participate in a conversation without bringing content related to the topic of the conversation. **There is no digital strategy without a content strategy.**[4] The content we are talking about here is not the

[3] *The Cluetrain Manifesto*, by Rick Levine, Christopher Locke, Doc Searls, and David Weinberger.

[4] A company can have its own "digital" strategy without having a content strategy, if it intends to improve its current products and services. However, this company will have difficulty attracting the attention of its customers to new offerings. This distinction is central to *Designed for Digital*, quoted in the introduction.

message associated with the future transaction (the product message of 20th-century marketing), it is the content that allows us to get a small part of the customer's attention (in the rest of this chapter, the word "customer" refers to the prospect, the future customer and the established customer). I quote Marco Tinelli: "*We bet on the strength of the content made available so that consumers pass on information to each other by e-mail, Facebook or simply by word of mouth.*" Building a content strategy requires knowing the interests of your customers (which is done gradually, hence the metaphor of conversation) and the places of exchange (digital or physical media) where customers are accessible with some level of availability. The 20th-century customer would come to find the message where the company had chosen to position it (for example, a television commercial), whereas it is the company that goes to meet the 21st-century customer where she is. The presence on social networks is, therefore, a formidable challenge of digital transformation, but this presence must be manifested as a conversation, not as a "*push*" of sponsored content.

1.1.3 Each Customer Is Unique

To build an effective conversation, it is necessary to understand the specific contexts of each customer and to personalize all interactions. Digital tools allow for a very strong personalization of content, services, and products. For example, all content can be geolocated. The core of the message can be precisely adapted according to everything that has been collected in previous interactions. Remembering the customer, never asking the same question unnecessarily, and taking their answers into account are the minimum expected in this digital age. It's not just about personalizing the sales or associated experience: the digitization of processes enables the personalization of services, while the digitization of manufacturing invites personalization into the products themselves.

One of the most important concepts to master in order to succeed in the digital transformation is the *customer journey*. The *customer journey* is a slice of the customer's life, in which the places, actions, moments, and intentions are identified to develop a "conversation" according to a well-identified context.

To build these daily customer journeys, companies must learn to work with designers. We will come back to this throughout the book when we talk about *experience design* in the next section and *design thinking* in Chapter 3. To observe, formalize, and design the daily customer journeys, designers use *personae*, which are "prototypes" of customers, both representative and very specific. The persona approach is opposed to the qualification of the "average" or even segmented customer, obtained by statistical analysis. The "persona" is a representation of a possible customer, with her history, her specificities. Working on a persona makes it possible to imagine the daily paths, the different possible points of contact (*touch points*) with the company. I'll quote Marco Tinelli again: "*The digital marketing industry, more permeable to this new culture, has imported this approach and crossed it with historical elements of marketing thinking, making the persona a formidable tool for brands.*"

1.1.4 The Economy of Intention

A few years after the *Cluetrain Manifesto*, Doc Searls wrote a book called *The Economics of Intention*, a nod to Herbert Simon. His focus on intentions is the logical consequence of the search for relevance in a world of supply overload. The best way to develop a conversation and then a relationship with your customers is to understand their intention—that is, the "why" that produces their actions. You can always ask them, which is what good salespeople have been doing for centuries, but it gets boring fast, and it's not necessarily scalable. In the digital world, customers' actions produce digital traces, whether they are real actions, such as transactions or movements, or virtual actions, such as consulting a web page, interacting with a mobile application, or even watching a video. From browsing cookies to events captured on social networks, digital companies are equipping themselves with DMPs (*data management platforms*) to collect as many digital traces as possible. The dizzying fall in storage costs makes it possible to keep all these traces and to easily build large data warehouses. The spectacular progress in the performance of machines and "big data" algorithms makes it possible to process all these traces to extract *insights*, which will enable to fuel conversations with customers.

The economy of intention is one of the new battlefields of digital transformation; just look at the popularity of the term *insight* in recent years. The renewed interest in AI and ML only reinforces this race to analyze digital traces. The significant progress in text and sentiment analysis increases the relevance of this "synchronized marketing" approach that Marco Tinelli describes. This concept of synchronization represents the search for the right moment, the right context to start a conversation with a customer, using the best of technology to collect and analyze.

This construction of intimacy through the collection of digital traces must take place in the context of respect for privacy, customer data, and a form of transparency marked by consent. Trust has always been a fundamental component for the development of the economy, as Kenneth Arrow teaches[5] us, and it is even more important in the digital economy. In their book *Extreme Trust: Honesty as a Competitive Advantage*, Don Peppers and Martha Rogers make trust a central element of a company's digital strategy. The more relationships and transactions become dematerialized, the more trust is needed. This is why the digital economy is conducive to brands and platforms that serve to establish and verify reputations. Compliance with regulations, such as RGPD when it comes to data collection, transparency, and especially education on the purposes are essential to build this trust. We will come back to this in Chapter 5.

1.2 "The Customer Is the Architect of His Experience"

1.2.1 Customer Experience as the Focus of the Digital Strategy

Just as the end of the 20th century saw the shift from product to service, the beginning of the 21st century is marked by the predominance of the term "experience." Experience is a catch-all concept that brings together products and services but from the point of view of the customer or user. **Talking about experience represents a double shift: forcing oneself to consider the customer's point of view and taking a global and holistic approach, which includes the context in which the product or service is used.** To think and design experiences, companies call upon experience designers (*UX design*, for *u*ser e*x*perience). Where in the past we would have thought of a product and its functionalities, which the user can use in several contexts, each context of use becomes a "product experience" in which everything becomes important to ensure customer satisfaction.

[5] On this subject, read the book *La fabrique de la défiance*, by Yann Algan, Pierre Cahuc, and André Zylbeberg, in which we find this beautiful definition by James Coleman: "*An individual is trusting if he puts resources at the disposal of another party, in the absence of a formal contract, in the expectation of benefiting from them.*"

Making the customer the architect of their experience is the central idea of C. K. Prahalad and V. Ramaswamy's bestseller, *The Future of Competition: Co-Creating Unique Value with Customers.* This fundamental idea of putting the customer in charge of their experience applies both during the design of the experience and during its execution. In the first case, co-creation is the primary principle of digital product and service design, and we'll come back to this in Chapter 3 when we talk about *lean startup.* In the second case, it is a matter of recognizing that the customer is the master of his or her context and that the opposite approach, when the company wants to prepare and control everything, is doomed to failure (in the sense of lesser customer satisfaction). The success of Apple's iPod a few years ago is an example of creating an experience around the product designed by Apple but with content chosen and arranged by the user. The experience design of the iPod when it was released was far superior to competing MP3 players, even for users who were using their own music and not that of Apple's ecosystem. In the digital world, experience is a *mash-up* of content and services obtained from different sources. This is the message of C. K. Prahalad and V. Ramaswamy to companies: get ready to create experience elements that customers will combine in their own way. **This is the main breakthrough of digital transformation: to give control back to the customer and to build modular and composable value elements.** This is, of course, the basis of the ecosystem concept to which we will return: the ecosystem is a space in which elements can be assembled and recomposed. The authors insist on the impact in terms of the IS: the IS must necessarily become more open since the value chain is broken down in a multi-company approach.

This idea that the customer is the architect of his or her experience leads to the implicit principle, underlined by Thomas Friedman in *The World Is Flat*, that the best form of personalization is *empowerment* (i.e., giving control back to the customer). This is a very general principle that applies to digital products, services, or subscription experiences, for example. There is a subtle contradiction between the digital vision of "synchronized marketing" in which the company guesses customers' intentions and provides them with perfectly personalized experiences—and this principle of giving back control to the customer by providing them with the means and tools to design their own experience. This tension is essential to understand and defines a successful digital strategy: we must know how to use all the resources of digital traces and data analysis to avoid unnecessary choices (those whose answer is easy to know and which are not experienced as choices by the customer) while leaving the customer in control of the "real choices" (those for which data analysis will not provide a reliable answer). We know that too many choices are detrimental to the quality of an experience,[6] and we also know to be wary of predictive algorithms that are often biased or wrong—we'll come back to this in Chapter 5. The right approach to digital transformation is to give a client back control over a limited number of choices that matter to her, while using the power of digital tools to avoid burdening her with choices that don't interest her.

1.2.2 Co-Construction with Users

The functional richness of the digital world, and its perpetual extension due to the constant progress of technologies, makes it extremely difficult, if not impossible, to predict the success of a digital experience and to understand its usage and the satisfaction that this usage will provide. Another fundamental idea behind the term experience is the fact that the customer is at the center of value creation. One could say that this is always the case, but it is much more relevant when it comes to using a smartphone than a fork or a spade. In the words of one of my colleagues at Bouygues Telecom, "with digital services, the customer is part of the production environment." **The complexity of the user's behavior invites itself in the midst of the technological complexity, and it is the user complexity that matters the most.** The vast majority of digital services offered by companies fail because the customer does not use them as intended (interestingly, this is also what creates success from time to time). Fortunately, the complexity and richness of the digital world also provide a palliative: it is much easier to iterate design/development phases and co-construct with its users than in the traditional physical world.

As Henry Ford or Steve Jobs once said, customers don't know what they want, so you shouldn't spend too much time asking them. On the other hand, they do know what they like, so it is very useful and effective to get them to react to products or services. This is the principle of co-creation in the digital world: an iterative loop in which each generation of the experience builds on the *feedback* obtained from the previous generation. This principle is, of course, applicable in a broader way than in the digital

---

[6] Read for example *The paradox of choice—why more is less* by Barry Schwartz. Many authors address the "cost of decisions" such as Daniel Kahneman in *Thinking, fast and slow*.

world, but digitization allows to formalize, automate, and accelerate these iterations. In a way, this is the main topic of this book, the continuous loop from customer to code and from code to customer.

The other novelty of experiences built around digital products and services is that they are by construction generators of digital traces. The world of digital experiences is one of continuous observation and measurement. We will come back to this in more detail in Chapter 3. The continuous loop of co-construction with users is greatly alleviated by the fact that the continuous measurement of usage avoids many questions and that it is possible to make a good number of choices by being data-driven. The caveat from the previous section applies: not everything is obtained from data analysis and real conversations, the ones that go through an exchange, are necessary for co-construction.

1.2.3 Products, Services, and Ecosystems

The digital world is constantly giving rise to new opportunities for new connected, intelligent, or augmented products, from Withings's connected blood pressure monitor to electric scooters and connected tires for civil engineering equipment. Without going into detail,[7] here are five features that characterize the acceleration of the digital world as far as products are concerned.

- First, we are living a Moore's law for sensors, which allows the equipment of products with multiple measuring instruments, less and less expensive and smaller and smaller. The best known are temperature, pressure, light, and contact sensors, but there is a very large variety of them, which gives new "senses" to augmented objects.
- In the same way, advances in terms of computing chips, whether they are classic processors or specialized processors—for example, for *deep learning*—make it possible to embed significant computing capacities in products.
- The third axis concerns connectivity: objects are increasingly directly connected to the Internet or to intermediate objects (*gateways*) that provide access to the Internet and thus to an ecosystem of services and data. In the field of connectivity, progress has been made in many areas: circuit

[7] On this subject, I refer you to the book *Reinventing the Product: How to Transform Your Business and Create Value in the Digital Age*, by Eric Schaeffer and David Sovie.

size, power consumption, network progress (throughput, range) from the constant improvement of Wi-Fi to the upcoming deployment of 5G.

- The fourth area of development is that of technologies for building man-machine interfaces, those that allow interaction with these new products. Without being exhaustive, we must mention the progress of artificial vision (*machine vision*), which, combined with the decrease in costs and the miniaturization of cameras, makes it possible to use gesture, face, and situation recognition as a method of interaction. In a parallel way (because in both cases, they are applications of the spectacular progress of *deep learning*), the progress of voice recognition, highlighted by Amazon's Alexa or Google's Assistant, opens new forms of control and interaction with products. We should also mention the spectacular progress of screens (it is possible to incorporate screens in more and more products because of the decrease in cost, size, and consumption) and haptic technologies (pressure recognition and tactile feedback loop on control surfaces).
- Finally, it must be emphasized that objects become truly "intelligent" (and first and foremost, adaptive to their environment) when these different axes/technologies are combined.

Regardless of the product itself, the digital context lends itself remarkably well to the observed evolution from product to service on the one hand and from possession to usage on the other. When we talk about physical products, which already exist, digital transformation produces platforms that allow us to digitize usage in order to propose all forms of models that are similar to rental or exchange. Examples include Uber for cars and Airbnb for housing. The companion of this usage revolution is, of course, the smartphone, which allows the production of digital traces of usage that will be consumed by the platform. This trend toward *product as a service* is facilitated by new objects that integrate sensors and connectivity to provide digital traces of usage, such as self-service scooters or electric bikes.

As Eric Schaeffer and David Sovie point out in *Reinventing the Product*, **the choice of ecosystems in which the product will participate is decisive; it represents one of the most strategic decisions in the design of a new product**. In the context of a global experience in which several products and services participate, the ecosystem will determine the user's scope of action (the customer is the architect of her experience but within the perimeter of an ecosystem of services). The customer most often chooses this ecosystem (for example, iOS or Android on her smartphone for a consumer customer or the force.com platform for a corporate customer), so the choice of the manufacturer is also determined by the customers he wants to reach. Let's remember that in the digital world, it is the service that moves to find the customer, not the other way around. The choice of ecosystem is, in fact, a choice of interfaces and protocols to collaborate, combine, and increase the value proposition. This choice is thus associated with the ecosystem of partners with whom the company wishes to collaborate to build a new experience.

1.2.4 The Obsession with the Customer's Time

The overabundance of offers, products, and services in the digital world, combined with a hyper-connected lifestyle, means that time has become scarce and high-valued for most customers. In an era where customer orientation has become mandatory, digital transformation imposes to consider the customer's time with the utmost respect and to seek to minimize its consumption. More than ten years ago, when I was developing digital services at Bouygues Telecom, we used to talk about "giving back useful time to the customer." Useful time is time that allows the customer to do what she or he wants. Giving them time means working on the ergonomics and design of the experience—subscription, use, or assistance—but also allowing them to make maximum use of "useless" time (at night, during transport, waiting in a queue).[8] The obsession with useful time is accompanied by ATAWAD (*anytime, anywhere, any device*) access, which allows the customer to do as much as possible during her "useless time" in order to preserve her "useful time." The obsession with customer time must be a cross-functional mission, from the analysis of daily customer journeys and interface design to service execution.

One of the great lessons of the web giants is the obsession with performance, to consume as little of each customer's time as possible.[9] The performance of a technical system is traditionally measured along three axes: **availability** (the percentage of time in the year that the service is available), **latency** (the processing time, which determines precisely how long the

[8] These examples for a consumer customer easily translate into the world of B2B relationships. Sales *front offices* are also looking to optimize their agents' valuable time. For the company that wants to sell, it's about making the buying process as efficient as possible—that is, consuming the least amount of time possible for these agents.

[9] *The Web's Giants* is a collective work by OCTO, published about ten years ago, which offers a synthesis of the managerial, cultural, and technical operating modes of the very large web companies (in the broadest sense) on the American West Coast. Ten years later, the findings and analysis have not aged a bit and I strongly recommend reading it for managers of large companies.

customer has to wait to get the service), and **capacity** (the number of processes or customers that the company is able to provide per hour or per day). Large web companies, such as Google, Facebook, or Amazon, are famous for the care and resources taken to optimize these three dimensions of performance, as perceived by the customer. Amazon is among the first web companies to have established the correlation between a very low response time and customer satisfaction rate (rate of requests executed to full customer satisfaction). Google developed a set of techniques to increase the availability of its services more than fifteen years ago, which have become, thanks to *open source*, the foundations of modern, high-availability, high-performance computing. Facebook has become, by necessity, one of the world champions of scalability.

Quality of service must be both excellent and constant. I insist on constancy because the digital world is an uncertain and chaotic world (in the sense of complex systems). The demand in the digital world varies significantly because it is subject to multiple amplifying factors: the immediacy of information, the power of communities and social networks, the speed of ordering processes. When a product or service is available or when an external event occurs that makes this product or service particularly relevant, it is not uncommon for the amplification mechanisms of the digital world to transform an initial demand into an instantaneous bubble of tens of thousands or even millions of requests. We will come back to this in the following chapters, in particular in Chapter 6, but one characteristic of the digital world is that it knows how to consider demand bubbles as opportunities. **Variability is not an enemy but a friend of value creation.** This is why scalability is so important in the organization of digital companies. It is also why scalable[10] computing technologies, from *cloud-based* to event-driven architectures, are relevant and popular.

1.3 Reinventing Products in a Digital World

1.3.1 Digital Products and Digital Production

Reinventing the product in the digital world is not just about developing new connected products that exploit all the possibilities we discussed in

[10] I use the term "scalable" to refer to the ability of a service, product, or organization to adapt to a rapid growth in demand. The digital world is characterized by the famous *hockey stick* curve, with disappointingly low growth followed by very rapid acceleration. Scalability is what allows you to take advantage of the growth explosion when it happens.

the previous section. It is also about harnessing the full power of the digital revolution in all stages of product design, manufacturing, and distribution.

The digitization of design processes is a strong trend that started several decades ago with tools such as CAD (*computer-aided design*). The increase in the power of digital tools has allowed this assistance to be extended in two directions. First, in the direction of testing and validation, with multiple simulation tools. The digital component or object can be simulated and validated. What started as a local validation of this or that property becomes a systemic simulation. A digital object can be interfaced with other digital objects, which represent its environment or other components of a larger system. Over the last twenty years, the term "system of systems" (SoS) has become commonplace precisely because system design and validation tools have made immense progress. An intelligent building is a good example of an SoS, which assembles multiple-scale components with their own adaptive intelligence (the connected lock, the smart radiator, the camera with face recognition) to form assemblies (equipment, rooms, floors) that are, in turn, enriched with adaptive intelligence at the subsystem level (heating, security, etc.). The AI revolution, which will be the subject of Chapter 5, continues to expand the scope of CAD: generative methods allow the computer to participate in the design and "invent" new shapes, new materials, or new assemblies.[11] The use of ML allows the reinjection of knowledge from use into the simulation and thus into the design.

The second dimension of progress in digital design is digital continuity—that is, the ability to use digital description from end to end with successively the first phases of design, detailed design, production engineering, realization, and monitoring of the product during its use. The concept of PLM (*product life-cycle management*), which also appeared a few decades ago, has been transformed from a simple nomenclature repository (giving the same name to the same things during the life cycle) into a backbone to assemble the different digital stages of the product's life. This digital continuity means that the digital product model becomes a collaborative platform for all the players involved in development. This allows, for example, the upstream actors of the design phase to participate in the manufacturing engineering and the production actors to be involved in the design phase. It also allows, for a given development phase, to convene multiple partners in extended enterprise mode who work together on the same object.

---

[11] Read the Airbus example on the Autodesk website: www.autodesk.fr/customer-stories/airbus.

The digital revolution on products also affects the marketing and distribution phase. Not all new products are connected or augmented products. One of the recent popular items in the US is the *Munchkin 360 Cup*,[12] a baby cup that allows a child to drink without ever spilling liquid. The innovation is a circular silicone valve in the shape of a lid, which allows water to pass through when the child pinches it with the jaw (anywhere on the circle, hence the 360, and as soon as the pressure stops, the liquid can no longer pass). Munchkin has joined the collaboration of the association of American dentists to certify that the use of the product is recommended for the development of the child's mouth. If the product innovation is classic (and incredibly relevant), this product is a good example of a successful launch in the digital world, from the website—which perfectly illustrates the notion of conversation (see their blog) and content strategy, the presence on electronic distribution channels, the viral videos available on YouTube, and so on.

1.3.2 Continuous Product Discovery

Product development in the digital world has become a continuous and iterative process. The role of the customer or user is so important that we talk about continuous product discovery. The term "discovery" here is opposed to innovation in a laboratory; it is an extension of co-construction.[13] Discovery begins with the observation phase made possible by the digital world: digital reinforces the power of conversations, the use of digital traces that we mentioned above, but also practices such as ethno-marketing (the observation of *customer journeys* according to anthropological practices). Continuous discovery continues with the invitation of the customer in the development phases. It lasts during development but especially throughout the life of the product. The digital product—Tesla is an emblematic example—evolves continuously through the evolution of the digital, and especially software, capabilities it embeds. One of Tesla's engineers says that the revolution in the digital world comes from the fact that a product is never finished. The product evolves during its lifetime, based on feedback and usage collected from customers. The term "continuous product discovery" is borrowed from two excellent

---

[12] See this website: www.munchkin.com/feeding/cups/miracle-and-spoutless-cups.html.

[13] There is a rhetorical process in using product discovery. We will see in Chapter 3 that innovation, including technological and laboratory innovation, remains necessary. The use of the term "discovery" is an invitation to start with the customer and the observation of his uses and *pain points*.

books, *The Lean Enterprise* and *The Innovator's Method*, which we will discuss in Chapter 3.

The iterative dimension of product development lends itself to the introduction of different iterative development paradigms, such as agile methods, and to the optimization of a repetitive process by introducing *lean manufacturing* principles. Donald Reinersten's book, *The Principles of Product Development Flow: Second Generation Lean Product Development*, is a key reference, quoted by Eric Ries in *The Lean Startup*, to explain the importance of these *lean* principles. The first one is that fast feedback is the first key to product development. The second is to avoid unnecessary waiting by calculating the cost of delay to minimize the work in *process* (WIP). Very logically, development evolves through short and thus limited iterations, using the frequency of the cycle to learn faster and avoid diverging too much from the real uses or needs of users. In the book *Reinventing the Product*, working in small multidisciplinary teams in agile mode—for example, using the Scrum method—is at the heart of the new product development organizations.

1.3.3 Knowledge Engineering

Whatever the product, connected or not, the knowledge used for its design and manufacturing is the main differentiation axis for companies. This is obvious for complex and sophisticated products, including connected products, but it is true for most products, even simple consumer products. As most of the books we just quoted say, a product reflects accumulated experience and acquired knowledge. This knowledge comes from all phases of development, from research and development to after-sales service, and touches all aspects of the product, from its materials to its assembly or logistical distribution. The technological acceleration of the digital world reinforces the importance of knowledge because it can be partially automated in its construction (we will come back to this in Chapter 5), because digitized knowledge can be more easily shared and distributed geographically, and because digitized knowledge is the support of a wider collaboration, within the company or in extended mode.

The use of digital tools for knowledge engineering is an old topic and one that has not always been successful. In the late '90s, everyone swore by *knowledge management*, being convinced that knowledge capture and sharing tools would revolutionize the world. The knowledge-base approach, with tools that were too heavy and not powerful enough, was a disappointment, and it was rather the notion of a community of practice, associated with social networking tools that allowed women and men to connect around topics, questions, and practice sharing, that emerged. During the past twenty years, digital knowledge sharing has been redefined as an open network of expertise in which testimonials are exchanged in the form of texts, photos, and especially videos.[14] Social networks have become the backbone on which knowledge elements are aggregated in response to the conceptual and disembodied vision of *knowledge management* of the past decades.

The digital model of the product is also an extraordinary candidate to serve as a backbone for knowledge sharing. A *digital twin* is what we obtain when the model is sufficiently rich and thus captures the dynamic properties of the "real" product being represented. The digital twin, as its name suggests, is a virtual double that closely resembles the object being modeled. It not only describes or visualizes but also simulates the operation of the object. Digital twins can be combined and used at all scales, from the simplest objects to systems of systems. The concept of a digital twin is old, but its practice has grown recently because advances in the digital world make building and simulating a digital twin easier and more relevant. A significant portion of testing can be performed on the digital twin, which is profoundly transforming both research and development and manufacturing engineering. **The digital twin becomes a collaborative platform and a knowledge engineering platform.**

The development of digital twins is accompanied by the development of augmented reality and virtual reality techniques. Augmented reality allows the superimposition of the information from the digital twin into the field of vision, on a helmet, glasses, or the screen of his smartphone. Recent progress in terms of artificial vision makes it possible to detect the parts of the product that are being viewed and to retrieve the corresponding parts of the digital twin and the information that corresponds to the problem at hand (assembly, inspection, repair, etc.). Augmented reality transforms the physical world into the navigation interface for the product knowledge base, materializing the "clickable environment" introduced more than ten years ago by Joël de Rosnay. In a dual way, virtual reality consists of using immersive visualization techniques, from 3D projection to HoloLens-like

---

[14] The best way to learn more about some of the technical topics that will be discussed in this book is to open YouTube and watch online knowledge shares or to sign up for MOOCs.

headsets, to observe and inspect different aspects of a variant of the digital twin. Virtual reality is combined with the ability to explore and produce product design variants.

1.3.4 The Role of Objects in the Materialization of Services

The concepts of "connected objects" and "IoT" are the topics of many conflicting conversations. On the one hand, we have been predicting a spectacular take-off and growth for the last twenty years. For instance, each generation of cellular network technology claims to support the future explosion of *machine-to-machine* traffic. Connected objects seem to be an unstoppable trend with unquestionable value. As a side note, for many digital services, the materialization by an object is indeed a plus in terms of ergonomics. This is why some connected objects, such as rotary volume control buttons (for example, the one proposed with the Devialet amplifier), cohabit with smartphone interfaces. We may also think of the connected labels proposed by Amazon, allowing one to reorder laundry detergent in one click. By placing the label in the right place (on the machine), the user builds his own intelligent environment (clickable); the connected object plays both a materializing and a service-enhancing role (giving "useful time" back).

On the other hand, the vast majority of connected objects that have been proposed to us over the last twenty years, especially for our homes, have failed. Those that have arrived in our hands have provoked very little use once the discovery period is over. *Machine-to-machine* traffic is barely visible next to the explosion of video traffic on our networks. It would, therefore, be tempting to adopt a very cautious, even cynical, attitude toward the development of IoT and connected products. However, as with most "exponential" developments in the digital world, the excitement about the technology happened too early, while the problems of embedded computing power, sensor costs, power consumption, connectivity, and so on were not solved, while progress is now very significant and on a steady pace. We must, therefore, learn to detect the *hype* of the famous Gartner curve[15] but prepare ourselves for a revolution that is well underway.

---

[15] Gartner's curve shows the evolution of the popularity of new technologies, starting with a phase of over-interest (the hype), then a sharp drop—when it is clear that the possibilities had been oversold—before slowly rising again over time, when that technology successfully spreads. The parallel with the Dunning-Kruger effect curve that shows the relationship between real competence and self-assigned competence is striking.

The journey toward connected objects is not as simple nor straightforward as it may seem. During the quest for connected and intelligent products opportunities, each additional level of functionality comes with a number of additional constraints. The simplest level, which consists of embedding sensors in its product, already forces to consider the problem of power supply, and most often, that of battery autonomy and the recharging process.[16] When computing capacities are added, consumption increases and the question of updating the software also arises, whether it is a simple *firmware* or an embedded AI. As soon as we talk about updates, we get the first level of cyber security risk, and a new class of constraints appears. When connectivity is added, the risk of cyber vulnerability becomes high, and power issues increase. Some of these constraints are passed on to the customer and will thus degrade the value of the solution. As Eric Carreel, founder of Withings, says, a real usefulness test of a connected object at home is to see if the user manages to reconnect it when a new Wi-Fi router is installed in his home.[17] Genevieve Bell, an anthropologist at Intel, talks brilliantly about the mental load that each of our connected objects imposes on us, often noisily demanding to be powered during the day. Transforming a current object into a connected object must, therefore, be done with an economy of means so that the value produced is clearly greater than the cognitive burden imposed on the user (not to mention the additional cost, but experience shows that product teams are sharp on costs optimization, while they often underestimate the constraints of use).

However, there is one connected object that is involved in almost every digital experience: the smartphone. Understanding the digital world means understanding the smartphone, its place in the "daily customer journey" and the time spent by our customers on their smartphones.[18] Inventing an experience around a new product means thinking about the role of the smartphone, even if the digital product has its own screens and interaction capabilities. The smartphone represents the quintessential connected and

---

[16] While waiting for the generalization of *energy-harvesting* technologies.

[17] This test is cruel because the documentation or the packaging has disappeared. The procedure of re-parameterization of the Wi-Fi network is more complex than the one of the first installation, and this happens one or more years after the purchase, when the excitement of the discovery is long gone.

[18] Those who tell you that the smartphone is outdated in terms of interfaces most often have something to sell you. In particular, the advent of voice assistants has seen some people talk about "the end of the smartphone," but voice is an interaction channel that is added (when it is convenient, for example when it is a command without much feedback) instead of replacing the smartphone screen.

personal object. It provides authentication, connectivity, and parameterization (because its touch screen is often far superior to those of connected objects) to most of the intelligent objects that surround us. If the use of the smartphone's capabilities is almost unavoidable, it also has its own constraints: the smartphone's autonomy is not infinite, access to frequent services has good usability, but access to occasional services can be slow and complex, and the conceptualization that is implicit when an object has to be manipulated through a smartphone's interface can be off-putting. We will return to these topics when we talk about experience design in Chapter 3.

1.4 Producing in a Digital World

1.4.1 The Ambition of Digital Manufacturing

The digital revolution is, of course, at the heart of the transformation of production. To take up the distinction proposed in the introduction, one part of digital transformation is concerned with the company's own function (how to produce better and be more effective and efficient), while the other part of digital transformation impacts production by addressing customer expectations (more velocity, more flexibility, and more variety). As for the rest of the company, the transformation of *manufacturing* is a combination of internal transformation potential thanks to digital technologies and continuous adaptation to a changing environment. The term "Industry 4.0" emerged in 2011, particularly in Germany, to refer to the large-scale integration of digital technologies (measurement, communication, computing, visualization) into industrial production. The development of Industry 4.0 is a major competitive challenge because one must meet customer expectations by producing a greater number of product types faster and more flexibly without increasing manufacturing costs.

Digital transformation is at the heart of the Industry 4.0 challenges. It profoundly changes the way we work and the horizons for reinventing business processes. This transformation—also known as *digital manufacturing*—is not easy to grasp because it is a revolution disguised as an evolution. It has three major components.

- The first is the ability of digital and exponential technologies to go even further in automating factory workstations. At first glance, this is a development in perfect continuity with what has been happening for many decades, namely the automation of production. If we take a closer look, which we will do in Chapter 5, the capabilities of AI and ML, such as image recognition, allow us to go much further and automate, or assist in the optimization of, much more complex tasks than what we knew how to do ten years ago. **Digital transformation allows us to control manufacturing capacities in a reactive way and to adapt production capacity to customer demand.**[19]

- The second component of *digital manufacturing* is the construction of digital twins, both for the product and for the entire factory and its manufacturing processes. Building a digital twin, as we saw in the previous section, is not simply building a digital model. It is the combination of modeling, capturing data from the real world (objects that are the physical instances of the model), being able to simulate the operation of the objects, and calibrating these simulations against what has been observed. The digital twin then allows—through simulation, forecasting, and optimization—to reinvent and redesign the factory processes. The digital twin of the product plays a key role in its design and development. The digital twin of the factory serves to transform and optimize manufacturing.
- Finally, the third component of *digital manufacturing* is the creation of an active workspace that acts in symbiosis with the operators in a principle of augmentation (the entire environment becomes an intelligent tool, thanks to the progress of all the technologies: sensors, miniaturization of actuators, new materials, etc.). The augmented environment of *digital manufacturing* aims both to automate some of the actions and to allow operators to better perform the others. It is one of the foundations for making production "intelligent" in the sense of continuous adaptation to the company's environment. For an increasing number of products, this adaptation goes as far as the customization of products on the production line.

The German Academy of Technology, Acatech, has proposed a maturity model for *digital manufacturing*[20] that is very useful for understanding this ambition (Figure 1.1). This model is based on a foundation that is a

[19] We will see in Chapter 5 that the combination of digitalization and AI applies to production, supply chain, and demand management, which is revolutionizing the marketing profession.

[20] The document *"Industrie 4.0 Maturity Index—Managing the Digital Transformation of Companies,"* by Günther Schuh, Reiner Anderl, Jürgen Gausemeier, Michael ten Hompel, and Wolfgang Wahlster (eds.), can easily be found online.

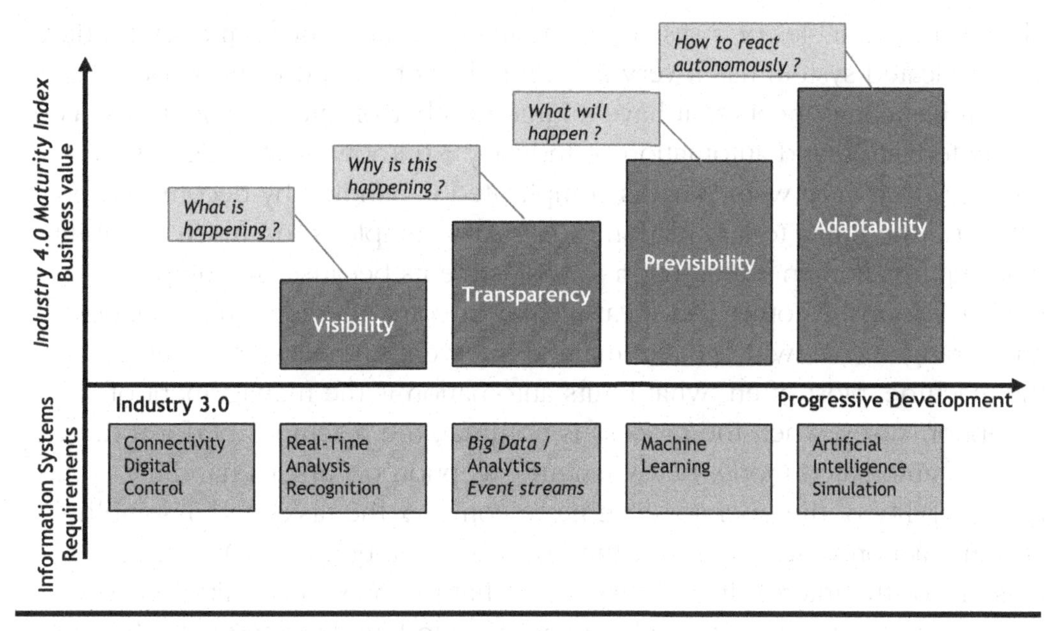

Figure 1.1 ***Digital Manufacturing*** **maturity levels.**

prerequisite, the digitization of production resources, both in the form of software automation and in the form of connectivity, which makes it possible to link all the production tools in the factory. Above this base, there are four levels. The first is visibility, the ability to know what's going on through sensors and the ability of automated machines to produce the right events. The second level is understanding—that is, the ability to produce *insights* and analyses from the collected events. The third level is reached when this capacity of understanding is projected in a predictive way—that is, when the analysis of events allows us to know in advance what will happen. The most frequently cited example is predictive maintenance, which is the capacity to launch a proactive maintenance operation on a machine before downtime occurs. The last level is adaptive self-optimization, when the automated production tool is able to control its operation in a reactive way according to the production objectives.

1.4.2 Artificial Intelligence as a Complexity Absorber

From a technological perspective, the main revolution in *digital manufacturing* is the introduction of AI and ML to absorb complexity and expand the frontier of what is automatable.

Why talk about complexity? Complexity is what connects things to each other; it is the set of multiple interdependent relationships between the objects and variables of a system. Complexity is different from complication: a complicated system has a very large number of components; a complex system has components that have a large number of interdependencies. The computerization and automation of Industry 3.0 know how to deal with complications very well. What is complicated is handled by decomposition.[21] What are the limits to automation today? An example is too much variability that requires human intervention for adjustments because of multiple feedback loops. Another is a great wealth of components, in their shapes and arrangements, which make manual intervention necessary to guide the machine. Most often, what limits automation is the management of exception cases: when the process is nominal, the machines perform their tasks in automated mode, but when an exception occurs, its handling is the responsibility of the operator. The more complex the tasks and assemblies are (interaction-wise), the lower the nominal operation rate. One of the reasons for the interest in Industry 4.0 is that the new possibilities of AI are moving the boundary of what is possible to handle in terms of the complexity of production processes.

We will talk about AI in detail in Chapter 5, but for the moment, it is sufficient to define it as a software modality that allows to perform or to assist in the accomplishment of tasks considered as difficult, requiring an important cognitive effort for a human. AI is a set of techniques that allow software to solve problems of classification, information retrieval, diagnosis, forecasting, and planning. The renewed interest in AI is linked to the spectacular progress, during the last ten years, of deep learning methods on sound, image, or situation recognition problems. AI is not an isolated technique; it is implemented in the form of software and requires data. The more data there is and the better understood it is, the wider and more relevant the toolbox of techniques becomes.

The deployment of AI in the enterprise or in the particular case of *digital manufacturing* is a component of digital transformation. The deployment of the Industry 4.0 maturity model is, first and foremost, an IS project and the implementation of the infrastructure for connecting all equipment and collecting all events. The first level, visibility, calls for data analysis capabilities and, in particular, for analysis and recognition of situations in near-real time. The spectacular progress in image, sound, and situation recognition means that AI plays an important role in this level of maturity. The predictive level of Industry 4.0 relies even more clearly on the

[21] On this subject, read *Processus et Enterprise 2.0*, by the author.

predictive capabilities of the *manufacturing* IS. To be able to analyze the digital traces of the past to detect abnormal situations or to predict when something abnormal will happen is neither a new idea[22] nor an idea specific to *manufacturing*. The use of learning and time series analysis algorithms is also applicable to the detection of problems in finance (fraud) or in IT (failures). Finally, reaching the last "adaptive" level is also conditioned by the integration of a large number of AI skills in the production IS.

1.4.3 Augmented Humans and Augmented Environment

The level of visibility referred to in the Acatech maturity model consists of increasing the level of information available to operators in charge of production. It is a matter of monitoring, detecting, and sensing what is happening and making this information accessible and useful to the operators. We find here the concepts stated previously: the IS uses a digital twin of the manufacturing process and "augments" the latter with information collected on the former. The information is accessible through usual software interfaces, but it is much more useful and relevant if it is provided in the operator's physical environment. This can be immersive augmented reality solutions for specific situations (e.g., glasses for troubleshooting) or, more simply, the provision of the right screens and interfaces on production sites and tools. This concept of the augmented and "clickable" physical environment is an important step in the development of the IoT. Ten years ago, we were talking about *web squared*: the digital world is constantly enriched by the flow of data from physical objects, while physical objects are constantly enriched by the digital capabilities of their digital twins. This paradigm allows for the gradual introduction of AI capabilities, both at the local level (making the object "intelligent") and at the global level (optimizing the system), without cognitive stress.

One of the most obvious aspects of augmentation is visualization. Advanced data processing techniques include methods of visualization and analysis, by and for the operator, of collected data. AI, more often than not today, accompanies the human rather than replaces him. The combination of global event collection and advanced visualization methods[23] allows

---

[22] This was already one of the active themes when the author was preparing his thesis in the AI department of the Marcoussis Laboratory, more than thirty years ago.

[23] "Advanced" methods should not be at the expense of simplicity and usability. Read the article "*The US Navy will replace its touchscreen controls with mechanical ones on its destroyers*," published in *The Verge* on August 11, 2019.

operators to better understand the system they are running. There is an interesting parallel with the use of visual management techniques from *lean manufacturing*, which we will discuss later. Another form of augmentation of human operators is the augmentation of memory. The collection of all the data, past and present, makes it possible to use "intelligent" data analysis techniques to find similar situations in the past, whether it is a question of making an adjustment or a diagnosis. This search in the history of the system can be quantitative, starting from numerical data, or qualitative, since the text-analysis techniques allow one to take advantage of all the reports of intervention on the machines.

1.4.4 Optimize with Digital Twins

The last level of maturity, the global optimization of the system thanks to the digital twin of the complete system, can take multiple forms. It can be a reaction to detected events in an adaptive form of self-control, which is the main case described in the Acatech document. It can also be a global reoptimization of the process, thanks to the accumulated data. The optimization of production processes from data collected in production is not a recent practice. For decades, operational research, planning, and scheduling algorithms have been applied to manufacturing processes to optimize them on multiple criteria: to save time, to reduce costs, to reduce inventory, and so on. What is new because of the progress of ML methods is that it is now possible to study much larger problems (using the whole set of data collected for a plant) and with different analysis approaches. In the book *The Mathematical Corporation*,[24] there is an example of a Merck vaccine production line. The use of a global digital twin, which required the constitution of a massive and complete *data lake*,[25] made it possible to optimize macro-parameters of the manufacturing process by simulation and to significantly increase the overall yield. This optimization, which takes into account external environmental factors such as weather, is profoundly different from what we would have done twenty years ago because of the volume of data used and the "implicit" approach to optimization (driven by data and not by the intuition of the production model creator).

---

[24] *The Mathematical Corporation: Where Machine Intelligence and Human Ingenuity Achieve the Impossible*, by Josh Sullivan and Angela Zutavern, is an excellent collection of examples of the application of AI to business problems.

[25] We will return to the concept of a *data lake* (a data warehouse designed to facilitate the flexibility and efficiency of ingesting new data) in the second part of the book.

The change that is taking place with the use of massive data and the new application of data analysis algorithms is that it becomes possible to optimize without forecasting. The techniques of previous decades relied on clear modeling of the production problem and on the ability to collect or predict the data on which the explicit optimization algorithms were applied. The practice was, therefore, to understand the problem in order to optimize and then to propose solutions. The approaches of searching for *patterns* in very large volumes of data make it possible to extract heuristics that improve performance without necessarily understanding why they work. In the abovementioned book, we also find the example of the FAA, which analyzed takeoff and landing data for three years to find key situations in order to minimize delays and especially accumulations in "avalanche" mode. What makes this example very interesting is that the data was far from perfect and that serial propagation of delays is a non-linear phenomenon that is very difficult to predict. The approach was not to build a prediction model but to analyze the data to extract *patterns* that characterize risky situations, for which remedies are possible to reduce the risk.

To conclude this chapter, it is important to highlight the fundamental role of cybersecurity in digital transformation in general and for *digital manufacturing* in particular. Digital twin data is extremely sensitive for two reasons. First, it represents an increasingly important part of a company's knowledge and intellectual property. When the digital model was just a digital bill of materials, most of the knowledge was in the heads of experts. But as the digital twin becomes a dynamic object and a collaborative platform, it grows significantly richer until it becomes the main knowledge base of the company. This is precisely the ambition we described in the previous sections since it facilitates sharing and deployment, but of course, it raises the question of protecting and securing access. Second, the "self-adaptive" operating model described in the latest maturity level of the Acatech model assumes the possibility of complete control of the machines by the algorithms, which raises further security issues if a malicious actor enters the system. Again, the shift from local automation of machines by automata—the common approach a few decades ago—to global automation means that the risk of cyber-attacks grows exponentially, both in probability and impact. Several Industry 4.0 experts, some of whom are quoted in the book *Reinventing the Product*, make cybersecurity the number one issue in *digital manufacturing*.

Summary

1. There is no digital strategy without a content strategy (1.1.2).
2. Talking about experience represents a double shift: forcing oneself to consider the customer's point of view and taking a global and holistic approach, which includes the context in which the product or service is used (1.2.1).
3. One of the main disruptions of digital transformation is to return control to the customer and to build modular and composable value elements (1.2.1).
4. The complexity of the user's behavior invites itself into the middle of the technological complexity, and it is user complexity that matters the most (1.2.2).
5. The choice of ecosystems in which the product will participate is critical; it is one of the most strategic decisions for the design of a new product (1.2.3).
6. Variability is not an enemy but a friend of value creation (1.2.4).
7. Product development in the digital world has become a continuous and iterative process (1.3.2).
8. The digital twin becomes a collaborative platform and a knowledge engineering platform (1.3.3).
9. Digital transformation allows us to control *manufacturing* capacities in a reactive way and to adapt production to customer demand (1.4.1).
10. The change that is taking place with the use of massive data and the new application of data analysis algorithms is that it becomes possible to optimize without forecasting (1.4.4).

Chapter 2

Homeostasis: *Continuous Adaptation to Change*

2.1 Digital Homeostasis

2.1.1 Change Comes from the Customer

When I joined AXA a few years ago, I had the chance to listen to a masterful presentation by Henri de Castries on the need for digital transformation, explained as a consequence of the changing environment. He reminded us of the accelerated changes of this early 21st century in terms of technology, geopolitics, complexity, uncertainty, the power relationship with customers, new customer uses, and the organization of networks of influence in society. He then posed the challenge of digital transformation as the "simple ability" to follow customers and their expectations in this new world. This approach echoes the often-stated observation that we experience the digital revolution faster as consumers in our homes than as employees in our companies. This presentation suggested the term "digital homeostasis." **Homeostasis**, simply put, is the ability of living organisms to continuously adapt to changes in their environment. Talking about digital homeostasis is a way of forcing ourselves to look outside to consider our own digital transformation so as not to make it an *internal* transformation.

The change dictated by the outside of the company is faster than the change that the company spontaneously generates internally. This is why the organization of 21st-century companies must be organized *outside to inside*, built to promote flows of information that originate outside and propagate

DOI: 10.4324/9781003272816-3

inside the company. This acceleration of change, both with customer usages and service expectations, is obvious in the B2C market for the general public, but it is also true in the B2B market between companies. The digital revolution, the digitization of business processes, is driven by the borders, the "edges of the company," the exchanges with its stakeholders. The company is the master of its own internal time and decides the pace of its transformation; it is not the master of its ecosystem's time and must adapt its transformation to the pace of change of its environment.

The digital revolution, since the arrival of the Internet and more recently of the *smartphone*, has profoundly changed the usages and expectations of customers. The level of service quality and performance of the tools they use in their daily lives has raised the bar on what they expect from a digital experience. This is neither a coincidence nor a surprise. Consumer digital ecosystems are benefiting from all the things that are necessary for continuous innovation and the development of excellence: volume, speed, openness, and community networks. For example, smartphone volumes have driven the cycles of manufacturing, improvement, and innovation of phone *chipsets* to the point of making them the dominant model on the planet.[1] According to Wikipedia, homeostasis is a regulatory mechanism that allows a given factor to adapt to the fluctuating demands of the environment of a system. **Digital homeostasis is the process of digital transformation that keeps the digital experience up to the expectations of the company's customers.**

2.1.2 Accelerating Change, from Uses to Technologies

The concept of accelerating change is a difficult topic, as it is so mundane and yet it plays a critical role in managing digital transformation. Some aspects are easy to qualify, such as the speed of penetration of new products in the digital world. The time it takes for a significant part of the population to adopt a new product has dramatically decreased over the last century, from the television to the smartphone.[2] This is even more striking with purely software products, such as services delivered via the Internet, mobile

[1] It is often more efficient and cheaper to use a smartphone chip (or a derivative) for another connected terminal than a functionally simpler solution better suited to the need because of the volume effect.

[2] There is a wealth of literature on the subject. For example, even though it is from 2012, the article "*Are Smart Phones Spreading Faster than Any Technology in Human History?*" from MIT Review is very interesting.

applications, or social networks. The diffusion acceleration of products and services is accompanied by the same pace of change in usage. This ties in with the previous section: it is because usages are changing rapidly that we need to understand them and to involve customers in the co-creation of new products. Another way of quantifying this acceleration of change is to monitor the metrics of content and service consumption on the Internet.[3]

Without going into detail, a few factors that contribute to this acceleration of change are worth mentioning. The first factor is, of course, the exponential progress of digital technologies. Even if it is starting to show signs of slowing down, Moore's law is one of the main factors in the acceleration of digital technologies. Similar laws have been observed in the evolution of storage and in the capacity and performance of networks. We will come back to this in Chapter 5 since the progress, in terms of computing power and storage of large amounts of data, is part of the spectacular acceleration in performance observed in AI since 2010. The permanent increase in connectivity, in all dimensions, has an impact that is much stronger than mere technical capacity. It is a societal accelerator because it reduces the time it takes for information to spread and helps create global broadcasts. The digital time, the time it takes for an idea, a product, a practice to spread around the world, is shrinking under the effect of technology, networks and globalization, both from an economic and cultural standpoint. The changes induced on our culture and our usages are so vast that they exceed the framework of this book. For example, the individualization of our behaviors is another factor of acceleration: behaviors normalized by society evolve more slowly than those of the individual, with the paradox that the connected individual changes faster than the isolated individual.

2.1.3 The Multitude Is an Opportunity

In a book that is a bit dated but still totally relevant, *L'Age de la multitude* (*The time for many*), Henri Verdier and Nicolas Colin explain that the digital revolution is marked by three upheavals:

- Reduced costs of digital technologies—which fuels disruption because new players can do what was done before digitization at significantly lower costs

---

[3] For example, it is useful to follow Mary Meeker's annual State of the Internet report, or Akamai's or Cisco's reports on network traffic.

- The principle of "unfinished" innovation—a product is never finished and is constantly evolving
- The ability to innovate externally, thanks to the contribution of the multitude

This multitude is made up of customers, prospects, developers, partners, innovators, and so on. This third disruption is so important that it gives the book its title. It is the combination of two profound ideas that reinforce each other. First, there is always more talent outside an organization than inside. In a complex world with difficult challenges, you need to be able to collaborate with external crowds. The second fundamental idea is that digital technologies enable the self-organization of crowds and the emergence of platforms—an important topic that we will cover in Chapter 8. One of the reasons the power relationship between companies and consumers is reversing in the 21st century is that consumers have organized themselves into connected crowds. Thanks to social networks, forums, and platforms, consumers talk to each other and act with group coherence, which gives them much more power than the isolated consumer of the previous century.

This reversal of power in favor of customer communities is sometimes a challenge, but it is also a real opportunity for companies to get to know them better, as we saw in the previous chapter. The use of voting, opinion sharing, and reputation platforms allows the "wisdom of crowds" to emerge (i.e., the relevance of the average opinion of a large number of people). This wisdom of crowds is both an established phenomenon[4] and a trap since the conditions necessary for this wisdom to be expressed are often not fulfilled, and digital tools can, on the contrary, provoke *groupthink*,[5] which is the opposite of the wisdom of crowds when different opinions add up to erase extreme positions. Knowing how to talk to communities of "stakeholders" is, therefore, one of the important challenges of digital transformation to enrich the company's innovation.

We will see in the rest of the book that we need to go further than knowing how to discuss—remember that markets are conversations—with self-organized communities, we need to know how to help stakeholders

---

[4] Read *The Wisdom of Crowds*, by James Suriovski, or *Supercollective: The New Power of Collective Intelligence*, the more recent book by Emile Servan-Schreiber.

[5] Groupthink is what happens when the desire to be part of the group and to be accepted by others leads to an "irrational" decision—that is, one that is not supported by the majority *individually* (if one asks each person separately).

self-organize into digital communities. The success of an innovation depends on the creation of a community of ambassadors for the product, which can then grow. In the same way, an open innovation strategy, which consists of building an ecosystem of partners, is a platform development strategy.

2.1.4 The "Letting Go" of Digital Transformation

A little more than ten years ago, I had the chance to participate with the Bouygues Telecom management committee in a study tour of the innovative Swedish digital ecosystem, including a visit to Spotify. Its CEO explained to us why Spotify had replaced its strategic plan with a monthly iterative approach: its customers' usages are unpredictable, and they change very quickly, as do competitors' offers. The CEO sets a strategic direction that aligns the month's "first steps," but a month later, the executive team meets to analyze customer feedback and reassess its strategic direction and product strategy. Strategy is built incrementally through regular observation of the environment; it is not decided in advance. The implementation of this notion of "small steps" naturally leads to the adoption of agile methods,[6] but this is the consequence of an agile perception of the business. As we will see in Chapter 6, agile practice is most effective when applied to the entire enterprise. **What transforms a company is not adopting an agile method for the development of its digital platforms or its IS; it is adopting agility as a strategic approach.**

What the CEO of Spotify described to us is a "chaotic" market of usages, in the sense of complex systems. On the one hand, there are many reasons a new service or feature may not work or may not fit in with the actual usage of customers. This is the consequence of the complexity of the digital world due to—for example, very rich hardware/software ecosystems in which elements are incompatible with each other or the complexity of interactions in the coexistence of all the competing services for music content consumption. Another factor of complexity is the impatience of users in a world where offers are overabundant. On the other hand, there are multiple loops of success amplification through social virality (from word of mouth to social networks), the fundamental role of "attractive" content, and the reactions of the music world. All this makes the success of

[6] Spotify is famous in the agile world for the quality of its large-scale agile practices. Much of it has made its way around the world in the form of videos. Just type "*Spotify engineering culture*" into your browser.

a new service unpredictable. The right pricing model, the right subscription ergonomics, and the right interface elements that allow social sharing of emotions emerge through iterations of testing and observation.

This idea that success *emerges* from a complex system is not new in the digital world. In his 1995 bestseller, *Out of Control*, Kevin Kelly already explains that intelligent systems are not designed but grown. They emerge if the right conditions are met, their management is no longer linear (where actions are logically deduced from goals) but holistic, based on observation, adaptation (trial and error), and constant effort on "favorable conditions." What characterizes the digital world is the need to "let go" because success is no longer the result of a "simple" objectives/efforts equation. Success is co-constructed with the environment. This is striking in the digital domain, but it is a more general principle stemming from the complexity of the modern world. Frederic Laloux, in his bestseller *Reinventing Organizations*, writes,

> The deep challenge here: it requires letting go of **our beautiful illusion of control**, our comforting illusion of control. The illusion that we've done our job as leaders: we've done all the analysis, we've got the plan, things are going to go according to plan, we are in control.[7]

2.2 Anticipation and Agility

2.2.1 Situational Potential and Anticipation

"Letting go" is not synonymous with inaction or *laissez-faire*. Giving up control is not a renunciation of ambition or strategy. It is a matter of thinking differently about one's actions and the role of the environment by invoking elements of Chinese strategic vision and the fundamental concept of situational potential.[8] The classical world, which could be described as linear (each action has a proportionate consequence) or predictable (like the world of mechanics), lends itself well to a voluntary approach to strategy, where the objective defines the plan and the plan generates the action. In this model, which can be associated with Greek thinking of which we are

---

[7] The emphasis on « illusion of control » is mine.

[8] I borrow these elements of language from François Jullien's fundamental book, *Conference on Efficiency*. Readers of my blog or of my other books know that François Jullien has been one of my main sources of inspiration for the past fifteen years. The discourse of his book *Conference on Efficiency* is taken from a richer work, *Treatise on Efficiency*.

heirs, man imposes his will on the world. The Chinese strategic model[9] considers that the world imposes its will on man and that we must play with the elements in an opportunistic way. The right action is the one that allows one to obtain a gain with the minimum of effort because it draws its strength from the context. To prepare one's ability to be opportunistic is precisely to build one's situational potential.[10] Thinking about a strategy then means building this situational potential, usually in a slow and methodical way, so that when the opportunity arises, you are in the best possible position to take advantage of it. This approach lends itself formidably well to emergence management because it corresponds to an "agricultural" vision of human action, which separates preparation (of the ground) and active adaptation (when the plant grows). The proverb quoted by François Jullien, "you can't make a plant grow faster by pulling on the stem," is a great illustration of this idea of abandoning the illusion of control.

This approach to strategy is not new since it is the heart of Sun Tzu's *The Art of War*. The main message of this military treatise is to win one's wars by developing one's situational awareness without having to fight.[11] This military strategy is, above all, a strategy of anticipation, but it is not a strategy of forecast. The general of which Sun Tzu speaks does not know where or when the confrontation of the battle will take place or under which form. Instead, he anticipates the conflict and matches his actions to the shape of his environment so that when the battle comes, the situation becomes an opportunity. The American military has exported the term "VUCA" into the vocabulary of corporate strategy as an acronym that associates volatility, uncertainty, complexity, and ambiguity of situations. Even though this text is almost three thousand years old, *The Art of War* is well suited to a VUCA world. It is not a manual for action but a manual for transformation. The more the environment has VUCA characteristics, the less forecasting, planning, and voluntary action (control) work. Instead, one must use the environment as it presents itself (VU), work on the factors favorable to situational potential (C), and play with ambiguity as an element of surprise (A). Coming back to our digital topic, precisely in this line of thought, Marty Cagan—one of Silicon Valley's experts on digital product

---

[9] This designation is of course a shortcut, there is no "one" Chinese model, but multiple axes of thought.

[10] The technical term "situational potential" can be replaced by "situational awareness," which is more common in the business literature.

[11] Even if this comparison has become a commonplace, there is an interesting parallel between the game of go (preparing the potential) and the game of chess (finding the decisive actions).

development—explains about *roadmaps* that 50% of what they contain will not be used by customers and that the remaining 50% will require multiple iterations before becoming useful.

2.2.2 Short Time and Long Time

Chinese thinking allows us to characterize a fundamental idea of the digital world, the duality between short and long time. All the literature on the digital world and digital transformation talk about the acceleration of time, speed, velocity, TTM (*time to market*), the time it takes to bring a new service to market), the time it takes to deploy a line of code,[12] and so on. The digital world is a fast-paced world, and only the fastest survive. Actually, the dominant players in the digital world demonstrate multiple strategic, organizational, and technical prowess in their ability to quickly bring value to their customers. But this is about the time to react to opportunity. Just like in *The Art of War*, the reaction must be as fast as possible. But what makes it possible to react quickly is the preparation work that has built the quality of the situational potential. The short time is that of the realization of the situational potential; the long time is that of the construction of this potential.

This is well known when talking about Chinese military strategy but less understood when talking about digital skills and digital transformation. This is one of the key topics of the rest of this book: how to build situational potential to be agile and fast afterward. The subtitle of the book, "from customer to code and from code to customer," and the principle of the double arrow proposed in the introduction are precisely references to building the skills, processes, and practices that allow the execution of these two "arrows" in the fastest and most agile and secure way possible. The reduction of the TTM is nothing more than the application of process optimization methods (like *lean*, of course) to reduce the *lead time* of the macro-process that these two arrows represent.[13] Everything that makes us admire the ability of a Spotify, a Netflix, a Google, or a Facebook to quickly launch a new service, to make continuous updates, to copy a competitor's feature, and to observe and listen to its customers as quickly as possible is the result of execution excellence (which is situational potential).

---

[12] This metric measures the time it takes to deploy an elementary change (a single line of modified code) to users.

[13] In a process, the *lead time* is the beginning-to-end elapsed time, the *takt time* the delay between the output of two results.

We will go into more detail on the construction of the situational potential, of which the IS is a fundamental component, in the second and third parts of the book. Nevertheless, there is a more general systemic vision that permits us to understand the time horizons of digital transformation. The short term is the time for action, and the long term has two horizons: the medium term is the time of capabilities that will allow the speed of action, and the long term is the time of development of *skills* that are necessary to obtain the excellence of capabilities.[14] Practice makes it perfect: it is by building digital capacities that one develops one's skills. When the fast time of action comes, it is no longer the time to learn, but the long time of the construction of capacities contains this loop of skills learning. The notion of capacity is fundamental; it is the elementary brick of the situational potential, which we will use in the rest of the book. The notion of *roadmap*, which is rightly criticized when it comes to services, makes sense when we talk about capabilities because capabilities are built over time. This borrowing from Chinese thinking gives full meaning to the expression "digital transformation": **it is the transformation, over time, of the company's digital potential, in order to support agile, rapid, and opportunistic action when the customer opportunity arises.**

2.2.3 Cultivating Innovation

The term "innovation" is omnipresent in the literature about digital transformation, and this is no accident. Customer-driven innovation is a necessity in the digital world. We have already outlined the reasons. The digital world is highly competitive; innovation is a fundamental tool for differentiation. In the race for the customer's attention, innovation provides the first reason to open a conversation. The digital world is a changing world, which is why "innovation is never finished." Innovation is mandatory to keep the product, the service, or the experience relevant for its customers. Continuous innovation is, therefore, part of the natural paradigm of the digital product life cycle until it is withdrawn from the market.

Innovation in the digital domain is the combination of talent, creativity, and several methods, practices, and capabilities. We find very precisely the agility/situational potential decomposition of the two previous sections,

[14] A fundamental idea of *The Digital Playbook* is that having the right digital capabilities allows you to be a *fast follower* and not get "disrupted." It's not about always being first, but you have to be able to follow if a competitor innovates in a significant way.

without surprises, since innovation management is also emergence management. This has been known for a long time since Pasteur said about innovation: "Chance favors the prepared mind." Chapter 3 will deal with the creation of the potential situation (methods, practices, and capacities) for innovation in the digital world, but there remains a part of chance and creativity that escapes rationalization.

What is unique to the digital domain is that much of the innovation is done by "osmosis," by contact with its stakeholders. As we mentioned before, these are the company's customers, its partners, the ecosystem of startups in the business domain, and so on. This is why digital transformation requires two things: an orientation of the organization from the outside in and a sustained effort on the "borders" to make them as porous and open as possible. The ability to "listen" to one's environment is part of the company's situational potential. The *technical and cultural* work on the borders is essential for the company to function as a partner in an ecosystem. This metaphor can be applied to the organization, as we will see in the rest of this chapter, or to the IS, which will be the subject of Chapter 4.

2.2.4 Customer Orientation as a Compass

The term "customer orientation" comes up a lot in books on digital transformation, and this one is no exception.[15] This term, which globally means "making customer satisfaction a compass for strategic and operational decisions," is especially relevant in the digital world. We will highlight three important reasons to build a digital strategy around the customer.

The first reason was mentioned in the previous chapter: the complexity of digital experiences and the difficulty of predicting what will be useful and satisfying for the customer require a co-creative approach. Customer orientation is a marketing compass, from thinking about the market in terms of a conversation to the iterative product development cycles of the *lean startup.* Customer orientation is an active practice, which includes looking at topics from the customer's perspective instead of the company's.[16]

---

[15] I refer the reader to Ram Charan's new book, *Rethinking Competitive Advantage: New Rules for the Digital Age*, which main principles echo this second chapter. What he writes about the difficulty of customer orientation for established companies is very insightful.

[16] The practice of the empty chair representing the customer during meetings is one of Jeff Bezos's famous requirements at Amazon. Read, for example, the web article "*Why Every Amazon Meeting Has at Least 1 Empty Chair*," by John Ketsier on the Inc. website.

The practice I have used over several years of meetings about digital topics—launching new products, services, sites, or mobile apps—is to measure the CCI[17] (*customer-centricity index*), which is the percentage of sentences during the meeting where the subject is a customer, and the verb is an action verb. A sentence of this type implies considering the customer's point of view and talking about their experience. This percentage is high in a digital startup (more than 20%, according to my observations); it remains above 10% in leading digital companies. This is an "acid test" for most large established companies; self-measurement is a good practice to become aware of the path to take.

The second reason is more specific to the digital world and its complexity. Customer orientation is a compass to avoid creating too much unnecessary complexity in the company. In the short term, customer orientation is an effective filter: we should only do what is directly useful to the customer, what responds to her expectations, needs, or difficulties. In the medium/long term, from the perspective of anticipating and building situational awareness, these choices are more difficult. Experience shows that the construction of "capabilities that could one day be useful" is one of the first sources of complexity in the company, especially in the IS. We will come back to this subject in Chapter 6 when we talk about architecture, but we can already stress that this permanent perspective of customer satisfaction is also a relevant criterion for long-term choices.

The last reason is the most essential one; **customer orientation is the best way to align various actors or functions in the company toward a common goal**. I can speak from my own experience here: I have seen many times the power of working on "customer cases," whether they are user stories or service failure analysis, to "break down the logic of silos" (organizational and functional) to produce true "end-to-end" collaboration, which is the only perspective that makes sense from the customer's perspective. The larger the company, the more complex the services it offers—in the sense that the end experience relies on the availability and smooth functioning of multiple components produced by different entities—and the easier it is to lose this end-to-end global vision.[18]

---

[17] No need to Google "CCI"; the use of an acronym for this "performance indicator" is a wink.

[18] In his book *Reinventing Organisations*, Frédéric Laloux shows through numerous examples that customer satisfaction most often derives from the initiative that is the consequence of the autonomy left to the teams. The example of FAVI provides many anecdotes in which customers are exceptionally satisfied because of a local and unexpected initiative of the team. The examples from Buurtzorg show the importance of *empowering* the team to be responsible for their own business objectives.

2.3 Scalable Organizations Adapted to Continuous Change

2.3.1 Exponential Organizations

The term "exponential organization" (ExO) became famous in 2014 with the release of the book *Exponential Organizations: Why New Organizations Are Ten Times Better, Faster, and Cheaper Than Yours (and What to Do about It)*, by Salim Ismail, with Michael S. Malone and Yuri van Geest.[19] Salim Ismail, in collaboration with Singularity University, has done extensive work analyzing which companies, particularly in Silicon Valley, are making the most of new technologies to establish their leadership or to "disrupt" their markets. An exponential company is, in their words, *"a company that is at least ten times more impactful or successful than its peers because of organizational methods that allow it to better take advantage of technological acceleration."* The concept of exponential technology is broad; it encompasses all areas where acceleration is strong, continuous, and established, with an overrepresentation of digital areas such as AI, ML, sensors, or virtual/augmented reality. The question raised is, therefore, precisely that of digital transformation: how to evolve managerial organizational principles so that a company can benefit from the continuous flow of technological innovations in the digital world? In the book *Exponential Organizations*, we find some of the ideas we encountered in the first chapter: the importance of the capacity to process information flows, letting go of a priori control, giving up 5-year plans, the plea for technical and cultural openness of the company, and the importance of measurement and *data-driven* decisions.

The first thing that characterizes an *exponentials organization* (ExO) is the presence of a very ambitious and transformative mission—that is, with a strong societal impact, understood by all, and the capacity to energize both internally (the employees) and externally (the ecosystem of partners). The MTP (*massively transformative purpose*) plays a key role in the coherence of the distributed organization. The other characteristics are summarized by the acronym SCALE: *s*taff on demand, *c*ommunity and crowd, *a*lgorithms, *l*everaged assets, *e*ngagement. The S and the L consist in favoring the variability of resources, both human and technical, by taking advantage of the ability of platforms to make resources available dynamically according to needs. This constant desire to leverage variable

[19] The term "exponential organization" is often used, for example, in the previously mentioned book *Reinventing the Product*, but I warmly recommend you read the book by Salim Ismail. It seems to me to be part of mandatory reading for a manager in the digital world.

resources is both a consequence of the strong desire for scalability and a strategic desire to maximize agility. The two Cs echo what we described in Chapter 1: knowing how to develop and work with communities around its products, taking advantage of the wisdom of crowds. The A represents the massive use of data science and AI techniques. The importance of algorithms is illustrated by numerous examples in the book. **The constant appropriation of the continuous progress of intelligent data processing methods is one of the strategic challenges of digital transformation**. The E means to work intensely to maximize customer engagement and build experiences that participate in viral marketing of products. We will come back to this in the next chapter.

Similarly, the book proposes the acronym IDEAS (*i*nterface, *d*ashboards, *e*xperimentation, *a*utonomy, *s*ocial technologies) to describe the main organizational techniques that are common to ExOs. The term "interface" is very generic here and represents what we could call "service architecture" to implement the SCALE approach. We find in it the notions of API, modularity, and agility by orchestration that we will develop in Chapter 6. The D represents data-driven enterprise management, while the E emphasizes the importance of experimentation, iterations, and a culture that celebrates trial and error. The book makes an important part of *lean startup*–type approaches: "*We define Experimentation as the implementation of the Lean Startup methodology of testing assumptions and constantly experimenting with controlled risks.*" The term "autonomy" means "*the organization into self-organized multidisciplinary teams working with decentralized authority.*" The S stands for the use of digital technologies for sharing, communication, and collaboration within the enterprise. ExOs make the most of *software as a service* (SaaS) technologies available in the cloud.

2.3.2 Networks of Autonomous Teams

I will now focus on the network organization of distributed autonomous teams because it is the cornerstone of all modern organizational theories.[20] The starting point is the observation, shared by all, that the bureaucratic and Taylorized way of working, which has worked wonders to meet the challenges of previous centuries, is finding its limit in the face of

---

[20] This is a common theme in all the books on organization I cite here, and one that I developed in my previous book *Process et Enterprise 2.0*. Autonomy must be real and often requires reinventing budget and resource allocation processes.

the complexity of the 21st century. The steering mode of hierarchical organizations, "command and control," must be transformed into "recognition and response." The world's complexity produces a large variety of situations that invalidate the notion of *command.* It is up to the team to *recognize* the situation. The issues we saw in the first chapter require rapid action, so it is no longer possible to work with a centralized command function (the heart of hierarchical management). The *response* must be decided quickly and locally (both to move quickly, but also because the complexity of the context means that recognition is not easily transported to an external control center). **What characterizes complex situations is that recognition and reaction are intimately intertwined, even indistinguishable because they are part of the same process**. The shift from "command and control" to "recognize and respond" is the central theme of Langdon Morris's 1995 book *Managing the Evolving Corporation.* It is fascinating to see the parallel evolution in the way operations are managed in the military, a theme found in many recent books.[21]

As we have seen, complexity means the presence of strong constraints linked to multiple dependencies. It is not enough to set up autonomous teams that work in R&R mode; they must also be organized in networks. The art of this network organization is to provide the greatest possible autonomy, but it is not total.[22] This organization is also a way of distributing the company's capacity to listen and to observe: all the teams have, by virtue of their recognition function, sensory capacities: to listen, to see, and to touch the customers and the environment. This list of sensory capacities should be extended to the digital world. The requirement that we formulated earlier, that a company should constantly listen to its environment, finds its solution in a distributed organization that multiplies interaction capacities. This way of thinking about the organization of companies, very much inspired by biology, has been masterfully theorized by the BetaCodex group.[23] Among the principles of network organization, we can retain the cellular organization, with a membrane and a nucleus, which brings to light the notion of a border in contact with the environment and the movement of information between

---

[21] Many management books refer to changes in command patterns in the military, but the book to read is *Team of Teams: New Rule of Engagement for a Complex World*, by General Stanley McChrystal.

[22] This need for a network is obvious for a large company, but it also exists for a startup that, if its objective is a complex TPM, needs to interact with a network of stakeholders.

[23] To discover the BetaCodex approach, whose motto is *"Bringing the Necessary Organizational Renaissance to Life,"* and the many supporting documents that have been made available for many years, see this website: https://betacodex.org.

the nucleus and the border. The "biological" organization combines the capacity of the global network to connect the entire company (paths exist between all teams, as in a hierarchical organization) with local connectivity that remains weak (not all teams talk to all teams) but is "situational" (teams that participate in the same customer situations are connected). Another principle from biology that distinguishes the new networks from hierarchical organizations is the existence of multiple (redundant) paths. Local connectivity (the number of other teams or actors connected to the "autonomous" team) remains low (to favor autonomy and speed) but favors short paths between teams working on the same customer experiences.[24]

2.3.3 Enterprise 3.0

I use the concept of Enterprise 3.0 to synthesize ideas common to most of the published works that deal with new forms of organization, capable of adapting to complexity.[25] After reading the books cited in the bibliography, it appeared to me that we could summarize these forms of organization with six principles, which find resonance and explanations in the theory of complex systems.[26] Here is a quick overview of these six principles:

1. A single vision, understood and shared by all, distributed to all components of the company. A single goal (holacracy) that each person can apply locally according to his or her context and means, in accordance with the **holomorphism** principle of complex systems.

---

[24] This topic is beyond the scope of this book. I refer you to my previous book or to my blog in which I talk about "small world" structures, these graphs that allow both greater resilience and better speed in the transmission of information. Network science considers *scale-free* networks, whose degree distribution is a *power law*, because they have the desired properties (resilience and small diameter) and they emerge in multiple situations, from biology to web networks. On this subject, read *Linked* by Albert-Laslo Barabasi, from which I reproduce here one of my favorite quotes: "*The power laws emerge—nature's unmistakable sign that chaos is departing in favor of order. The theory of phase transitions told us loud and clear that the road from disorder to order is maintained by the powerful forces of self-organization and is paved by power laws. It told us that power laws are not just another way of characterizing a system's behavior. They are the patent signature of self-organization in complex systems.*"

[25] There is an interesting parallel with the concept of Management 3.0, developed by Jurgen Appelo in his book *Management 3.0: Leading Agile Developers, Developing Agile Leaders*, that I will quote when I talk about agile governance. If the convergence on the "3.0" designation is fortuitous, the convergence on the diagnosis and principles is not, since I share the vast majority of my bibliography and part of my professional experience with Jurgen Appelo.

[26] The reader who wishes to deepen this concept of Enterprise 3.0 will find several online resources: the video and the slides of my presentation to X-SHS (the X-Sciences of Man and Society Group) or various explanatory posts on my blog.

2. This vision involves **co-developing** an experience with the **customer** that brings them true satisfaction. This is the central message of lean startup: in a complex environment, satisfaction and true innovation are co-constructed in an iterative way, in order to bring out a solution to a "problem" that is revealed progressively, as opposed to the complicated world for which the specification of the problem is accessible.
3. This co-development is ensured by a **network** of autonomous and cross-functional **teams**. These teams operate in a synchronous way (i.e., by applying a real physical collaboration with place and time unity).
4. "*Command and control*" is replaced by "*recognize and respond*"; forecasting is replaced by measurement and reaction. Enterprise 3.0 adopts the agile approach: working in small batches and constantly readjusting its actions according to the evolution of the environment.
5. Enterprise 3.0 is part of an ecosystem of partners, which is centered on a shared vision of its mission to the customer. Enterprise 3.0 is a **platform** that knows how to attract contributions from outside: it brings out a form of open innovation. To do this, it favors simplicity and excellence: doing few things but doing them as well as possible.
6. Enterprise 3.0 is **antifragile** because it continuously learns from changes in its environment. It organizes itself so that teams learn as much as possible from the problems they encounter. These difficulties are both opportunities to continuously enrich business skills but also chances to strengthen collaboration.

These six principles and their relationship to Salim Ismael's ExO are illustrated in Figure 2.1.

We have already met these principles; I will just comment and deepen the first and the last one. The concept of holomorphism represents the fact that a complex system is defined by its purpose. Holomorphism means that the global purpose of the system is reflected in the different components, in a local form, but keeping with the global vision. In other words, the strategy must be holistic and declarative, in the sense that the mission is unique and understood by all but locally declined and interpreted. We find the unifying principle of the MTP. We also find the warning of Isaac Getz: autonomy without (shared) vision is chaos.

The other concept that plays an important role in understanding digital transformation is antifragility, due to Nassim Taleb. A system is fragile if too much stress breaks it; it is antifragile if it becomes stronger and more resilient as a result of this stress. Biology provides us with many examples

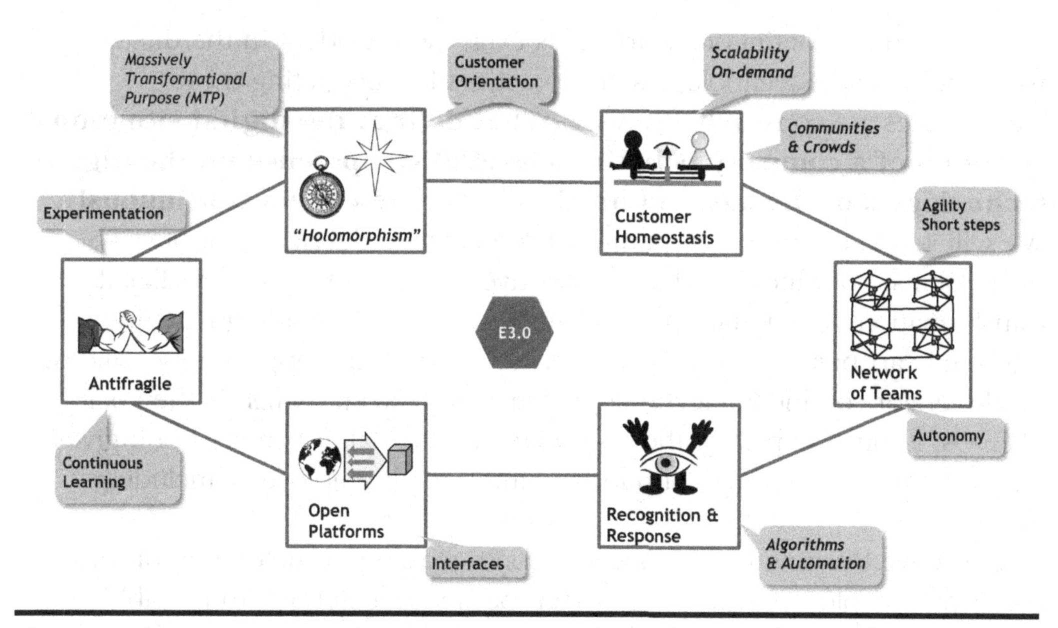

Figure 2.1 Enterprise 3.0—key features of an ExO.

of antifragile systems—I am thinking, for instance, about the growth of muscles, which is a reaction to the micro-breaks of effort. I encourage you to read the book *Antifragile: Things That Gain from Disorder* to understand all the interest and the scope of this concept. In a digital world full of uncertainty, hazards, and over-solicitations that are impossible to predict, antifragility is a sought-after property for both digital and human systems.[27]

2.3.4 Continuous Learning

The main mechanisms that make a system antifragile are learning and reinforcement. For the system to be antifragile, all "shocks"—over-solicitation, aggression, unforeseen incidents, failures—must be opportunities to learn and to reinforce, as opposed to wear and tear that would lead to a breakdown. A system that learns and develops by reinforcing itself from the difficulties encountered without its environment is more resilient, more adaptable, and thus better adapted to its environment. This is the desirable behavior for a company in a VUCA environment. Continuous learning is a necessity for companies in the modern world.

---

[27] To simplify, we can say that antifragility is illustrated by the saying "what doesn't kill me makes me stronger," a saying that applies to living systems and not to mechanical systems.

The need for continuous learning is even more evident in the digital world because the technologies and practices for integrating these technologies are constantly evolving. **What defines the digital situational potential of a company is both its level of competence on the digital technologies of the day and its ability to renew them continuously.**[28] We will see in the next two parts that the iterative development of digital skills, both individual and collective, is part of the core of digital transformation. Let's remember this analogy: the skill-building machine feeds the capability-building machine, which feeds the opportunity-building machine. For continuous technology learning to work, which is the goal of ExOs, it must be part of the corporate culture. Salim Ismail's book gives an important part to the continuous training of all employees, including managers.

Collective learning is not conceived on a closed perimeter, that of the company's employees, but on the open perimeter extended to possible partners. *ExOs* insist on *staff on-demand*—that is, the ability to seek out skills and talents from outside, in all forms: service providers, freelancers, skills marketplaces, and so on. The collective learning dimension is a compass for the internal/external balance of skills. Focusing too strongly on the internal side deprives the company of external talent and slows down its ability to absorb new technological waves. The open world learns and adapts faster by design. On the other hand, an approach that relies too much on external skills makes organizational and collective learning more difficult. A pool of *gig economy*[29] talents who come to join projects and leave as soon as the task is done does not have the long-term permanence needed to capitalize on what is learned during the build.

Learning is not only based on real events; it also develops during simulated situations. In his book *The Black Swan*, Nassim Taleb insists on two things: it is not possible to predict the major events that will disrupt the company, but it is possible to train to deal with the consequences. By practicing multiple crisis scenarios, the collective organization develops learning, reflexes, which will be useful if and when a situation similar to the scenario occurs. More generally, this practice will develop resilience

---

[28] We should not become extremist and say, as we sometimes hear, that today's skills and experts are no longer necessary or valued since everything is constantly changing and only the "ability to learn" counts. A quick tour of the Silicon Valley champions shows that today's technical skills are necessary, developed, and highly valued.

[29] "Gig" is a colloquial word, which comes from the entertainment world and refers to a (small) temporary job.

skills that will be useful even if the event that occurs is different from the training scenario. This is the tradition of *war games*, where the objective is not to prepare for a battle scenario that may occur or not but to develop the collective skills of the organization.

2.4 Culture Change and Change Management

2.4.1 Which Change for a Digital Transformation?

These two chapters have enabled us to characterize the challenges of digital transformation. They have shown that it is a profound transformation of the company's objectives, organization, and working methods. We can summarize the major points that create a change in the daily functioning of the company by the following list:

- The voice of the customer is invited into the product development cycle, and this voice is amplified by the power of crowds and communities.
- The profitability of a new service or product is an emergent property, which cannot be planned in advance.[30]
- The continuous and accelerated renewal of the underlying digital technologies challenges the company in terms of the necessary skills.
- The rapid but uncertain acceleration of the potential of digital technologies, such as AI, implies risk-taking.
- The direction of information flows is reversed because what happens outside the company is more important than what happens inside.
- Decisions must be made mostly "on the ground" (i.e., in the presence of their context) instead of reasoning about abstractions.

The change we have just outlined with this summary list is complex; it is difficult—especially for managers—and it takes time. In almost all large companies, this change is underway; it is not finished. For managers, it is a double change about the meaning of the word "strategy" and their operational role. Strategy is changing in meaning because it is adapting to the unpredictability and complexity of the digital world and because it is becoming holomorphic—that is, the declarative form

[30] Because of the central role of usage, even if, of course, some economic dimensions, such as pricing or resource consumption, can be planned.

of a vision that is interpreted locally in order to take action. Operational management changes when applied to a network of autonomous teams; the manager becomes a referent of the strategy, a coach for the team and a pivotal element of the company network.[31] The change in practices, tools, and working methods will be the subject of the next chapters. In a way, because this book seeks to explain the "why" of digital transformation and to describe the practices and capabilities to be put in place, it constitutes a tool for change management.

The term "digital transformation" is not insignificant; it is indeed a transformation, in the medium and long term, as we saw in Section 2.2, of the company's culture, practices, methods, and even values. The associated change management is not that of a "project mode," with a beginning, an end, and clear objectives; it is about transformation management, day after day, over an open period of time. As in all transformation programs, the two essential dimensions that must be supported and nurtured are motivation and commitment.

2.4.2 Resistance to Change

One of my favorite books on change management is *Change or Die: The Three Keys to Change at Work and in Life* by Alan Deutschman.[32] Its mission, as described in the title, is to replace three biases about change drivers (3F: *facts, fear, and force*) with three principles (3R: *relate, repeat, and reframe*). To summarize, **facts** are not enough to trigger change unless they are personally related to the individual. **Fear** is a negative emotion, and it does not fuel change in a sustainable way. It is essential to create positive emotions, desires. **Force** does not work: change must always start from the individual—from a management point of view; it is, therefore, necessarily

[31] The topic of changing the role of the manager is beyond the scope of this book. It is extensively covered in the works I cite in the bibliography and in my previous book. Because of the connected network structure of teams, the manager is not only a coach; he is also an ambassador: he represents his team—a task shared with other roles—to other teams and other actors in the company.

[32] This is an exciting book about change, with poignant examples from medicine and offender retraining. The introduction begins with this question: what would you do if change were a matter of life and death? In the case of a category of patients who are on their third (or more) cardiac event, lifestyle change determines their survivability. Change is possible, with proven spectacular results, yet more than 90% refuse the change after a few months and return to their habits that lead them to death: *"If you look at people after coronary-artery bypass grafting two years later, ninety percent of them have not changed their lifestyle. And that's been studied over and over and over again. And so we're missing some link here. Even though they know they have a very bad teasing and they know they should change their lifestyle, for whatever reason, they can't."*

a *bottom-up* approach! What can be *top-down* is the creation of favorable conditions for change, the management of emergence. The first R in *relate* means that a strong and aspirational **relationship** must be created with the individual who needs to change. The change manager must "sell you this aspirational state and convince you that you are capable of achieving it." The importance of motivation and commitment is essential to change; it is primarily a personal process. Dean Ornish has a beautiful saying in the book: "People do not resist change, they resist being changed."

Repeat logically indicates that change involves **repetition**, learning, developing new habits and skills: "change involves learning." *Reframe* means that change involves **rebuilding** the way you think about yourself, your situation, and your life—*you have to rebuild your mental models.* As with methods of projecting into the future, change involves looking at the world in a new way, from the point of view that is made possible when change is accomplished.

One of the recurring themes of the book is the importance of action and activity as a source of thought education: "*It is obvious that what we believe and what we feel influences how we act. This is common sense. But the equation also works in the other direction: the way we act influences what we believe and feel.*" Activity is what makes it possible to develop a new point of view: "*Reframing is not something that happens just by listening to another person explain a new way of seeing things. You have to do things in a new way before you can think in a new way.*" One of the experts interviewed in the book is even clearer: "*Change is a verb and should remain so. Change happens in action. You have to act to change.*" This brings to mind the famous quote from Confucius: "*What I hear I forget, what I see I remember, and what I do I understand.*" Change management is an essential subject. I refer you to the leading book in the field, *Leading Change*, by John Kotter, who writes, "*Change management is important. Without competent management, the transformation process can go off the rails.*"

2.4.3 Motivation and Commitment

Motivation in a transformation situation, and more generally in a complex situation, must come from the individual and not from the system. There are multiple scientific experiments that show that extrinsic motivation, whether it is rewards, such as performance bonuses or pressure through sanctions for failure, works well on simple tasks but no longer works on complex tasks. Daniel Pink, in his bestseller, *Drive: The Surprising Truth about what Motivates Us*, shows us that what works in complex situations is to develop the intrinsic motivation of the employees of the company. Intrinsic motivation is fueled by three factors: the **purpose** (meaning of the work, the fact of participating in a collective work that goes beyond individual action—this is why ExOs use MTPs), the **autonomy** allocated to each person in the achievement of his or her objectives, and the **mastery** of his or her professional skills.[33] Daniel Pink's term "mastery" evokes the pleasure of the musician or the professional athlete in mastering the quality of his or her gesture—one could speak of developing professional excellence through the development of skills. Daniel Pink's book is a little dated, but it remains a reference for understanding and developing intrinsic motivation in employees. His recommendations are valid in any complex environment; they are essential and remarkably relevant in the digital world.

To go from motivation to commitment, I am greatly inspired by the book *Stratégie Modèle Mental: casser le code des organisations pour les remettre en movement* (*Mental model strategy: break organization codes to reset them in motion*), by Philippe Silberzahn and Béatrice Rousset. Motivation is a condition, but it is not enough to get people moving. The mental model, which we mentioned above, is the representation that we make of reality based on beliefs and hypotheses. In order to change, it is necessary to leave some mental models and adopt those that allow us to work differently. For example, in the case of digital transformation, to emulate winning companies, such as GAFA or digital unicorns, it is not enough to adopt their practices or tools; we must appropriate their mental models.[34] The *Mental Model Strategy* book proposes five "new models" that correspond remarkably well to the change management challenges we posed at the beginning of this Section 2. The first model is to learn to start (right now) with what you have rather than making plans for what you should have to get started. This is one of the pillars of effectuation, an approach we will discuss again in the next chapter. The second model is the *affordable loss* model, which replaces

---

[33] The importance of lifelong learning and the joy of learning that contributes to engagement is beautifully illustrated in the book *The Progress Principle: Using Small Wins to Ignite Joy, Engagement, and Creativity at Work*, by Teresa Amabile and Steven Kramer.

[34] Here we find a classic idea from books on change management, such as those by A. Deutchsmann or J. Coplen: in order to change, one must start thinking as if the change had already been accomplished. Deutchsmann or J. Coplen's *habits*: in order to change, one has to start thinking as if the change had already been accomplished. The book by P. Silberzahn and B. Rousset goes further and proposes new mental models that are very well suited to the implementation of digital transformation. The concept of mental model is one of the nuggets of the bestseller *The Fifth Discipline*, by Peter Senge.

business models and their returns on investment for digital projects whose value creation, as we have pointed out, is emergent. Since we don't know if the value will be there, we must work with a constrained budget, a quantity of time, effort, and money that we are willing to invest "to see" but with a great deal of freedom within those boundaries. The third model focuses on the possibility of obtaining commitments from one's stakeholders, while the fourth model invites one to "take advantage" of surprises and to accept the unpredictability of the world as an opportunity. Here we recognize the idea that the company that has succeeded in its digital transformation has a new "relationship with the world" and lives in homeostasis with permanent change. We also find the antifragility concept: taking advantage of hazards is a strategy for development and resilience. The last model consists of "creating your context"—that is, building an environment favorable to the development of your products and services. It is precisely a model of "gardening by small actions" to manage emergence. We recognize here the Chinese model of building the potential of a situation. Employee commitment to digital transformation is an emergent property,[35] which is *cultivated* and not *designed* in a change management program.

2.4.4 A Culture without Borders

If the challenge of digital transformation is important, we must not rely solely on the internal resources of the company. The concept of homeostasis is part of the solution: transformation can be achieved in part through osmosis, through contact with the external environment. In these two chapters, we have insisted on the importance of opening the borders with external stakeholders, of learning to listen to them better in order to be able to collaborate. This openness is an important factor in transformation. Co-creation with customers is an opportunity to reinvent the business in the digital world. Contact with business partners is an excellent way to learn how to build platforms. Collaborating with an extensive network of external talents and developers is a continuous learning opportunity to develop one's own technical skills. Participation in *open-source* communities is the most efficient way to develop your own best practices for software. Digital transformation must, therefore, resemble the company's target organization:

---

[35] On the subject of engagement in large companies, read also *Scaling Up Excellence*, by R. Sutton and H. Rao, which identifies the specific difficulties linked to the size of companies, in particular disempowerment and standardization.

it must be distributed, it must be based on autonomous teams, and it must be oriented from the outside in.

The development of software and technology culture is essential. It concerns both the actors of the company's digital production (for example, all the IT and service development professions) but also all the company's employees and especially their managers. This culture is what makes internal and external exchanges more fluid, reduces transaction costs in the sense of Coase,[36] and increases trust, thus accelerating exchanges. Many companies that profess to put a lot of energy into recruiting and training new digital talents do not understand that they already have these talents but that the rigidity of the culture and organization prevents them from expressing their skills. This is especially true for younger employees, as the vast majority of engineers coming out of school have a well-developed digital life of their own and often already have some experience. This also applies to external hires: very often employees who are poached from digital companies do not succeed in integrating and then resign because the company does not have the necessary conditions to use their talents.

This book, like those cited in the bibliography and in particular *Exponential Organizations*, seeks to describe a target organization and the ideal processes, methods, and tools for the company to succeed in its digital transformation. But all of this is not enough to succeed. Culture, which is more difficult to grasp—a combination of mental models, shared knowledge, and values—plays a fundamental role. Bringing in external talents doesn't work if the culture doesn't allow them to thrive and contribute. That's why general education—especially in technology and software—is a critical component of digital transformation. I'll close here with a quote from the *Lean Enterprise*[37] book we'll encounter in the next chapter, which highlights the role of culture and management: "*The only path to a culture of continuous improvement is to create an environment in which learning new skills and becoming better at what you do is seen*

[36] The lack of a shared technical culture leads to over-contracting. This is particularly important in France, where the project manager / project owner scheme is strongly anchored in our mental models and perpetuates a Taylorism that considerably slows down the penetration of digital transformation.

[37] I will often quote two books with similar titles but different content: *Lean Enterprise*, by Barry O'Reilly, Joanne Molesky, and Jez Humble, and *The Lean Enterprise: How Corporations Can Innovate Like Startups*, by Trevor Owens and Obie Fernandez. The former talks more about lean startup and digital transformation, while the latter addresses more digital systems and the DevOps approach.

as value creation in itself and is encouraged by management and business leaders, thereby reducing learning anxiety."

Summary

1. Digital homeostasis is the process of digital transformation that keeps the digital experience up to the expectations of the company's customers (2.1.1).
2. The reversal of power in favor of customer communities is sometimes a challenge, but it is also a real opportunity to allow the company to know them better (2.1.3).
3. What transforms a company is not adopting an agile method for the development of its digital platforms or its IS; it is adopting agility as a strategic approach (2.1.3).
4. Digital transformation: over the long term, to build the company's digital potential in order to support agile, rapid, and opportunistic action when the customer opportunity arises (2.2.2).
5. Customer orientation is the best way to align various actors or functions in the company towards a common goal (2.2.3).
6. The constant appropriation of the continuous progress of intelligent data processing methods is one of the strategic challenges of digital transformation (2.3.1).
7. What characterizes complex situations is that recognition and reaction are intimately intertwined, even indistinguishable, because they are part of the same process (2.3.2).
8. What defines the digital situational potential of a company is both its level of competence on the digital technologies of the day and its capacity to renew them continuously (2.3.4).
9. The change associated with digital transformation is complex, it is difficult—especially for managers—and it takes time (2.4.1).
10. The development of software and technological culture is essential. It concerns not only the actors of the company's digital production but also all the company's employees and especially their managers (2.4.4).

Chapter 3

Lean Startup

Lean Principles Applied to Co-Creation

Lean startup has been mentioned several times in the previous chapters. We will dedicate this chapter to it because it is a remarkable and complete model of innovation in the digital world. *Lean startup* is both a concept and a book, due to Eric Ries,[1] but it has deeper roots. *Lean startup* is the result of a combination of (1) a formalization of a number of principles that pre-existed in Silicon Valley, notably in the writings and courses of Steve Blank, which Eric Ries followed, and (2) a remarkable work of modeling and analyzing successes and failures through the *lean* approach, which is Eric Ries's essential contribution. The first section of this chapter will focus on the roots of lean startup, which are the principles of innovation in a digital world that we have already started to discuss. The next section will focus on the core contribution of lean startup: the systematization and optimization of the *customer insight* discovery process. The last two sections will offer a more practical description of the implementation of *lean startup* in a large company, based on my own experience.

[1] The book *The Lean Startup: How Today's Entrepreneurs Use Continuous Innovation to Create Radically Successful Businesses* was published in 2011 and has grown considerably, turning into a practice carried by many authors and speakers. I will have the opportunity to cite a few other books, but I encourage the reader to discover the wealth of associated educational content and books on the web. Of course, we must start with Eric Ries's book, for which I had the pleasure of co-writing the preface with Michael Ballé, for its French edition. Steve Blank's book *The Four Steps of Epiphany* was published later (2013) even if his ideas precede those of Eric Ries.

DOI: 10.4324/9781003272816-4

3.1 Innovation in the Digital World

3.1.1 Innovation Is about Execution

I was lucky enough to take over the responsibility of services at Bouygues Telecom in 2006 and to be able to observe this digital innovation ecosystem for several years. I worked in very good conditions, with excellent teams within an extended ecosystem of partners. Thanks to an outstanding innovation team, we have designed and developed a large number of innovative services, each of them coming from a jubilant phase of creativity. Looking back, two things stand out: all our colleagues at other telephone operators, in France, Europe, and the United States, had more or less the same ideas, at more or less the same time. Moreover, ten years later, a good part of these ideas exists successfully as applications on our cell phones; on the other hand, they were not brought by telephone operators but by innovative digital players, most often startups. In the digital world, the idea doesn't matter; it's the execution that counts. Innovating is not a matter of producing ideas; innovating is doing. What characterizes the execution of excellent digital companies is software competence—in the broadest sense, from design to production—and speed of execution, allowing multiple iterations.

In *Lean Enterprise*, we can read a similar testimony from Eric Boulanger, CTO of Neopost: "*Anyone can have ideas. What makes the difference is the execution. People tell you: 'I had an idea, but someone else did it.'*" The difference is precisely the action. This idea that in the digital world, with all the complexity and richness we have discussed in the previous chapters, value creation requires to act, instead of trying to anticipate through thinking, is old and precedes *lean startup*. In 2009, a group of innovators produced the *Pretotyping Manifesto*,[2] which states in particular that "innovators are more important than ideas," "it is better to do than to talk," "now is better than later," and "data is more important than opinions." Similar mottos can be found in GAFA or in the famous IETF formula:[3] "*We believe in rough consensus and in running code.*" The value creation of digital innovation is a learning cycle, and you have to jump in

[2] I recommend that you read the *Pretotyping Manifesto* on the web—for example, at https://sites.google.com/a/pretotyping.org/www/the-pretotyping-manifesto-1. This idea of a pretotype is the opposite of a prototype and is the ancestor of the MVP. A pretotype is simpler than a product, but it works "for real" in the hands of real users.

[3] Read the Wikipedia article (https://en.wikipedia.org/wiki/Rough_consensus) on the motto of the Internet Engineering Task Force, which is the organization that governs Internet standards.

quickly to learn from your customers. This idea that innovation happens in execution is more disruptive than one might think for countries with a conceptualization culture, such as France. We shall see in the rest of the chapter that this does not detract from the importance of creativity and the techniques used to generate ideas, but what matters is access to real users, to future customers.

This idea is remarkably illustrated by numerous examples in Furr and Dyer's *The Innovator's Method.* They cite Intuit, which created its Intuit Labs **to give innovation teams direct access to real customers.** Access to customers is often an insurmountable barrier in many large companies due to the Taylorization of roles between different departments. Yet all digital innovation experts agree with this statement: "Teams need to conduct experiments with potential customers if they hope to discover the *job-to-be-done* and then build the right solution—*nail the solution.*" Giving access quickly and easily to different types of customers facilitates a rapid experimentation cycle. This access needs to happen as early as possible, before the solution is developed, including in the form of a website that allows for "smoke tests"—making it seem like the product already exists to gather initial feedback.

3.1.2 Innovation Requires Iteration

The second fundamental idea of digital innovation is that no one is clairvoyant enough to guess the experience that will bring true customer satisfaction. Only an iterative process of trial and error in contact with the customer will allow this experience to emerge. This is the principle of co-development described in Chapter 1. The complexity and uncertainty of the digital world mean that innovating is fundamentally risky. The goal of iteration is to rapidly accumulate experiences that reduce uncertainty. It is, therefore, necessary to iterate quickly but methodically to capitalize on advances as well as failures. As the authors of *Lean Enterprise* point out, "*conducting experiments is difficult and requires great discipline. Developing the right experiments requires being innovative and thinking things through. By nature, people tend to jump to solutions instead of first agreeing on the goals that define the problem.*" This idea that iteration and rapid exploration of paths is a necessary condition for innovation is also not new. Thomas Watson, founder of IBM, had this famous quote: "*If you want to increase your success rate, double your failure rate.*" What is specific to the digital world is that, on the one hand, this advice is becoming mandatory—a consequence of complexity—and that the exploration process has been formalized, precisely by the *lean startup* approach.

One of the favorite aphorisms of the digital world and startups is "fail fast," made famous by large Silicon Valley companies. It is often misunderstood and used to justify giving up quickly if a project doesn't succeed—all the more so because we operate on a Greek model of thinking that seeks to make an impact on the world. "Fail fast" is a principle of systemics, which applies to *cycle time* and not to *lead time*. In other words, the aphorism is to be understood in a world of continuous iterations, and it means that one must know how to fail as quickly as possible because one must iterate several times to succeed. The more what we try to achieve is ambitious, the more we need to shorten the duration of iterations.

In 2008, while participating in a conference organized by a Silicon Valley venture capitalist, one of the most experienced partners explained to me that after twenty years of experience in software startups, he saw no correlation between the quality of the solution, at the time the startup came to raise money, and future success, but that the latter was instead strongly correlated to the ability to continuously adapt this piece of software to the feedback of the first customers. I could pick examples in each of the books cited in this chapter. I will talk about *Hacking Growth: How Today's Fastest-Growing Companies Drive Breakout*, by Sean Ellis and Morgan Brown, because it analyzes methods—which we'll come back to in Section 3.4—used by famous companies like Twitter, Facebook, Pinterest, Uber, or LinkedIn. Each company is different, but there is a common body of methods for designing and developing digital innovations, and iteration is part of that foundation: "*It wasn't the immaculate design of a product that was going to change the world, nor was it a single insight, a moment of extraordinary luck, or a touch of genius that allowed these companies to achieve spectacular success quickly. In fact, success was achieved by the methodical application of idea generation and rapid testing, for the development and marketing of their product, and by the use of data on the behavior of their users to select the ideas that brought growth in usage.*"

3.1.3 The Business Model Is an Outcome, Not a Prerequisite

The business model—the *business case*—only exists when usage is established, and this emerges from the innovation process and cannot be presupposed. This is the consequence of the complexity and the multiple reinforcement loops we mentioned in Chapter 1. **A working value**

creation model is the result of the innovation process, whether it is a startup or a product or service line from a large company and not a prerequisite to launch the innovation project. Of course, there exist value-creation hypotheses (to be validated or invalidated), as well as a budget to be respected at the beginning of the innovation process, but a *business case* produced too early is a fantasy, to quote from the book *The Lean Enterprise*: "*The business model becomes a science-fiction story based on a universe that is poorly understood—or simply does not exist!*"

The alternative practice, in order to manage expenses and resource consumption in an uncertain situation, is to reason in terms of *acceptable loss*. The acceptable loss is the budget that you can allocate to an experiment, an investigation, or the development of a product, without complete failure being a problem at the end. The idea of managing investments with acceptable loss is not new in the world of venture capital. What is new is to use it as a method of managing investments in innovation and services for large companies that are used to the business model and the return on investment. The practice of *affordable loss* is combined with portfolio management, which allows for the allocation of "tokens" of varying sizes based on risk analysis (potential gain vs. difficulty).

Acceptable loss management is also one of the entrepreneurial practices highlighted by the theory of effectuation that we encountered in the previous chapter.[4] Effectuation was theorized by Saras Saraswathy, based on the analysis of forty-five successful entrepreneurs. Through in-depth interviews and role-playing, she was able to define four characteristics of the way entrepreneurs think, solve problems, and act. **Acceptable loss management** is one of these principles; **starting immediately with one's own resources** is another. Effectuation can be seen as the rational and scientific foundation of the fundamental axiom that to innovate is to do. I quote Philippe Silberzahn: "*More than the idea, it is the action around it that counts . . . The experience has been confirmed many times. The origin of the entrepreneurial project is not the idea, it's you.*" On this point, there is a total coherence between effectuation, *pretotyping*, and *lean startup*. But

[4] On effectuation, I recommend reading the book *Effectuation: Entrepreneurship Principles for All*, by Philippe Silberzahn. This book is a reference for understanding the effectuation paradigm, which seems to me to be the most concrete and effective way to absorb a part of the entrepreneurial culture in the company. The four principles of effectuation are traditionally described as follows: "*Bird-in-Hand: You have to create solutions with the resources available here and now,*" "*Lemonade principle: Mistakes and surprises are inevitable and can be used to look for new opportunities,*" "*Crazy Quilt: Entering into new partnerships can bring the project new funds and new directions,*" and "*Affordable loss: You should only invest as much as you are willing to lose.*"

there is even more to the first principle of effectuation: you have to start from what you are and what you have, in the broadest sense: "*Effectuation does not consist in starting from the goals to determine the means necessary to reach them, but on the contrary in considering the means you have to determine the possible goals.*" This should remind us of François Julien's ideas about efficiency and situational potential. The entrepreneur is "Chinese"—he adapts and takes advantage of opportunities in the environment—and not "Greek"—he does not try to impose his plan on the world.

3.1.4 The Playing Field Is Determined by the Skills

As the fable says, "there is no point in running; you have to start on time." It is not enough to launch into action, to repeat the iterations, or even to carry out all the steps of the *lean startup* process that we will detail later, to succeed.[5] To succeed, you must also carefully choose your playing field, the one in which you are uniquely qualified. In the book *The Lean Enterprise*, the authors propose to think about an *innovation thesis*, which is the perimeter of ideas or services for which the company has a strong interest (immediate or strategic, in the long term), markets on which it is legitimate and can use existing positions as levers, and important competitive advantages for the realization: resources, experience, skills, and so on. This approach allows, on the one hand, to concentrate and filter innovation ideas to identify groups with a critical mass of value (for the client) and, on the other hand, to ask the question of differentiation—that is, how to value or build or even acquire the skills and knowledge that will form a decisive and sustainable competitive advantage. This approach is, of course, linked to the notion of capabilities: it builds on existing capabilities and guides the construction of future capabilities. To come back to our fable: running is about short time; it means churning quickly iteration cycles to innovate; "leaving on time" means having built the capabilities to win the race that is earned over the long term. Capabilities determine the speed of execution as well as the ability to learn, so the long-time perspective is essential for the success of the short-time opportunity.

This idea of the playing field is found in a key tool, the *lean canvas*, or its ancestor, the *business model canvas*,[6] whose use has become

[5] A number of authors, including my friend Philippe Silberzahn, criticize *lean startup* because it is too often presented as "the method to succeed in digital innovation". This method does not exist because the uncertainty is too great and because it is necessary to succeed in finding the environment in which the innovative actor is uniquely qualified.

[6] About this tool, I recommend reading *Running Lean*, by Ash Maurya.

a best practice of digital innovation. The lean canvas proposes nine questions and organizes how to structure the answers on an A4 sheet, which is easy to share and to continuously improve. One of these questions is "What is my unfair advantage?" The *unfair advantage* is the advantage over my competitors that I have gained in a non-repeatable way. It is unfair because competitors cannot acquire it by simple effort or investment. The presence of this question forces the digital entrepreneur to enter the race only if she has unique differentiating advantages: a patent that can be protected, a unique skill, exclusive content. This question is essential because the digital world is deeply competitive, with a high level of excellence. This excellence is twofold: on unique and differentiating domains, which have just been said here, and also on all the technological domains of the digital world that are mentioned in the book, from data processing or AI to the fundamentals of web and mobile site design.

3.2 Lean Startup: Formalizing the Knowledge Creation Process

3.2.1 A Machine for Validating Insights

The *lean startup* approach consists of applying the optimization principles of *lean manufacturing* to the repeatable part of the innovation process. To put it simply, applying *lean* consists of eliminating what does not bring value (this is called *value stream mapping* and leads to the elimination of waste designated by *muda*), working on reducing cycle time (the *lead time*), and using the continuous improvement methods of total quality management (*A3 problem-solving, PDCA,* and *kaizen*). The generic innovation process consists of making a hypothesis about what the customer expects, producing a creative solution to meet this expectation, producing the product, putting it in the hands of the customer, and observing that the use of the product corresponds to the expectation postulated as a hypothesis. To consider the "innovation starting point"—whether it is the detection of pain points or latent needs—as a hypothesis requires to be humble in a complex and uncertain world. Waiting for confirmation through customer usage is the realistic consequence of what we saw in the first chapter. Very often, this process will fail and deliver a product that does not satisfy the customer. The *paradigm shift* proposed by Eric Ries is to consider that this process is a factory for producing *validated insights*, in all cases, whether or not the product meets customer expectations. The objective of the innovation process is to better understand the needs and expectations of its customers on an ongoing basis. The *lean* approach will then allow us to shorten and formalize this process, to iterate more quickly in order to better understand our customers. This is a "small batch" approach. Decisions are validated thanks to data through getting in touch with the customer as quickly as possible. In response to the lack of *business case* and the fact that traditional product development metrics do not allow us to manage the innovation process in the digital world, Eric Ries proposes the principle of *innovation accounting*, which consists of formulating hypotheses about customer expectations, formalizing the observations that validate or invalidate these hypotheses with metrics, and building the *innovation ledger* with positive inputs (an experience validates a customer need) and negative inputs (another experience teaches us that a particular solution does not meet a customer need). More precisely, Eric Ries proposes to formulate value creation hypotheses for the customer. As in any scientific experiment, the ability to learn is directly linked to the care taken in formulating it. The sum of the validated elements of value creation models will feed the business model of the solution

Lean startup consists in iterating, to accumulate knowledge, in order to progressively build a product, a service, or a satisfying experience for the customer and the associated value creation model. However, this process does not necessarily converge, especially if the negative experiences outnumber the positive ones. If the outcome is mostly negative, the entire effort should be viewed as a learning step in a learning curve and move on. But if the outcome is mixed, it is possible to extract a new value-creating hypothesis from the accumulated knowledge. This is what Eric Ries popularized under the name of "pivot," which has become an inescapable term in the world of startups and innovation. Among the various books cited in this chapter, I recommend *The Innovator's Method*, which contains a very interesting chapter devoted to the art of the pivot, with lots of practical advice backed up by metrics. You may read about the story of Aardvark, which illustrates the tension between the mission of the startup (or the product) and the feedback of the users. In the case of Aardvark, customer demands conflicted with the "strategic positioning" of the product. This caused a delay in addressing some requests—and lost an opportunity to a competitor. I appreciate this testimonial because it is a situation I have experienced. The testimonies of the first users are full of "nuggets," which are often rejected for so-called "strategic" reasons (they do not fit the original vision of the product), whereas those who manufacture the product would know perfectly well how to carry out these evolutions.

3.2.2 Three Steps: Design, Pretotype, and Grow

The innovation process can be broken down into several stages, which are also iterative processes. It is, therefore, a big loop, made up of small loops. To simplify, I suggest you start with the decomposition in three steps, which correspond to the PDC of the PDCA:[7] the **design**, which poses the hypothesis of value creation for the customer and defines the experience of the associated product; the **pretotyping**, which consists of making a minimal product, with just what is needed for the customer to use it and give his opinion; and **growth hacking**, which consists of listening, analyzing, and working with its customers.

This first *design* step is twofold: the customer problem must be characterized, which is often referred to as the job-to-be-done before moving on to the solution design. All experts insist on the fact that one should not launch into the design and realization of the solution without having properly characterized the problem (i.e., the *pain points* that one wishes to solve). For example, I quote Furr and Dyer:[8] *"Although it may feel 'slower' to start with the customer problem rather than the solution, you save time by deeply understanding the customer's job-to-be-done."*

The most popular term in the lean startup approach is MVP (*minimum viable product*), which corresponds to the notion of pretotype.[9] Every word of MVP count: the MVP is a *product* that can be put in the hands of a customer (it is not a prototype, it can be simple, but it should not be fragile). An MVP is *viable* if it solves the customer problem identified in the

[7] *Plan, do, check, act.* Here, *plan* means "design," *do* means "pretotype," and *check* means "listen to customers and measure usage." The *act* part consists of deciding on the next iteration level, going back to the pretotype, going back to the design or pivoting.

[8] In this book, we find the interesting concept of *pain-storming*, the application of brainstorming methods to the characterization of pain points: *"Pain-storming involves creating a customer's journey line to understand how customers now complete a task and identify their main pain points (and emotions) along the way"*. On the job-to-be-done, read *Competing Against Luck: The Story of Innovation and Customer Choice*, by Clayton Christensen et al.

[9] The term "MVP" has become so popular that it is used in multiple ways. In this book, I use it for the product phase (second stage) and not for the prototypes that are made in the first design stage—hence the reference to the (older) concept of pretotype, which is opposed to prototype. Here, MVP refers to a real product.

first phase. Its role is to initiate the process of collecting customer feedback, which can only happen if the customer sees the practical value of the MVP from day one. The MVP is *minimal* because it is "as simple as possible, but no more," to paraphrase the Albert Einstein quote. The M represents the *lean* application of cycle time minimization.

There are several possible ways to break down the third part.[10] One of the key moments in the overall process is *product market fit* (PMF), the moment when usage is strong enough and growing to validate the value creation model. This is also known as traction, the point at which the product's relevance is such that it "pulls" the market (and attracts customers). The first way to break down the process is to consider that the MVP grows until it achieves this traction, in which case the third phase is growth, or how to use *growth hacking* techniques to accelerate the natural growth observed. In terms of investment, this approach makes a lot of sense: the initial phase is low-cost and most often involves hidden costs; the pretotyping phase is an entrepreneurial phase based on the principle of *affordable loss*—you have to know how to stop—and the last phase is an investment phase, facilitated by the existence of the PMF (which is what most venture capitalists ask for in order to invest).

There is another way of organizing—the one in Figure 3.1—by grouping everything that concerns the analysis and use of customer feedback in the third "*growth*" step. This second approach has a double logic. On the one hand, it identifies very clear milestones from the development viewpoint: we enter MVP mode at sprint zero when the development team begins work, and we leave it when the product is released. This brings to mind the famous quote by Reid Hoffman, the CEO of LinkedIn: "*If you're not embarrassed by the first version of your product, you've launched it too late.*" On the other hand, the set of methods for analyzing customer feedback and continuously improving the value proposition—which we will discuss next under the name of *growth hacking*—is quite similar before and after obtaining PMF.[11]

[10] During my experience at AXA's Digital Agency, we used both variants. The first one is due to my colleague Stéphane Delbecque, and it is the one that received the most interest on social networks because it better fits the market vision. I personally use the second one because it is better adapted to the internal vision, from a large company's viewpoint.

[11] In the book *The Innovator's Method*, there are five phases: *insight* and *problem* correspond to our first phase of design, *solution* corresponds to the realization of the MVP, *business model* represents this first stage of growth hacking to obtain the MVP, and *scale* corresponds to the second phase of growth hacking.

3.2.3 Running Lean: Keeping the Promise

One of the fundamental tools of lean startup is the notion of *unique value proposition* (UVP), which is the statement made to the customer about the problem to be solved and of what the solution will bring him. The parallel with *unique selling propositions*, which are a classic marketing concept, is obvious, but the focus is on usage, experience, and the story to be told to the customer. A good UVP should tell the world what you do, offer a *pitch* that target users can understand in ten seconds and finally offer an immediate benefit and make it clear why this proposition is unique and different. An important part of the *running lean* book is dedicated to UVP and the care with which they must be identified.[12] Ash Maurya defines the UVP as a promise you make to the customer. Finding your UVP is a big job, requiring an iterative approach and a lot of questioning. According to Ash Maurya: "*UVPs are difficult to produce satisfactorily because you have to distill the essence of the product into a few words that will become the hook of the online communication tools—especially the landing pages.*"

UVPs form the link between the *design* phase in which they are produced and the second phase of MVP realization. In the words of Ash Maurya: "***The role of your UVP is to produce a compelling promise. The role of the MVP is to deliver on that promise.***" Because MVP mode of development is iterative, and because the agile methods we'll discuss in Part 2 provide a lot of flexibility, it's easy to get sidetracked during development. My experience of more than ten years of service development is that it is very frequent that the numerous stages of backlog rewriting and the creativity, which is natural in iterative development, lead to forgetting the initial ambition. The UVP is a compass during this phase of development. The main lesson of Ash Maurya's book is not to start developing solutions during the design phase and even more so when starting the MVP until the problem and the UVP are perfectly characterized and validated with future customers. In other words, lean startup is not just about "going fast"; **it's about validating stages where iterations are easy and low-cost before moving on to stages where each iteration is more expensive**. In my personal experience, as a developer and as a manager, this is what requires the most discipline.

---

[12] If Eric Ries' book is the founding "textbook" of lean startup, Ash Maurya's *Running Lean* is the indispensable "tutorial book" for putting it into practice. I also strongly recommend the online courses of Oussama Amar, as part of *The Family*'s MOOC, which details with many examples what is a UVP and how to build it.

The UVP promise must be unique, that is, original and differentiating. As Guy Kawasaki points out in the bestseller *The Art of the Start 2.0: The Time-Tested, Battle-Hardened Guide for Anyone Starting Anything*, you have to describe your promise in a way that is opposite to what your competitors are proposing, in order to differentiate yourself; otherwise, the positioning is incomprehensible and therefore useless. Guy Kawasaki also recommends working carefully on your message and choosing a precise target, focusing all your energy on one subject: "*While it is already difficult to create and communicate one message, many startups make the mistake of producing several for fear of being categorized as a niche product.*" This message must be transformed into a story to touch its audience through its emotions. We will come back to the role of emotions for design in the last section. The communication of the promise is much more than a rational approach; it must provoke emotion and adhesion. I quote Guy Kawasaki again: "*People want more than information. They are already overwhelmed by too much information. They want to have 'faith'—faith in your company, in your product, in your success and in the story you are telling. It's faith, not facts, that moves mountains.*"

3.2.4 Nail It, Then Scale It

The MVP's solution must have solved the problem perfectly before moving on to deployment and growth investments. This is what the phrase "nail it, then scale it" means, taken from the book *The Innovator's Method*. This is one of the development mottos of Silicon Valley startups. The authors suggest using the NPS (*net promoter score*)[13] as a metric and verifying that you have exceeded the value of 10 before wanting to grow the customer base: "*So start by shooting for a 9 or 10 NPS score with 10 people, and then you can think about progressing to the hundredth.*" NPS works at all scales, with a small user community and a mature product. Investments in communication and viral marketing should wait until the NPS for these first users is really good (above 40, which is not easy when you start). Reaching this NPS value is the first step toward the PMF we mentioned above and marks the beginning of important investments.

[13] We recall here that the NPS is the difference between the percentage of very satisfied users (a vote of 9 or 10 on a scale of 0 to 10) and unsatisfied users (0 to 6). Starting at 10, it is necessarily to have an enthusiastic user in the first test group.

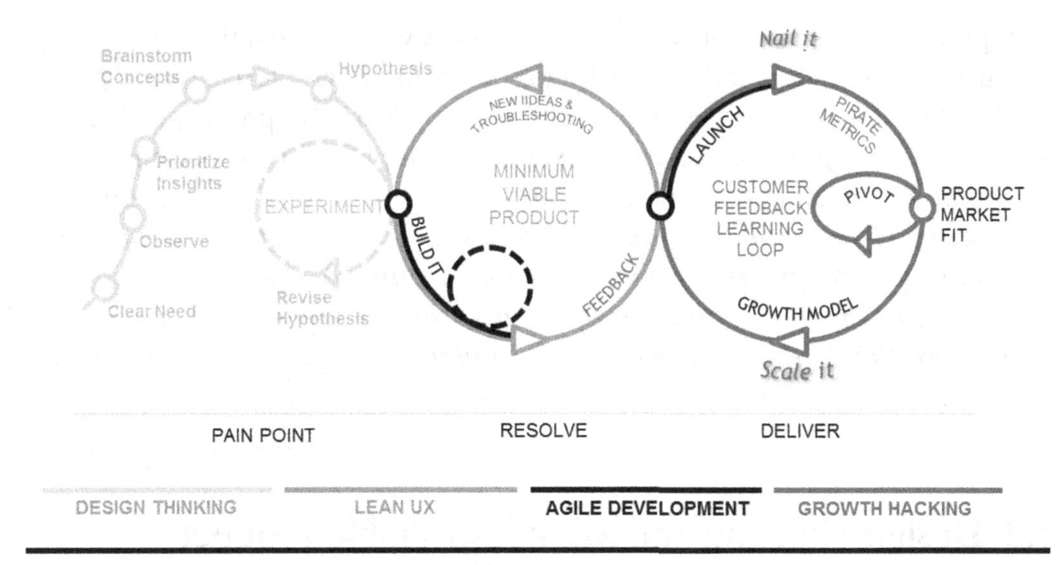

Figure 3.1 The three loops of lean startup.

Figure 3.1 represents the lean startup process as we have implemented it at AXA's Digital Agency. I use here the three-stage version, centered around the MVP, from sprint zero to launch. This illustration is an extension of a diagram by Dave Landis[14] (the first two loops), which illustrates the complementarity between *design thinking*, *(lean) UX design*, and agile development methods. The "nail it, then scale it" principle is explicitly represented on the drawing because the temptation is strong to want to compensate for disappointing results during the launch of a product by increasing, at best, communication and, at worst, resources (to add more *features to* the product). You don't fix a digital product that doesn't work back with more spending but with better listening.

Lean startup is often associated with disruptive innovation—inventing a new product—in the B2C world of the general public. In fact, this approach is much more general and applies to the majority of product and service developments in the digital world. Many of the startups whose analyses led to the formalization of *lean startup*, by Steve Blank and by Eric Ries, come from the world of enterprise software. There is no "size effect" that would make the principles we have just presented—and that we will detail later—valid only for a large number of customers. *Lean startup*, in particular *design thinking* and *growth hacking*, can be applied with a handful of customers. In the same way, even if *design thinking* is particularly suitable for inventing

[14] See the original diagram on Dave Landis's blog: https://lithespeed.com/lean-ux-dont-part-1-3–2/.

new products, it is also suitable for designing new functionalities for existing products and services, and especially for designing new interfaces or digital modalities (experiences) around a traditional product. The process described in the previous figure, therefore, has very wide applicability, especially as a support for digital transformation. This is confirmed in the book *Lean Enterprise*: "*However, the founding principles of Lean Startup can be applied to all kinds of activities in the enterprise, such as internal tool development, process improvement, organizational changes, legacy system replacements, and governance, risk management and regulatory compliance management programs.*"

3.3 Design Thinking and Minimum Viable Product

3.3.1 Design, Observation, Anthropology

Design has the dual objective of facilitating the experience—we talk about "reducing friction"—and increasing the satisfaction it produces, the pleasure of the experience. The importance of design in this complex digital world is well established. In the pages of *L'Age de la multitude*, Henri Verdier and Nicolas Colin write, "*We have entered a cycle dominated by design, that is to say, work, not on the appearance of things, but on the intelligence of objects and situations, their proposal to the market, the user experience, the manageability of the complex.*" This last point is particularly important: design serves to tame complexity. Design has always been an essential component of product development, but the complexity of the modern world, from the digital dimension to the multiple interactions of products and services mentioned in Chapter 1, makes design critical to success. The most common cause of failure of the services I have contributed to for fifteen years is not the weakness of the UVP. It is the complexity of the appropriation of the experience by the customer—what is called *onboarding* in the world of digital innovation.

Design starts with the observation of future customers or users. In the book *The Innovator's Method*, there are several examples that show that the first step in finding the problem to be solved is to go out into the field, to meet the users in their surroundings and places, and to observe. One of the most exciting stories in the book is that of ChotuKool. The goal was to create a refrigerator for the Indian market. After the first idea of making a fridge "as usual but smaller and cheaper" (a *top-down* idea that actually failed in the face of practical constraints), the authors tell the story of the ethno-marketing approach, consisting in going on-site to live the life of the future customers, hour by hour, for a few days. This part reminded me of a fascinating presentation I heard more than fifteen years ago about the use of this ethno-marketing practice at Leroy-Merlin and how "living the life" of a few customers (professional craftsmen) had allowed the detection of weak signals that the analysis of receipts by big data (already!) had not found.

The use of the term "ethnography"—for example, in the section "Ethnography to Explore Assumptions"—is not neutral: it really suggests observation "in the customers' home," in her context, and with a difficult objective of neutrality and non-disruption. We also find in the literature the use of "anthropology"—as in the role of *product anthropologist,* dear to Richard Sheridan[15]—with a similar objective. User stories and observations are collected and made available to the entire team using the power of visual management (i.e., wall posting). This underlines the importance of serendipity in design: it is not just about collecting *feedback* to validate or invalidate hypotheses; it is about listening. The construction of hypotheses, *behavioral insights* that will be used to propose UVPs, is done in an emergent way.

3.3.2 Design Thinking

Design thinking is a process proposed by IDEO,[16] for creative problem-solving with a focus on users. *Design thinking* is a non-linear process with loops and iterations, which presents the "*build, measure, learn*" pattern of lean startup. It can be broken down into five stages as follows. The first phase, **empathy**, is a phase of observation and research of user needs. The objective is to understand, in an empathetic way with the users, their problems, their aspirations, and their needs. The second step consists in defining the **job-to-be-done** (i.e., the problem to be solved). The third step is the **ideation** phase, when as many solutions as possible are generated and where the different creativity techniques are used. The next step is the **prototyping phase**, during which solutions—often rough ones—are created, allowing for experimentation with users. The last step is that of

[15] Richard Sheridan is an iconic American entrepreneur. His book *Joy, Inc.: How We Built a Workplace People Love* is a reference on how to lead a deep digital transformation around customer orientation, symmetry of attention and software excellence, in particular thanks to a particular form of agile methods (*extreme programming*). We will come back to this in Chapter 7.

[16] See for example the IDEO website: www.ideou.com/blogs/inspiration/what-is-design-thinking.

user testing, collecting opinions, and observing usage, which will most often lead to a return to ideation to create a new prototype. The general framework is illustrated in the first loop of the previous figure.[17]

Design thinking plays a fundamental role in the lean startup process: it formalizes the observation and definition of the problem, most often by producing a list of *pain points* (the key points,[18] the problems to be solved), then iteratively produces the UVP or UVPs, as well as the *user stories*[19] that materialize this UVP and that will be the starting point for the development of the MVP. The book *Lean UX* sets the collaboration between designers and developers as the foundation of digital innovation and defines a *user story* as follows: "*The smallest unit of work expressed as a benefit to the user, according to the following pattern: as a <type of user>, I want to <accomplish something> to get <the next benefit>.*" The distinction between the value proposition (UVP), which represents the "essence" of the promise, and the *user stories*, which represent how the promise is realized by the product, is fundamental. Each prototype of the *design thinking* cycle is used to develop the UVP, in co-creation with the users, and to test the *user stories*. A good practice that we have developed at AXA is to build and maintain the dependency graph between the *pain points*, the UVPs, and the *user stories* (Figure 3.2). This graph must be shared between the different teams and roles; it ensures consistency (the MVP holds the promise of the UVP that addresses the problem) and, above all, provides a shared context. **It is easier and more efficient to develop the prototype or later the product code that implements a *user story* when the problem to be solved is understood.**

The *design thinking* phase must also allow us to define the promise of the UVP through the customer results, the *outcomes* (we distinguish between *outcome*, which is the consequence of what is produced, and *result*, which is the produced result). The *Lean UX* book insists on defining

[17] On the use of experience design and *design thinking* in the lean startup process, I recommend the book *Lean UX: Applying Lean Principles to Improve User Experience*, by Jeff Gothelf. This book allows you to appreciate that *design thinking* has a much wider applicability than digital product development; it is a fundamental tool for the development of any value proposition: "*every aspect of a business can be approached with design*."

[18] It is customary to focus on the *pain points* and to consider that an innovation solves a problem and removes "difficulties," as this is indeed the most frequent case. It also happens that the innovation brings something very different and "creates its own need." This is called a latent need: "you needed it but you didn't know it yet."

[19] A *user story* is what replaces specifications in agile methods. As its name indicates, a *user story* describes the result as seen by the user, without going into detail about how this result is obtained.

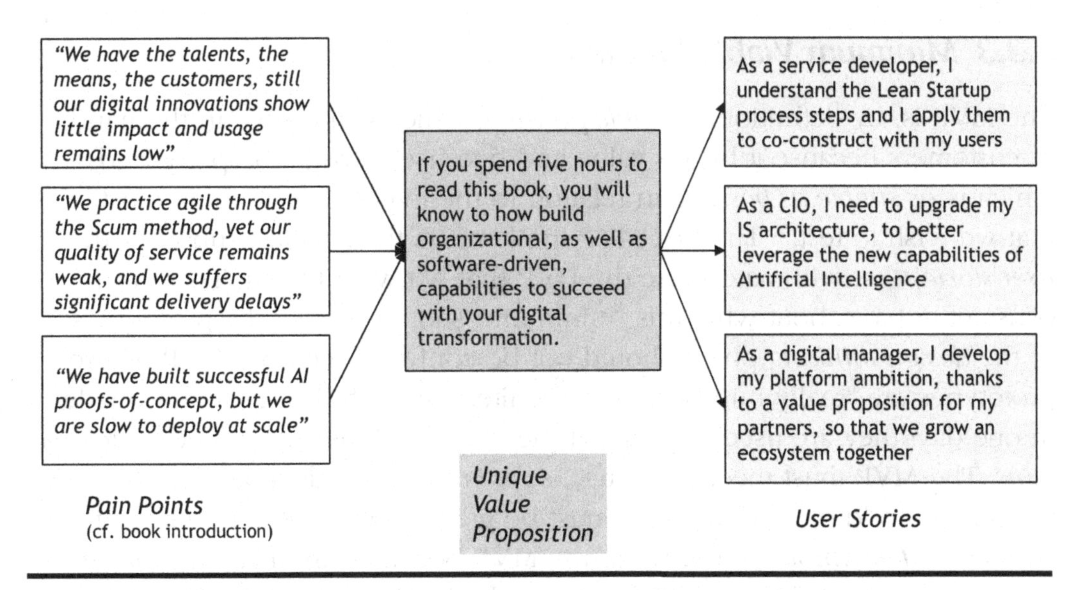

Figure 3.2 The *pain points/UVP/user stories* dependency graph.

success from customer satisfaction and, therefore, from the experience, and not from what is produced: "*Our goal is not to create a product, it is to change something in the world—to create an outcome. We start with a vision of the world and the user instead of specifications. We create and test hypotheses. We measure whether we have achieved these desired outcomes.*"

One of the key principles of lean startup is to include the learning loop from customer feedback as early as possible and at all stages of the lean startup development process, from *design thinking* to *growth hacking*. From the beginning, you need to talk to future users continuously and repeatedly. Ash Maurya writes, "*The fastest way to learn is to talk to customers. Not by putting code into production or by collecting and analyzing usage data, but by talking to people.*" Ash Maurya puts a lot of emphasis in his book on the right way to talk to and observe customers, along with the ethnographic guideline defined in the previous section. He encourages being wary of *surveys* that assume you already know the questions to ask and to avoid *focus groups* because your clients cannot articulate their needs.[20] Moreover, group work produces *groupthink*: a collective thinking process that converges too quickly and misses the nuggets because of the pressure of "peer judgment."

[20] Here we see the link with the classic quote from Steve Jobs: "*It's really hard to design products by focus groups. A lot of times, people don't know what they want until you show it to them*".

3.3.3 Minimum Viable Product

The MVP is, by definition, a *viable product*, which can be put in the hands of customers because it brings value and because it works properly, and which is *as simple as possible* in relation to the hypothesis of value creation that we wish to test.[21] The first MVP implements the smallest subset of the *user stories* that will materialize the UVP that we want to test. There is a constant debate about what this "minimum" should be, but the prototypes of the *design thinking* phase should not be confused with the MVP. These prototypes are "really minimal," and the literature is full of examples made in one day; they are used to perform the first iterations, also called *concierge runs*. The MVP must meet a real use, so it is a real product, and to convince users in a world of abundance, it must be great, to use the expression of the authors of *The Innovator's Method* (the MVP becomes an MAP: *minimum awesome product*). This point is very clearly explained by Ash Maurya: The MVP is minimal because it embeds few UVPs, but it is great because every UVP must be great. One should not enter sprint zero that marks the beginning of the MVP if the UVP is mediocre: "*about 90% of the first solutions we invent do not satisfactorily solve a significant problem.*"

MVP development is a doubly iterative process—represented in the previous figure by the nested loop: several iterations are necessary, in agile mode, to build the first version, and other iterations come afterward to evolve the MVP according to customer feedback. During the MVP improvement cycles, features must be pulled, ***not pushed***, from user *feedback*. Without going into the details of agile methods, which we will review in the second part, the construction of the MVP is characterized by sprints (iterations in the form of small batches), by the use of a *backlog* of *user stories*, and by the various rituals that allow a cross-functional team to work together in a synchronized manner. These cross-functional teams, which we mentioned in the previous chapter as a marker of new forms of organization, bring together development, design, product design, marketing, and quality assurance. True collaboration between designers and developers is one of the keys to success, according to the authors of *Lean UX*: "*A shared understanding is the common knowledge of the team that is built up progressively. This understanding encompasses the space, the product, the customers . . . without this cross-functional collaboration, there is no*

[21] This is viability from the customer's point of view, not product viability from an economic point of view.

shared understanding and therefore a lot of documentation and formalized handovers must be used."

The MVP development process evolves into a product development process. **The MVP is not a prototype that is replaced by a "real product"; it is a simplified product that is co-constructed and evolved with customers.** This statement has two consequences: the MVP must be built with discipline and by taking advantage of the best continuous deployment approaches because the life of the product will be a succession of deployments with high frequency. We will return to CICD approaches in Chapter 7. One of the main messages of the double arrow presented in the introduction is that the MVP must be built with the state of the art of development methods because simplicity is not an excuse for mediocrity: DevOps must be mastered for the lean startup process to work to the end of its logic of continuous product development. This message is echoed in the *Lean Enterprise* book, which also notes the dual popularity of CICD and lean startup approaches and how they reinforce each other. In addition, the MVP must be fully instrumented to automatically provide the usage data that will be used to learn (validate/invalidate *insights*) and evolve it.

3.3.4 User Experience Design

Experience design plays a fundamental role in the success of the digital product innovation and development process. Even if the *design thinking* phase produces a UVP that works with target customers, and even if the MVP succeeds in "delivering on the promise of the UVP," there are two challenges that must be overcome that cause most digital innovations to fail.

- The first is *onboarding* (convincing future customers to "get on board" the experience): We have a promise. We have a product. How do we get the customer? Does she understand the promise? This is to realize that the product will fulfill this promise and to embark on the adventure of using it.
- The second is usability, the ease of use. From the beginning of use to the realization that the promise is fulfilled and the value has been produced (often referred to as the *aha* moment), experience design must, as has been said, reduce the "friction" of use as much as possible and make the experience as pleasant as possible.

The subject of experience design is beyond the scope of this book and beyond the scope of lean startup in general. In addition to the *Lean UX* book mentioned above, I also recommend *Designing Experiences*, by J. R. Rossamen and M. Duerden. This book proposes a segmentation of experiences into different types, from the simplest (prosaic) to the richest (transformational) according to a number of characteristics, such as user engagement, energy required, frequency and impact, and type of customer benefit. This is where we find the key role of the *personae* and *customer journeys*, which we mentioned in Chapter 1 about building a new experience. This construction is formalized by an *experience map* that positions the *touchpoints*, the transitions, the assumed intentions, and the expected reactions. The experience map is a structured form of the "story" that the experience tells. It is critical to think in terms of *storytelling* to capture emotions and take advantage of the richness of the narrative motifs that the experience can evoke.

One of the key dimensions of experience design is emotional design, which consists of both understanding and anticipating the emotions that the experience will provoke, and playing on this palette to reinforce the experience (i.e., improve the design).[22] The principle is to annotate the experience plan with the emotions, those felt by the users during the tests, and those that the designer would like to arouse. The "chronography" of the experience plan—knowing precisely how much time the user spends for each sequence, in front of each interface or touchpoint—is essential to play with the attention without over-soliciting it (just like a magician who alternates strong and weak moments). Emotions such as surprise, anticipation,[23] *ownership* (cf. Don Norman—allowing the user to feel "this is mine"), and sharing are part of the interaction palette. Those like serenity, satisfaction, trust, and empathy are rather part of the palette of artifact

---

[22] The reference book on the subject is *Emotional Design*, by Don Norman. He distinguishes three levels of perception that correspond to three types of design and three types of emotions: the visceral level (what affects our reptilian brain: the senses [touch, sight, smell], pleasure, desire ["*Visceral design is what nature does*"]); the behavioral level (what affects the mammalian brain: the functioning that satisfies us); and the reflexive level (what affects the cortex—the experience of the object or the rationalized pleasure). All three levels should be used in emotional design: "*Iterative human-centered approach works well for behavioral, but is not necessarily appropriate for either the visceral and the reflective side. When it comes to these levels, the iterative method is designed by compromise, by committee, and by consensus. This guarantees a result that is safe and effective, but dull.*"

[23] The emotions of surprise and anticipation play a symmetrical role, controlling our desire to learn and anticipate.

construction (colors, shapes, sounds, use of images,[24] etc.). It's all a question of balance, since, for example, allowing the user to express their emotions—in a give-and-take logic, allowing them to give creates an engagement—very easily goes from enriching to weighing down the experience.

Another important ambition of digital experience design is to nurture habit creation and encourage the viral practice of sharing[25] so that the product or service participates in its own marketing, which is the basis of *growth hacking* that we will explore in the next section. A successful experience must limit the choices offered to the user because each choice has a cognitive and emotional cost. Different experiences show that many products and services reduce their value, or even fail, because they are too rich and offer too many choices to the customer. There are multiple references in digital viral marketing to Cialdini's six principles[26] that deal with persuasion and influence. These principles—in particular reciprocity, which consists of obtaining small "commitments" from the user to solidify the relationship with the product or service or "social proof," which summons the opinion of other users who are popular or whom we trust—are already part of our digital experiences.

3.4 Growth Hacking

3.4.1 AARRR Metrics and Data-Driven Steering

The term "growth hacking" has recently become popular in the world of digital innovation and products. **It refers to a set of digital marketing practices that use data, the product itself, and network effects to accelerate growth in usage and customer base**. The word *hacking* is important; it means that we are talking about active marketing, based precisely on the *plan-do-measure-learn* cycle mentioned earlier. The *hacking* is done either on the digital product itself—one of the key ideas of *growth hacking* is that the product is its "own distribution channel"—or

---

[24] For example, studies show that a photo of a person is more empathetic, but a drawing is easier to understand. The role of emotional design is to know how to choose.

[25] Seth Godin notes that *"virality is not a marketing feature that is added to the product launch, but an intrinsic characteristic of the product."*

[26] Robert Cialdini wrote a book, *Influence: The Psychology of Persuasion,* over thirty years ago on persuasion and influence, in which he explains the following six principles: reciprocity, commitment and consistency, social proof, appreciation (the like of today's social networks), authority, and scarcity.

on tools that participate in the diffusion and promotion of the product. An emblematic practice of *growth hacking* is to practice *A/B testing* on features of the product, or the website, to determine which of two approaches is more appreciated by customers. Since the principle is to make decisions based on measurements, the *growth hacking* phase begins with the strategy of collecting usage data. In the context of the three-step *lean startup* process, this means that the MVP must carry the analytical tools that will provide its metrics. If *growth hacking* is applied to existing products and services, the first step is to get the tools to collect the data. In the reference book *Hacking Growth: How Today's Fastest-Growing Companies Drive Breakout*, authors Sean Ellis and Morgan Brown give several examples, such as Walmart and Facebook, that show the importance of the infrastructure for collecting and processing usage data, which we will discuss in Part 2.[27]

The most commonly used metrics for *growth hacking* are the AARRR (*acquisition, activation, retention, referral, revenue*) metrics, also known as pirate metrics. There is an implicit order that corresponds to the customer life cycle: **Acquisition** measures the number of leads that come to the product or service. **Activation** measures the number of customers who have become active (completed their enrollment process). **Retention** measures how many customers leave or stop using the service after a certain amount of time. Good practice is to do a cohort analysis (grouping together users who activated at the same time) so that the attrition rate (called *churn* rate) is more meaningful, based on the customer's lifetime. **Referral** metrics are used to evaluate virality (i.e., the propensity of users to recommend the service or product). Finally, **revenue** metrics measure revenue creation. In the logic of the *lean* process, the metric that receives the most attention is retention, which is obviously linked to user satisfaction. The first step is usually to check that the *onboarding* process is working, which is measured by the activation/acquisition rate. The second step is to make sure that the customer is creating value, which is measured, among other things, by the retention rates. Only then can we work to promote the virality of the product.

The *growth hacking* step in the lean startup process is used to drive the evolution of the product through data to bring out "growth models" through successive experiments. In their book *Hacking Growth*, the authors

---

[27] The example of Facebook is interesting because it is a leading digital player. The systematic use of *growth hacking* came gradually: "*in January of 2009, they took the dramatic step of stopping all growth experiments and spending one full month on just the job of improving their data tracking, collection, and pooling. Naomi Gleit, the first product manager on Facebook's growth team, recalls that 'in 2008 we were flying blind when it came to optimizing growth.'*"

propose the following definition: "*Mixing powerful data analysis methods, technical know-how on the product and clever marketing methods to create combinations that accelerate growth. Through rapid testing of multiple ideas that are measured and evaluated against goals, growth hacking makes it possible to discover much faster which ideas work and which ones should be abandoned.*" The ability to modify the product very quickly and easily is, of course, a unique feature of the digital world, as is the rich stream of data produced by the use of these products. There is complete continuity between the principle of *innovation accounting* of the lean startup and the validation/invalidation of the "growth models" produced during the stages of *growth hacking*. In both cases, it is a "hypothesis/development/validation based on user feedback" loop. **It is the same loop, with the same support product (the MVP) that goes through different stages of maturity: we progressively validate the hypotheses on the problems to be solved, the creation of value for the client and then the creation of value by the company**.

3.4.2 Product Market Fit: Finding Traction

We have already introduced the essential concept of PMF, the moment when the "product has met its market" is proven based on usage, satisfaction, and growth. According to Wikipedia, "*growth hacking* is particularly common among startups, when the goal is to find the *product/market fit* or demonstrate rapid growth." We saw earlier that the *growth hacking* loop applies to both getting the PMF and then ensuring the fastest possible growth by optimizing both virality and product communication effectiveness. Experience shows that it takes many iterations between the first version of the MVP and the one that achieves PMF. The first step on this road to PMF is to ensure that the customer receives the experience promised by the MVP. This is called the *aha* moment, the moment of recognition, where the user becomes aware of the value provided by the product or service. The first phase of MVP iteration aims to ensure that this moment is reached, that "the MVP delivers on the promise of the UVP." The notion of "*growth*" is not yet present, but the learning loop on the data collected—and on the testimonials—allows to correct and optimize all the steps of the *experience map* that we introduced earlier. In concrete terms, it is most often a matter of "making the experience smoother" and eliminating the friction points at the points that are pointed out by the collection of detailed usage metrics (so it takes more than just AARRRs).

The growth dimension of *growth hacking* really begins with the appearance of *aha* moments. To quote Sean Ellis and Morgan Brown, "*no amount of marketing and advertising—no matter how clever—can make customers like a mediocre product, so the cardinal rule of growth hacking is to only move into the steady pace of growth experiments when you're sure the product is a must-have and you know why.*" Sean Ellis has given his name to a test that provides an indication of whether the PMF has been achieved. Based on the analysis of a thousand startups, he looked for an indicator of whether the much sought-after rapid growth phase was attainable or, in other words, when it was time for a startup to raise funds to scale up its communication. The indicator he found was the percentage of "engaged" users who said they would be "really disappointed" if the product was abandoned. The "Sean Ellis ratio test" is to verify that more than 40% of the product's users are engaged. Note that there is a certain symmetry: one can measure growth as an indicator of satisfaction and measure satisfaction as a predictor of growth.

It is important to understand that in the search for the PMF, you have to work as much on your communication (your *pitch*, your *landing page*, *embedded tutorials*, content to facilitate *onboarding*, etc.) as on the product itself. **More than half of the failures are not "bad products" but products that customers don't understand and, therefore, don't try.**[28] In Osama Amar's online course mentioned above, an important part is dedicated to the creation and optimization of UVPs, using *growth hacking* techniques. The segmentation of the market to find its ideal target is fundamental because universal products or services are not within the reach of startups: you have to pick a fight, always with the idea that you have to become an undisputed leader in your own market. For example, Oussama Amar shows how to use Google AdWords to improve your UVP (by detecting customer intentions and the importance of word choice). He also shows how to use Facebook's hyper-targeted campaigns to build and validate its segmentation analysis, producing a "sociology of future users."

3.4.3 To Create a Community of Regular Users

The success of a product or service in the digital world is most often achieved by creating a community of "enthusiastic" users

[28] In the highly competitive world of mobile applications, a significant portion of downloaded applications are not opened (a concrete manifestation of abundance and lack of time) and a large majority are only opened once or twice, showing the failure of the *onboarding* process.

who will act as ambassadors. *Growth hacking* is a story with three protagonists: the team, the product, and the community of early adopters. The product acts as a mediator between the team and the community. The user community is the preferred tool for extracting deep *insights* beyond what is possible with analytical approaches. For Guy Kawasaki, using feedback from early customers is essential to characterize and build *aha* moments. It is thus necessary to build this community of active and engaged users to combine a qualitative part with quantitative data analysis. This qualitative analysis of community feedback allows for a detailed understanding of user behavior: "*It's crucial to never assume that you understand why your users behave the way they do; instead, start by looking at usage data and then asking questions based on the observations you've made, which then allows you to direct experimentation efforts to have the greatest impact.*"

The way to build a large community of ambassadors is to start with a small community of satisfied users, work with them to further increase their satisfaction to the point of making them ambassadors, and then use viral techniques to grow this community. It is critical to offer an exceptional experience to your first customers. You have to "over-deliver in terms of experience to compensate for under-delivery on the product." As Paul Graham puts it, you have to take "*extraordinary measures to acquire early adopters and keep them as happy as possible.*" The same idea is found in Ash Maurya: establish an intimate relationship with the first fifty users and ensure their complete satisfaction before going after the other customers. The term "community" of users is important; it is not simply a group, so it must be equipped with communication and animation tools so that a sense of community emerges. It must become self-organized and develop its own recruitment capacity (one generation of ambassadors recruits the next), so we find the practices and tools of *growth hacking* applied to this community of fans (virality and exploitation of all digital tools to spread messages). They also need to be recognized and rewarded; Guy Kawasaki insists on the importance of small signs of recognition.

To create a community that will grow, the experience associated with the product or service must become a habit. This notion of habit is essential in a digital world marked by an overabundance of supply and low attention. I quote *Hacking Growth* here: "*The main mission of growth hacking teams is to build loyalty (increase retention) among average users by transforming usage into habit.*" This implies working on the experience to increase satisfaction progressively over time. *Growth hacking* and digital marketing methods make several borrowings from psychology, behavioral science, and the study of habit formation. For example, we often find references to Nir Eyal's *hook model*, which describes the habit formation cycle in four steps:[29] *trigger* (create the favorable context and propose a triggering event), *action*, *reward* (create the reinforcement loop by rewarding the action), and *investment* (create the conditions of commitment by offering feedback on the positive consequences of repeating this action, to create the *desire* that will feed the habit formation loop). *Growth hacking* methods focus on creating *triggers*, starting from *customer journeys* (the global context) and the *experience map* and, of course, on creating rewards. Sean Ellis and Morgan Brown note that "*intangible rewards are often the most effective in forming habits.*" We can see here that *growth hacking* work is strongly linked to the experience design mentioned above.

3.4.4 The CFLL Learning Loop

The CFLL (*customer feedback learning loop*) represents a global vision of learning loops. It has three components: the explicit dimension, which is the qualitative analysis of customer feedback; the implicit dimension, which is the quantitative analysis of all usage metrics collected by digital tools; and the social dimension, which covers the development of the user community. The CFLL concept was introduced at AXA's Digital Agency to remember that each of the dimensions is essential and that they are moreover complementary. Figure 3.3 represents the maturity model we have developed to ensure progress in the practices described here. The advantage of a maturity model, which is nothing more than a prioritized *checklist*, is that it capitalizes on best practices while promoting a sustainable rate of learning. We find the three dimensions and five classic levels of maturity. The content of the boxes was developed for mobile application development, but it is easy to adapt for other digital products. The progressive nature of the levels is explained by the need to develop analytical capabilities gradually and also because

[29] This cycle can be found, for example, in James Clear's best-selling book, *Atomic Habit*, which is an excellent resource for change management.

	Level 1 *Start*	Level 2 *Defined*	Level 3 *Measured*	Level 4 *Optimized*	Level 5 *Adaptative*
Implicit	Mobile Analytics (basic tag plan) Application monitoring (crash analytics)	Tag plan defined by *product owner*, step by step, leverage monthly analysis	Collect and analyze « *drop-off* » on all « *user paths* »	Add tags and digital traceds to measure virality	Measure and analyze the way users influence once another
Explicit	Collecter ratings from *AppStores* – for each release	Collect and analyze feedbacks ... and answer to them	Allow users to submit feedback directly from the application	Identify « *aha moments* » and let the user share them	Trace and analyze events / contents created by users
Social	Setup a beta-tester community, collect & analyze feedbacks	Start a dialog with users : answers to each request or suggestion	Create a "supporter" group for service and nurture that group	Collect user needs and requests thanks to a collaborative platform	Allow users to participate to the backlog management through votes about features

Figure 3.3 CFLL practice maturity model.

it takes time for the community of committed users to develop. One of the classic mistakes is to make a "*tag* plan" that is too ambitious and costs a lot in development when it is more efficient to develop the usage data collection strategy progressively, following the usage and its own understanding.

The CFLL practice and its model are the last step of the dialogue with customers in the *lean startup* process. It should be emphasized one last time that it is a constant obligation in all stages: observations, studies, and focus groups for prototypes in the design phase; tests with internal and external first users in the MVP development phase before launch. We used the CFLL at the Digital Agency as a diagnostic tool (Where are we now? What is the next step?) combined with an A3 action plan inherited from the *lean* culture. The A3 table is a list of macro-lines for each problem under analysis; we used the following columns: description of the problem, current solution hypothesis, action plan corresponding to this solution, who is in charge, current action plan step, expected date of results, conclusions (learning), and comments. The use of A3 PDCA tools is recommended by many authors, such as those of *The Innovator's method*: "*The customer feedback loop is critical to improving service quality . . . A3 charts are problem-solving tools that capture the most important information and define the team's issues and constraints.*"

Summary

1. Innovation teams must be given direct access to "real customers" (3.1.1).
2. A working value creation model is the result of the innovation process, whether for a startup or a product or service line of a large company, and not a prerequisite for launching the innovation project (3.1.3).
3. Lean startup consists in iterating to accumulate knowledge in order to progressively build a product, a service, or a satisfactory experience for the customer and the associated value creation model (3.2.1).
4. We need to properly validate the stages during which iterations are easy and low-cost before moving on to stages where each iteration is more expensive (3.2.3).
5. It is easier and more efficient to develop the prototype or later the product code that implements a user story when we understand the problem to be solved (3.3.2).
6. The MVP is not a prototype that is replaced by a "real product"; it is a simplified product that is co-constructed and evolves with the customers (3.3.3).
7. Experience design plays a fundamental role in the success of the digital product innovation and development process (3.3.4).
8. You need to know how to use *growth hacking*, a set of digital marketing practices that use data, the product itself, and network effects to accelerate growth in usage and the customer base (3.4.1).
9. More than half of the failures are not "bad products" but products that customers do not understand and, therefore, do not try (3.4.2).
10. The success of a product or service in the digital world is most often achieved by creating a community of "enthusiastic" users who will act as ambassadors (3.4.3).

EXPONENTIAL INFORMATION SYSTEMS

Chapter 4: The Information System as a Foundation for Digital Transformation

Chapter 5: Artificial Intelligence and Machine Learning

Chapter 6: Governance, Architecture, and Situational Potential

Chapter 4

The Information System as a Foundation for Digital Transformation

We said in Chapter 2 that digital transformation is the company's response to the digital revolution. This revolution was described in a famous post by Marc Andreesen titled "*Software is eating the world*." What Marc Andreesen explains is that digitization affects all human activities, all business processes, and that the management of these digital flows is carried out by software. For a growing proportion of business activities, there is no longer any operational excellence without software excellence.

The issues we mentioned in the first part, agility, speed, and innovation are all conditioned by the ability to develop software. Digital strategy is expressed on the playing field of IT systems and skills. The dominance of the digital giants is more striking from the point of view of their software excellence than by their strategic dazzle—once again, it is primarily a question of execution. This chapter focuses on the IS because it is where a significant portion of the company's software assets are concentrated. We will see how the ambitions of digital transformation impact the IS, which must be open, built for continuous change, while ensuring excellent quality of service to its users.

DOI: 10.4324/9781003272816-6

4.1 Exponential Information Systems

4.1.1 Which IT for an Exponential Organization?

The ExO is an evolution of the company's organization in order to make the most of extremely rapid changes in technology. This applies doubly to the IS. First of all, it must also evolve to adapt to exponential change. This means being open to the constant influx of new technologies and being able to transform itself at an accelerated pace. Second, the IS is the foundation for absorbing and implementing new technologies. This is what makes the IS the foundation of digital transformation. Even if this transformation leads to the addition of new digital capabilities and new technologies outside of the IS, the IS remains a backbone. The IS provides common services such as access and flow security, transport and sharing of business data, integration architecture, and service orchestration, to give just a few examples. The way in which the IS provides these services, in terms of reliability, performance, and speed, has a strong impact on the capacity for digital transformation. A large part of the ambitions expressed in Chapter 1 are based on the capabilities of the IS.

What characterizes the digital world is the dramatic acceleration of change. Twenty years ago, elements of the IS, or large technical systems, had many years of life ahead of them, even one or two decades, before they were replaced. The life of the system was punctuated by a cycle of maintenance and evolution, but the rate of change was relatively low. At a component level, software modules had a relatively long life span. This stability has a strong impact on the way a system is built: one can invest in the quality of the specification; a strong specification means that the system can be designed as a black box assembly. This "black box" approach determines the way in which systems are tested and integrated and also enables the distribution of work, offshoring, outsourcing, and so on. **The radical change in digital technology is that this *refresh rate* of technical systems is multiplied by an order of magnitude.** If the code of the new digital system changes continuously, this profoundly changes the way it is built, as we shall see in Section 4.2.

Salim Ismail's book emphasizes the importance of experimentation. Developing your digital transformation means knowing how to experiment continuously to explore opportunities and acquire new skills.[1] These

[1] We remember that, especially in the digital world, capabilities come from skills and skills are developed through practice. I quote Salim Ismael: *"Constant experimentation and process iteration are now the only ways to reduce risk. Large numbers of bottom-up ideas, properly filtered, always trump top-down thinking, no matter the industry or organization . . . As Nassim Taleb explains, 'Knowledge gives you a little bit of an edge, but tinkering (trial and error) is the equivalent of 1,000 IQ points.'"*

experimentation skills are critical to import new innovative technologies from outside, but it goes much further: they are essential to implement continuous adaptation. It is not a question of being able to experiment "on the side," in a laboratory, but of being able to experiment on the production system. Digital systems are built through continuous learning—see the previous chapter—and through trial and error in real life, on the production environment with real customers. The practice of *A/B testing* is a perfect illustration of this principle.

The two acronyms SCALE and IDEAS, which we saw in Chapter 2, contain the essential features of the exponential IS: the variability of resource use, the significant use of external skills and resources, the importance of algorithms (from data science to AI), continuous experimentation, and the importance of interfaces, especially APIs (*Application Programming Interfaces*, the "computer plugs" that a system exposes to others).

4.1.2 Outside to Inside Steering

Another characteristic that the exponential IS borrows from ExOs is that it is built and driven from the outside in—that is, by turning one's attention first to the "edges" or "borders." This might seem obvious since these edges, whether they are user interfaces or *system-to-system* interfaces (APIs), are the places where customers and partners meet. The edges are where value is created and where continuous adaptation must take place. Yet traditional systems engineering often starts from the core. In a stable world, this core approach makes sense and is effective; in a world of constant change, it is better to start at the edges.

We saw in the first chapter that in the digital world, customers are (often) the architects of their own experience. This means that control, especially of orchestration (in the sense of the conductor who drives the orchestra), is often external. This is a profound change in the architecture of the IS: orchestration is no longer a stable function, controlled by the enterprise and implemented in the core of the system, but a changing function, which is controlled by the user and often implemented externally, in the overall experience delivery ecosystem. The notion of a microservices architecture, which are self-contained elements of service delivery that are used and assembled by actors other than those designing the microservices, is a response to this outsourcing of orchestration. Assembly is a characteristic of a digital world in constant change (we speak of composite applications).

Just as for the business, change in the IS comes from outside. It is dictated by the permanent change of the environment, from customers to suppliers—this is the principle of homeostasis discussed in Chapter 2. To allow for a sufficient speed of change, for the IS to adapt quickly enough to support the necessary digital transformation, it must be able to differentiate itself like a living organism. It is not possible, and we will come back to this, for the whole system to evolve at the same speed, this accelerated speed imposed by the environment. On the contrary, it is necessary to build a differentiated approach by "layers," where the speed of evolution is high at the edge and slower in the center, to use an analogy with living cells.

4.1.3 An Information System Open to the Continuous Flow of Technologies

The exponential IS must make massive use of what is done outside. Of course, this means knowing how to use the constant flow of technological improvements, but the objective is more general. Since "software is eating the world," the company will mobilize more and more software to succeed in its digital transformation. The only way to succeed without an explosion of costs is to learn to use, more and more and better, externally developed software. This is especially true for open-source software not only because it is cheaper[2] but also because it is often of better quality and evolves faster. Open-source software benefits from multiple advantages described in this book: it is built by and around a community, it is developed with transparent exposure that favors quality ("thousands of eyeballs" that review the code), and it uses modern software factory approaches that we will discuss in the third part. In particular, open-source software is by construction an emergent product co-developed with its users.[3]

Openness to the continuous flow of technological innovations is first and foremost a characteristic of the technical system. Since we live in a world of software ecosystems, an exponential IS must be built on "technical stacks" that are constantly updated.[4] Modularity (which we will discuss later) and the use of APIs in the internal construction of the system are also necessary conditions for using new components or services. The choice of integration technologies and

[2] This statement is less obvious than it seems, because the acquisition of a line of code is only a small part of the complete cost of a software.

[3] A very simple summary of this book would be to say that the exponential IS must both use *open-source* software and be built in the same way.

[4] The *software* stack is a set of components that work together, from the lower layers (operating system, network protocols) to the application layers, including services such as middleware and databases.

the "white box" development culture are also important factors in being able to easily use new technologies. The remainder of this chapter will focus on the architecture and technological choices of the exponential IS.

If we take a step back, this openness to the continuous flow of innovation is a characteristic of the organization, the women and men who build the system, and their way of working. The exponential IS is, from a human perspective, a learning organization. Technologies change continuously and on an accelerating cycle, so it is the ability to continuously learn new skills that are important, more than the skills available at a given moment. Here we find the idea from Chapter 2 that continuous learning is a fundamental characteristic of digital transformation. There is a strong link with the previous point: what enables continuous learning is the combination of the culture (each employee receives the message from his stakeholders that learning new digital techniques is part of his mission) and the technical environment (which enables experimentation in an easy way) since digital learning happens through practice (*learning by doing*).

This imperative to know how to use technological improvements that come from outside is both a risk and an opportunity. We have just talked about the opportunity by listing the expected benefits in terms of costs, new functionalities, and increased agility. The risk is simply to be "disrupted by the barbarians" if the company does not move fast enough. Disruption is one of the common themes in many books on digital transformation: the revolution in technologies (from the collapse of hardware costs to the advances in AI and new approaches to distributed computing) makes it possible to reinvent yesterday's IS, to do the same things faster and cheaper.

4.1.4 An Antifragile Information System

We saw in Chapter 2 that ExOs must be antifragile. This concept of Nassim Taleb applies perfectly to the exponential IS. Here are four characteristics from his book *Antifragile*:

1. An IS in a digital environment is "alive," in perpetual evolution.[5] An IS is antifragile if its exposure to the hazards of its environment strengthens it instead of destroying it or reducing its capacities. This requires

[5] One of the fundamental corollaries is that the homeostasis (equilibrium) of such a system is defined with movement and perpetual change: "*For something organic, the only stable equilibrium (without movement) is death.*"

a double property of exponential systems: they are elastic—elasticity consists in absorbing hazards by scalability or in responding gracefully without loss of service—and they are learning systems.

2. One should not try to control/master complex systems by a single voluntary *top-down* governance. In the tradition of Kevin Kelly, Taleb insists on the disasters of the absence of humility when one wishes to pilot large systems in a hierarchical, command-and-control manner. Following Edward Deming ("*cherish your errors*"), Taleb declares, "*Thank you, errors.*" Hazards, unforeseen events, and efforts to adapt help educate and strengthen the system.
3. In a complex world, we must welcome and accept the random nature of events and not try to predict in order to control. This does not prevent us from being prepared, but it focuses on reaction rather than on the illusion of prediction (here we find again François Jullien's situational potential). An exponential IS placed in a complex environment is better controlled with simple[6] rules. Reactions must be quick, but decisions are made on the basis of reality, not anticipation.
4. In the conduct of operations, one must be wary of *narrative fallacy*, the desire to understand everything, often confusing cause and correlation. This illusion—what Taleb calls *the Soviet-Harvard illusion*—consists in mistaking the order of causal chains and confusing cause and effect. This behavior favors the model, then the analysis, over reality and leads to inferring a superiority of theoretical science over applied science, of technique over practice. Taleb is resolutely on the opposite side—which I naturally associate with *lean*—which places practice, action, and concrete reality at the source of knowledge.

To be more concrete, here is a list of best practices from the digital world that characterize the antifragile operation of an exponential IS. The first one consists in learning to change better (faster and with fewer errors) by changing more often. This is worth noting, it is counterintuitive, and we will come back to it. A second practice is to analyze each incident to look for root causes and incrementally add protection mechanisms that increase robustness. We must also encourage the evolution of the architecture based

[6] Nassim Taleb confirms principles drawn from systemics: "*A complex system, contrary to what people believe, does not require complicated systems and regulations and intricate policies. The simpler the better.*" Ashby's law of requisite variety tells us that homeostasis in a complex environment requires a complex system. Taleb's point, similar to Steve Wolfram in *A New Kind of Science*, is that emerging complexity is better controlled with simple rules.

on external demands (constraints on the edges). Externally visible computing capabilities, whether they are gateways or platforms, should be developed in the following way: starting with a simple approach and reinforcing what is overused. This is the strict application of the "grown, not designed" principle.

This antifragile approach is also suitable for developing cybersecurity capabilities. Protecting against intrusions and malicious actions is a complex domain (because of the system) and unpredictable (because of the opponents) domain. Without going into the details of an area that is beyond the scope of this book, note that the traditional approach of defending the IS with successive walls has given way to defense in-depth, with multiple interlocking zones. It is much easier to spot the adversary once he has crossed an initial border. It then becomes possible to observe and learn. Since the nature and strategy of attacks are constantly changing, good defense is a set of practices that adapt in a similar way, by learning. Each observed "attack" is an opportunity to develop and add a new protective behavior. This ability to learn from the behavior of the "intruders" naturally leads to the mobilization of observation, classification, and prediction skills of the IS in the service of its own security and to the use of AI and ML techniques for cybersecurity.

4.2 Information Systems and Perpetual Change

4.2.1 Multimodal Architecture

The multimodal architecture is a response to the tension we have already identified: on the one hand, the exponential IS must evolve at the speed imposed by its environment; on the other hand, this accelerated rate of change is very difficult to implement throughout the system. All of the approaches and technologies that we will see in the rest of the book, which we could call digital computing, cannot be deployed in one go on the entire IS. **The multimodal[7] approach consists of defining a service architecture in zones, organized according to the required refresh rate.** The zones that need to change the most regularly are those that will immediately adapt to new approaches and techniques and will

[7] I chose the term "multimodal" in reference to bimodal approaches. The zones operate with different modalities, whether it is the rate of renewal and refreshment (life span and rate of change), the openness to the outside world, and consequently the technologies used.

organize themselves into software factories, as we will describe in Chapter 7. Following the "outside-in" principle described in the previous section, multimodal architecture sets different rates of change: the boundary evolves fastest, the core more slowly. A particular case of this approach, made famous by Gartner, is the bimodal architecture, with a "core IT" zone that groups together the business functions often provided by older systems—the so-called legacy—and a "fast IT" zone that is built with newer software technologies. The bimodal approach has been criticized[8] because it has become synonymous with the juxtaposition of fixed legacy IT and new IT. The systems approach, like biology, teaches that all areas of a multimodal architecture must evolve. On the other hand, multimodal decomposition allows you to adapt your efforts, and above all, to achieve greater speeds of change at the organization's boundaries more quickly.

The multimodal architecture is a service architecture that defines different services that each zone exposes for the others. It is implemented by a technology that we have already discussed, that of APIs. In the famous metaphor of IS as a Lego box, APIs are the round studs that allow the different bricks to fit together. An API is both a functional object and a technical object. From a functional point of view, it is an interface and a service contract. The API encapsulates services (business objects sharing in the particular, but emblematic, case of REST APIs[9]) and must specify the expected quality of service: load capacity, availability, and response time. From a technical point of view, the rise of the web has produced and standardized various "plug" techniques that ensure interoperability and compatibility with network architectures and security constraints. The proper mastery of APIs is fundamental for the construction of a modern IS in the digital world. This mastery is both an architectural and technical skill. From a technical point of view, it is necessary to know the best practices and the usages associated with the tools that dominate the software world,

---

[8] An example of this debate can be found in the article "*Bimodal IT: Gartner recipe for disaster*," by Jason Blomberg, or "*Saying Goodbye to bimodal IT*," by Mark Campbell. In both cases, the bimodal approach is seen as leading to the creation of silos that separate a legacy that does not change with the new digital IT where the action is. This separation is deeply counterproductive, especially if the two modes are entrusted to different organizations (e.g. CIO vs. CDO). All areas need to evolve and change in-depth on an ongoing basis, and the core areas are often where much of the intellectual value is concentrated. The term "heritage IT" is used to replace "legacy" to avoid this negative connotation.

[9] REST (*representational state transfer*) is a method of querying and modifying objects that supports, using the HTTP protocol, the development of simple APIs, popularized by the development of mobile applications.

in particular the open-source world. The best way to write, present and deploy good APIs is to have a good experience of using other people's APIs. From an architectural point of view, the art of the API is to know how to make a service available to a user you don't know for a usage you don't know. It is, therefore, a work of encapsulation and a quest for simplicity. The interface must be minimal (from a functional point of view) so that the API plays its role of "expansion joint" between the different areas of the multimodal architecture or with regard to external partners.[10]

Figure 4.1 represents an instantiation of a multimodal architecture in an approach with four zones. This is only an illustrative example, but it allows us to see that the zones are both defined by the speed of change and the set of actors who determine the software and technological choices. The first core zone groups together the business capabilities of the classic IS as support for business processes.[11] This zone is, of course, itself multimodal, in a fractal way,[12] which enables the implementation of a continuous transformation—for example, with the introduction of microservices and internal APIs. The area referred to as the matrix is the service engagement and composition area. This zone, of the "fast IT" type, is designed for a higher rate of change.[13] It is separated here from an exponential zone that represents all the services provided by external suppliers for advanced functionalities. This separation emphasizes the even higher rate of change and the fact that the company uses these services as they are and does not control their evolution. Thinking of it as a separate area better visualizes the need for experimentation, testing, and integration protocol (you have to experiment to understand, and to understand before you integrate). The last zone, called the *edge*, represents the customer's software and digital environment, which is chosen by the customer and built by multiple actors. The company is only one actor among others, or even from time to time, a "parasite" (a small actor that

[10] To be more precise, there is a permanent tension between minimality (atomicity to promote use) and genericity (providing services at a higher level of abstraction to avoid each client doing the same work again). To go further, you should read the reference book *SOA: Le guide de l'architecte d'un SI agile*, by Xavier Fournier-Morel, Pascal Grojean, Guillaume Plouin, and Cyril Rognon.

[11] We find here the concept of the *operational backbone* described in the book *Designed For Digital*, cited in the introduction, in which the exposure of services that can be recomposed by means of APIs is considered as one of the cornerstones of digital transformation.

[12] An IS architecture, which decomposes a system into subsystems and compositional modes, is fractal in the sense that this decomposition applies recursively to the subsystems. See *Urbanization, SOA and BPM*, by the same author.

[13] Symmetrically, this zone corresponds to the *digital platform* described in *Designed for Digital*. We will come back to the different speeds of evolution in Chapter 6.

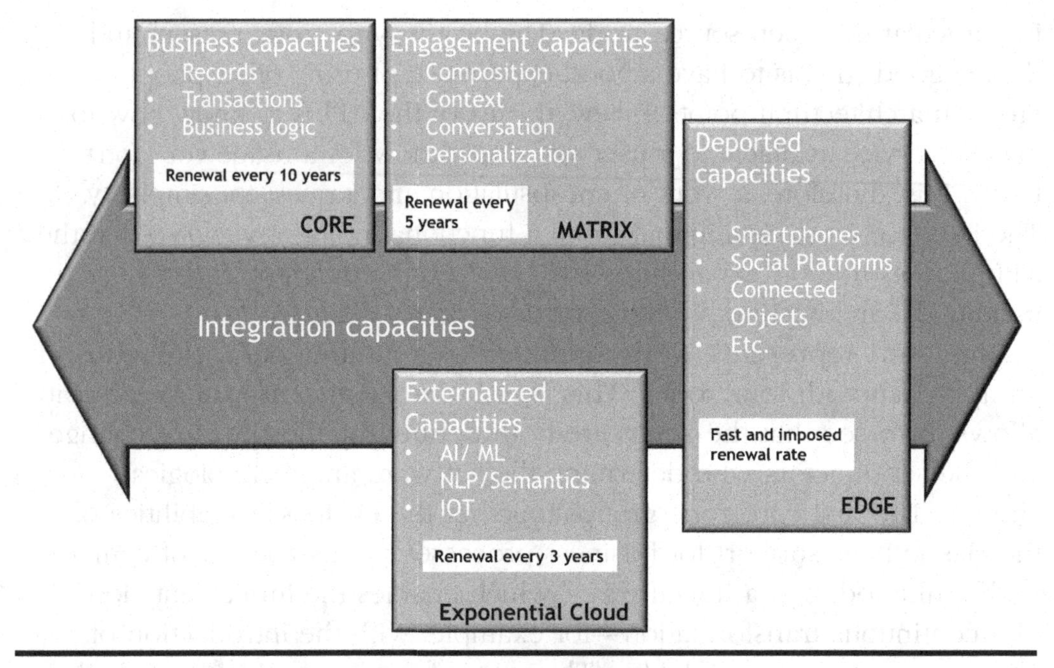

Figure 4.1 An illustration of a multimodal architecture.

takes advantage of the massive effort of larger actors). The exponential IS must develop in symbiosis with the digital environment of the company's customers,[14] taking advantage of the constant enrichment of its exponential capacities, illustrated by the constant progress of learning, artificial vision, or speech recognition on our smartphones.

4.2.2 The System as an Executable Specification

The notions of "white box" and "black box" oppose two conceptions of system engineering. The "black box" approach is associated with encapsulation: it is not necessary to understand the inside of a component; it is sufficiently defined by its interfaces to be integrated into the system. The specification, which is a description (a model) of the component, is what is used to assemble the system. In the "white box" approach, the ability to understand the functioning of the component in an abstract way is not sufficient; we want to be able to observe how things work. In a complex world that changes a lot, the "white box" approach becomes necessary

[14] In their book *Darwinism in a consumer-driven world,* whose tenets are very similar to the first part of this book, Erik Campanini and Kyle Hutchins write: *"the new name of the enterprise architecture game is symbiosis"*.

because the specification is not necessarily both complete and up-to-date (speed of change) and because there are interactions between components that require a fine-grained understanding of the behavior to be analyzed (complexity equals richness of interactions). This is not a binary distinction: most digital systems are assemblies of black boxes (which change little and are well encapsulated) and white boxes (which change a lot and have many interactions). This is not an exact dichotomy either; "white box" IS components combine specifications (e.g., interfaces) and "white box" access to source code.[15] **On the other hand, what characterizes digital systems is the return of the source code. The component, through its source code, becomes its own model, its own specification.**

Among the components of the system that are complex and often change, we find, first of all, integration subsystems and services. An important feature of exponential ISs is the use of *integration as code*—that is, replacing complex technical integration platforms with script pages, code that describes how the components fit together. Moving from a technical platform setting to a script page is the direct application of the executable specification. Where the parameters of an integration platform represented an abstract specification executed by an automaton (the technical platform), reverting to a general-purpose programming language increases the expressive power, and thus the agility, of the overall system. The term "X as code" appears in all areas of system construction: machine *provisioning*, system *configuration*, and the construction process are all elements that are both specified and executed by the same piece of code. *Scripting* languages have evolved to allow the writing of idempotent scripts[16] that specify the state to be reached rather than the sequence of operations to be performed.

This return of the "white box" approach has multiple consequences for system code. Code that serves as a reference for the component's behavior and that is intended to be read by unknown users must be as simple and readable as possible. Code that is intended to be constantly modified according to the frequent evolutions of the system must also be concise, to minimize the effort to be made (the number of lines of code to be

---

[15] To go deeper on this topic—how to leverage software architecture to adapt to various rates of change, one must read Robert C. Martin reference book, *Clean Architecture: A Craftsman's Guide to Software Structure and Design*.

[16] A script is idempotent if it produces the same result when applied one or more times (such as the idempotent function that checks f o f = f). This property greatly facilitates execution since it avoids keeping production states in memory, all scripts can be reapplied freely. See, for example, the documentation on Ansible playbooks (scripts, one of the configuration description systems).

changed). For several years now, we have been seeing a return of interest in more compact languages, such as node.js/JavaScript, more powerful functional languages, such as Scala or Erlang, and more flexible interpreted languages, such as Python. For example, functional[17] languages allow complex manipulations on environments to be described in a more compact and abstract way, resulting in code that is both easier to understand and to modify. Beyond the choice of language, we are also witnessing a return to the importance of the elegance of the code, respecting the rules of "good writing," naming conventions, and everything that makes it easier to come back to a piece of code written a long time ago or code written by others. In a word, digital computing marks the return of the "code culture."

4.2.3 Reactive Systems

Since the purpose of the exponential IS is to serve the ExO and its imperative of digital homeostasis, it is necessary to build an IS that is able to adapt permanently and react continuously. An exponential IS inherits the properties and architecture of reactive systems. Reactive systems are defined in the *Reactive Manifesto*[18] as *responsive*, resilient, elastic, and *message-driven*. The purpose of a reactive system is to interact continuously with its environment. Consequently, its first implicit characteristic is openness, its ability to open interfaces (APIs) on its boundaries in a modular and recomposable way. A reactive system must then be able to process the signals collected on the boundaries in a fast, robust, scalable, relevant, and continuously adaptable way.

To achieve scalability in the exponential system, it is not enough to have scalable computational resources—for example, by taking advantage of the *cloud* or external services as shown in Figure 4.1. It is necessary to use a scalable system architecture, which involves the distribution of processing and the event-driven approach, which is called *event-driven architecture*. Events mark transitions in the state of the system, so moving to an event-driven architecture means focusing more on what changes than on the steady state—which is a good start to building a reactive system: we will react to an event rather than asking whether a state has changed—and isolating, representing, and sharing these changes in the elementary form

[17] Functional languages inherit from LISP, a language associated with the beginnings of AI, and whose revival of interest provokes ironic smiles from the old-timers like myself.

[18] See the *Reactive Manifesto* at www.reactivemanifesto.org. We will address the dimensions of *responsiveness* and *resilience in* the next section.

of events. **One of the characteristics of modern digital systems is precisely their scalability, which relies on an event-based approach, massive distribution of processing, and tools for processing event flows.** The development of the web giants in the last few years has given rise to various event stream distribution and processing tools, of which an emblematic example is Kafka.[19]

The exponential IS is most often a complex assembly of multiple components. To make it robust, elastic, and resilient, it is necessary to introduce a multimodal approach with a weak coupling between the components of the system (we speak of *loose coupling*). The principle of *loose coupling* is very old, and the composition architecture by sending messages is a classic solution to build this weak coupling.[20] By associating components of the IS through asynchronous message sending, we create a temporal and load decoupling. Each system can implement its resilience, robustness, and *responsiveness* independently. As the *Reactive Manifesto* points out, message sending enables load balancing, elasticity, and flow control, as well as driving and managing message queues.

4.2.4 Rules, Reflexes, and Automation

The exponential IS, serving the digital ambition of the ExO, is an "intelligent" system, in the primary sense of intelligence, which is knowing how to adapt to a complex environment. This statement thus concerns both the composition and the purpose of the IS. The exponential IS assembles different components with AI capabilities because competition and digital transformation require it. This is also the thesis of ExOs: to know how to integrate the best of digital cognitive technology because it is a tool for better success in one's business. To say that intelligent capabilities are part of the system's purpose means that developing one's overall intelligence (of the organization as well as the IS) is a condition for being truly responsive and adaptable in a complex world. In the biological world, intelligence is built progressively through contact and reaction with its environment.

---

[19] Kafka is a distributed and scalable open-source data-streaming solution from the Apache Foundation that combines high availability and high performance. For a more in-depth look at the importance of event-driven architectures, read *Event Processing: Designing IT Systems for Agile Companies*, by W. Roy Schulte and K. Mani Chandy, in which we find this quote that makes the link with our first part: "*All companies and people pay attention to events because the real world is complex and dynamic, and no one has complete foreknowledge of what will happen.*"

[20] Read, for example, *Urbanization, SOA and BPM* previously mentioned, which describes the technologies of twenty years ago (EAI) but the principles are unchanged.

The same applies to the IS; **the "intelligent" capabilities are both an adaptive mechanism—what we said in Chapter 1 about AI absorbing complexity—and a tool for capitalizing on experience since the intelligence of the system is a form of knowledge**.

The IS calls upon a multiplicity of intelligent capacities, from the simplest to the richest, in a distributed manner throughout all its components. For example, the very concept of reacting to an external event can be applied to different time horizons. It can be to react instantaneously, without humans in the loop, to assist a human operator in making the best decision or finally, over a long time, enriching the memory of the system to improve future decisions. Even in the instantaneous or real-time domain, we can distinguish between "reflexes" encoded by simple rules and more complex "algorithmic decisions."[21] In an event-based architecture, we will find different event processing and routing techniques—often referred to as *complex event processing* when intelligent capabilities, such as rule engines, are added to routing capabilities. We also find this distinction between "hot" processing of events, in the form of a chain of operations on event flows, and "cold" processing, which involves storing events (the system's memory) and algorithms, which can access a larger fragment of the past.

The event-based approach can only be adapted to the complexity of the world and the challenges of digital technology if it is applied at multiple scales, with a hierarchical approach corresponding to the levels of abstraction of the subsystems. The notion of event is not *scale-free*. It depends on the level of abstraction at which we place ourselves. In a collaboration of systems, recursively composed of subsystems, all the events do not have to be shared everywhere. This would pose problems of cost, design complexity, and processing power. The multimodal approach we have seen above assumes that the services exposed between two subsystems are limited to events and objects that belong to a common abstraction level. To be responsive in a complex environment, a system must be designed as an SoS and must take advantage of this architecture both for the scalability (for load balancing) and for the variety that this approach allows.[22] This SoS approach is a key to combining different smart capabilities, which we will see in the next chapter.

---

[21] In the same way that Daniel Kahneman distinguishes between system 1 (producting reflexes) and system 2 (producing reflective thoughts) in the human brain, in his famous book *Thinking, Fast and* Slow.

[22] This approach of loosely coupled systems of systems collaborating for a single purpose naturally leads to the inspiration of biology in the search for models and architecture.

4.3 Managing Complexity and Technical Debt

4.3.1 Information System Complexity and Inertia

So far, we have explained the superiority of incremental and emergent approaches in a complex world, compared to classical methods where design precedes execution—in the words of Kevin Kelly, "*intelligent systems are grown, not designed.*" But there is an unfortunate downside of the iterative approach, which nature teaches us, as does the science of complex systems: adaptive incremental construction produces waste, redundancy, and overconsumption of resources. It produces additional complexity, which is both a strength (resilience and adaptation) and a weakness. **It is, therefore, essential to imitate nature and to add to any iterative process a process of cleaning and reorganization.**[23] In the world of ISs, we speak of application cleanup, technical debt management, and *refactoring* (reorganizing the software by regrouping what needs to be done).

This need to clean up and reorganize is not new in itself; however, it is becoming an imperative in the digital world because of the accelerating rate of change we have just outlined. We can formulate a revisited "Newton's law" about its evolution:

<Energy to adapt IS> = <System weight> × <Rate of change>

The weight we are talking about here is a global complexity, which depends, of course, on the number (number of applications, number of lines of code, number of function points, number of user interfaces, etc.) but also on the complexity in the essential sense: the number of interaction relationships between the different elements. Since the cost of adapting the IS is—at best—proportional to this energy and since IT budgets are under constraints for obvious reasons of competitiveness, it is necessary to control and reduce this weight if one wishes to change quickly. This is what makes Werner Vogels write on Twitter that the first job of the CTO is to simplify.[24] To illustrate the challenge of accelerating the rate of change, it is estimated

[23] I owe to my friend Pierre Haren the reading of the remarkable book, *La sculpture du vivant*, by Jean-Claude Ameisen. Nature builds by iterative additions, but it also uses destruction (hence the notion of sculpture), as well as inhibitions.

[24] Werner Vogels is the CTO of Amazon and one of the great voices in digital computing. Here's an excerpt from a tweet on September 6, 2019: "*Wanna be a CTO? Simplify. Focus on the business, what is the simplest, most robust Tech/Ops that makes the business succeed.*" We can also quote C. A. R. Hoare in his "*Turing Award Lecture*": "*The price of reliability is the pursuit of the utmost simplicity.*"

at Google that each elementary module is modified, rebuilt, and reintegrated at least once every two months. It is interesting to see that this "law" can be read the other way around: in a stable world where needs change little, the strategy of broad functional coverage through component accumulation can be justified. But this is the opposite of good practice in the digital world.

The burden of complexity is felt throughout the life cycle of the IS components. During the design of a component, the effort is more than proportional to the number of other components that may be impacted. Small changes (few lines of code) end up requiring significant impact studies, especially if the system is poorly documented and understood (another consequence of complexity). Once the component is developed, the cost of its integration into the rest of the system is directly related to complexity (number and difficulty of each of the interactions). This is why the practice of internal APIs is an effort to standardize these interactions. In the next phase of integration testing, we find both the complexity of everything that is impacted and everything that could be impacted, which leads to the need to perform important non-regression tests, the volume of which is proportional to the complexity and the lack of control over this complexity. Often, when one can no longer certify one's impact analysis, one is led to take large safety margins and replay a volume of tests that has nothing to do with the few lines of code of the initial modification.

There are other impacts of complexity in the operations phase, both directly on the support or indirectly as an increase in fragility, but what is interesting about the three factors we have just described is that they occur with each change. Each change produces a design/development/test cycle (not necessarily in order if you are working in agile mode) that triggers the complexity overhead, both time and money. It is easy to understand that if we start changing the IS constantly, an unnecessary increase in complexity becomes an unbearable burden, which is what the previous law expresses.

4.3.2 Minimize the Size of the Information System

We will, therefore, briefly discuss best practices for minimizing the weight of the IS, as mentioned in the previous equation.[25] To put it simply, it is a matter of increasing less (reducing the input flow), which we will cover

---

[25] I will not go into detail on a subject that is beyond the scope of this book. The reader can consult *Information Technology for the Chief Executive: Value Analysis, Organization and Management*, by the same author.

here, and reducing more (increasing the output flow), which we will cover by talking about technical debt in the next section. The increased flow of IS corresponds to a need to create value for the business, and this is the foundation of exponential IS (knowing how to absorb this incoming flow). Minimizing the impact on the size of the IS, therefore, comes down to making the most classic choice in IT management: choosing between *making, buying, renting* in SaaS mode (*software as a service*), and *shifting* (allowing the user to satisfy his or her needs without adding a component). Unsurprisingly, the best practices of the digital world consist of getting as far right as possible in this list while respecting the imperatives of rapid change (which leads to making as soon as the component implements a unique behavior specific to the company). The requirements of digital transformation lead to a double movement: to accumulate less code to be able to change it faster but also to better control the code that supports the core business, also to be able to change it faster, when applicable. The consequence is a double movement of more renting (SaaS) and open-source usage and a return to the production of custom code. This concern to avoid unnecessary growth applies at all levels of the IS, from application governance to the way code is written for these applications. The best "digital code" practices, which we will discuss again in Chapter 7, suggest writing as little code as possible, starting by not writing any code when it is not absolutely necessary or when a third party can provide the service and take care of the continuous management of change itself.

The general principle that it is better to measure in order to manage applies to the weight of the IS. It is important to measure the size of the IS systematically and over time. There has been a debate for decades on the right metrics, my experience shows that it is impossible to decide because it depends deeply on the software maturity of the company and the heterogeneity of the IS.[26] What matters is to choose a way to count and to stick to it. There are multiple *software asset management* tools—*application portfolio management*—and using them is a good way to be systematic and have shared definitions.

---

[26] In a homogeneous software environment, the number of lines of code is a good measure. If the software manufacturing process is under control, precisely calculated function points are even better. If the environment is very heterogeneous, "approximate" function points work well (there are many tools available to switch from lines of code to approximate function points). When the software process is no longer under control, one can simply cross-reference the number of applications with the cumulative investment costs (which works very well if it is done over a long period of time).

Once the practice of measurement is established, it is critical to share it with all the actors who are stakeholders in the decision-making process, particularly the business actors and the company's management. Here we apply another elementary principle of systemics: building a feedback loop to regulate an iterative growth process. The actors in the company who (rightly!) cause the IS to increase in size—and complexity—must be made aware of the consequences of their demands. The more we operate in a distributed organization with multifunctional and autonomous cells, the more this advice is superfluous or even useless. But the longer the decision chain, the more it is necessary to create a governance body for the management of the IS's assets. More than fifteen years ago, we created software asset management committees at Bouygues Telecom to observe together—business and IT, build and run—the main key metrics of the IS components (precisely with one committee per business domain) in order to share a strategy for the evolution of the software assets.

4.3.3 Manage Your Technical Debt

The concept of technical debt is attributed to Ward Cunningham, although it is easy to find earlier references to the same ideas. Debt is something one owes, with the option of getting rid of it by providing money (which represents effort) or keeping it by paying "interest" until it can be paid back. Similarly, a poor software architecture that is the result of too many iterative cycles or too many shortcuts—often called *quick and dirty*—is a burden. The company can either decide to keep this extra weight by paying "interest" in the form of extra cost (more effort and money for continuous adaptation of the system, as explained in the previous section) or "pay off" the debt by making the effort and expense of reorganizing and rebuilding the system.[27] It is worth noting that technical debt is expressed in terms of the need for change, and here I quote Ward Cunningham: "*We can say that code is of high quality if productivity remains high in the presence of change, both in the team and in the objectives.*" Debt is measured against a theoretical ideal standard of code quality and organization. As shortcuts and unnecessary complexity accumulate, the debt measures the effort it would take to return to the desired state. It is, therefore, most often measured as the time it would take to return to this state.

---

[27] For a more complete introduction to the concept of debt, I recommend reading the article "*Introduction to the Technical Debt Concept*," by Jean-Louis Letouzey and Declan Whelan, on the agilealliance.org website.

The interest that must be paid when retaining technical debt is anything but theoretical. While the measurement of technical debt is doubly subjective in nature—about what the standard is and about the time or effort to return to that standard—this deviation from the standard does have a cost, which we have sketched out for complexity and which is well documented.[28] In their article "Estimating the size, cost, and types of Technical Debt," Bill Curtis, Jay Sappidi, and Alexandra Szynkarski define five factors that are the main features of this technical debt and the consequences of unnecessary complexity: loss of robustness, loss of efficiency, increase in security holes, difficulty in changing the teams that own the code, and difficulty in changing the code. **Reducing technical debt decreases future costs and increases the situational potential.**

Reducing technical debt is beyond the scope of this book, but I'll borrow a few key ideas from Carl Tashian's recent article "Managing Technical Debt." First, there are the classic recommendations of a good service architecture: create and maintain areas of flexibility,[29] use APIs and intermediation, and seek to reduce dependencies as much as possible (in other words, seek modularity of the architecture). Intermediation, as its name implies, is a component that isolates two or more parts of a system. The incremental addition of code, links, functions, and so on tends to weave a network of exceptions over a modular architecture, which should be repaired by refactoring (putting the additions back in the right place and using intermediations instead of direct links). The second recommendation echoes this chapter: refactor to facilitate velocity—that is, prepare and facilitate future changes by eliminating redundancies (which require multiple efforts in subsequent changes) and by making the design intent more visible in the code. The third recommendation is to leverage usage statistics (the importance of which we emphasized in the previous chapter) to ruthlessly get rid of features or code that are little or not used. Reducing technical debt has a cost, but this can be reduced by automating the build and test cycle. *Refactoring* only works well if the team has acquired a high level of maturity in its continuous testing practice, as we will come back to in the next section.

---

[28] On this subject, you can read Samuel Mullen's article "*The High Cost of Technical Debt*," where you can find the impact of technical debt on development, maintenance, and support.

[29] Read this article available online on Medium. Carl Tashian draws a parallel with building a house: "*Design your software as you would design a building. You have slow moving parts and fast moving parts. Some components, like furniture or wall paint, are loosely coupled to the building. It's far harder to change the angles at which the walls meet. You have to pick your battles. Knowing what needs to be flexible isn't only about the current requirements, it's about future requirements too.*"

4.4 Resilience and Quality of Service

4.4.1 Site Reliability Engineering

Quality of service is one of the key attributes of the exponential IS. As we said in Chapter 1, performance is part of the quality of experience in our digital world. This performance is driven by technical systems, whether it is response time, availability, or scalability (i.e., resistance to load variations). The exponential IS must respond in a very short time, constant, and quasi-independent of the load (as far as the time perceived by the customer is concerned) and be available all the time, or almost. The acceptable annual downtime is measured in a few hours for most services and in minutes for critical services. The exponential IS must be efficient to give back time to the customer because this is a fundamental expectation of customers in the 21st century. It must also be efficient because it is indeed possible, because the web giants and small digital players are capable of achieving very high levels of performance and availability, and because they have thereby raised user expectations.

In an unpredictable and complex world, quality of service is associated with resilience. Despite the best architectures and technologies, unexpected incidents occur that stress system performance. Resiliency is about being able to return to a nominal mode of operation quickly and without too much effort. The development of resilience and business continuity plans is beyond the scope of this book. My goal here is to point out that in the digital world, there is a continuity between the search for performance, scalability in particular, and resilience. The highly scalable, high-availability architectures of the web giants are built under Werner Vogels's famous assumption that everything is fragile—"*everything breaks, all the time*"—which makes it easier to achieve resilience.

The term *site reliability engineering* (SRE) comes from Google and is the title of an excellent collective book by Google engineers on how they improve and optimize the quality and resiliency of Google services. I quote this book for two reasons. First, it is a rich collection of best practices for building and operating large-scale distributed systems in a robust way. The use of parallelism and distribution is the technical reason that large technical systems can be efficient, scalable, and robust. On the other hand, what has changed dramatically in twenty years is that the methods and techniques used by Google or Facebook are now widely available as open-source tools, and the associated know-how is easily available knowledge. This is what allows small disruptive players to build efficient and scalable systems and what makes it necessary for all companies to evolve their ISs to achieve similar levels of performance and robustness. Ben Taynor Sloss, who is the creator of the SRE approach, writes in the first chapter that robustness is the most fundamental property that users expect from a digital product.

Before discussing the system's capabilities and the core practices that the SRE approach proposes, it is worthwhile to outline the organization proposed by the book's authors, who insist that this ambition of "resilience and quality of service" is first and foremost a matter of people and culture. SRE teams are small cross-functional teams that orchestrate end-to-end operations processes, such as change management, and carry responsibilities associated with these processes, such as organizing "postmortems" (the analysis of the root causes of production incidents). The team is responsible for the performance of operations in the three dimensions we have already mentioned: availability, response time, and load robustness. The team develops and applies its methods in a flexible way depending on the context. For example, to arbitrate between the need to change digital systems and the risk inherent in any change in production, the team uses downtime budgeting,[30] which allows it to adapt the effort (and therefore speed and frequency) of changes to observed availability in relation to the SLA (*service level agreement*, the level of availability promised to the customer). Robustness is not a state of the system; it is a permanent search for improvement through continuous improvement processes (experimenting, analyzing, and capitalizing on errors, progressively building a better-shared understanding of the system we operate—in the tradition of the Toyota Way).

4.4.2 Automation and Monitoring

The two key capabilities of the exponential IS are automation and active self-monitoring. They are essential for several reasons—we'll come back to them in the rest of the book—but I'll quickly highlight here their contribution to

[30] The concept of *error budget* is an important contribution to the SRE practice. The SRE team "*balances reliability and the pace of innovation with error budgets, which define the acceptable level of failure for a service, over some period. . . . As long as the service hasn't spent its error budget for the month through the background rate of errors plus any downtime, the development team is free (within reason) to launch new features, updates, and so on . . . If the error budget is spent, the service freezes changes (except urgent security and bug fixes addressing any cause of the increased errors) until either the service has earned back room in the budget, or the month resets.*"

the quality of service.[31] The first virtue of automation is to reduce human error, which is one of the primary causes of incidents. The more frequently changes are made, the less interesting they are for the operators, and the more it is necessary to automate in order to move towards fully automatic deployment (which we will see in Chapter 7 with the concept of CICD. Second, automation saves time, which is useful for improving the speed of deployments (thus satisfying the objective of increasing the frequency of exponential IS) but, above all, for reducing the MTTR (*mean time to repair*). The automation (and testing) of *backup/restore* or *rollover* operations is essential for rapid incident resolution. Finally, automation aims to make the load of operations sub-linear to the size of the system, to use Ben Sloss's words, with the simple principle that the more you reduce the "mechanical" load of "simple" operations management, the more operators can focus on value-added operations: prevention, observation, and maintenance in optimal operating conditions. Automation is not a project; it is a recurring task. Automation code, like testing, is part of the system's software repository that needs to be updated continuously.[32] That's why an SRE team must include development and software engineering skills and must be able to work on systems in production.

Systems *monitoring* is the heart of robust operations management. I quote from the SRE book: "*Whether it's Google or any other company, monitoring is an absolutely essential component of the right way to manage your production. If you can't monitor a service, you don't know what's really going on, you're effectively blind and you can't operate in a robust way.*"[33] **Monitoring and automation work together and cannot be separated.** Monitoring a large system produces far too much information for these alerts not to be automated in the first stage of processing. The objective of proactive monitoring is that as many alerts as possible should not only be analyzed but also processed automatically, considering human

---

[31] These two topics are covered in detail in the book *Site Reliability Engineering*, and the analysis of QoS improvement is the subject of a chapter in my previous book *Information Technology for the Chief Executive* and in the eighth chapter of my course at Polytechnique, which is easily found online. You will find the classic explanations of MTBF and MTTR.

[32] I quote from the SRE book: "*Automation code, like unit test code, dies when the maintaining team isn't obsessive about keeping the code in sync with the codebase it covers.*"

[33] It should be noted that monitoring allows us to better understand and resolve incidents more quickly but also to find the systems at fault more quickly, which is fundamental when operations are distributed among several partners. It is both technical and functional monitoring (as explained in *Urbanization, SOA and BPM*). Functional monitoring is essential to establish effective communication with the business actors.

intervention only as a last resort. Symmetrically, automation requires strong instrumentation to ensure robust execution. Automation is not a panacea against human error since scripts are written (mostly) by humans. The only way to develop robustness is to put the development of automation in a continuous improvement cycle, which is based on observation.

Monitoring and automation are the two capabilities of the exponential system that are most likely to benefit from advances in AI and ML. The use of these "exponential" techniques to optimize IS operations is often referred to as AIOps.[34] The systematic practice of observing and recording events (*logs*) produces a massive amount of information and opportunities to apply modern methods of intelligent data analysis, including ML, to detect, understand, or predict incidents.[35] The toolbox of SRE teams includes classical *time series* analysis methods, as well as correlation and pattern detection tools. AI techniques are applied to both detection and processing automation (adaptive scripts and processing optimization, for example, with respect to resource utilization). The use of AIOps improves the robustness of operations by playing on the two factors of availability. The MTBF (*mean time between failure*) is increased by reducing errors through automation and by enabling early detection and prevention of incidents. In addition, the MTTR is reduced by an ability to establish the diagnosis more quickly (assisted analysis) and by a faster recovery (better automation).

4.4.3 SRE Practices

Change management is the main source of difficulties—including at Google—and thus needs to receive maximum care and attention, especially since exponential IS is characterized by a high rate of change. Google's SRE team found that approximately 70% of failures (leading to service unavailability) were due to change in production systems. This high number is actually fairly consistent across organizations. What changes between mediocre organizations and excellent organizations like Google is the number of occurrences (MTBF) and the speed of processing (MTTR), not the fact that most errors are due to a poorly controlled change. We have already

---

[34] Searching for "AI for IT operations" on your search engine will give you an idea of the scope of this field.

[35] About fifteen years ago, IBM introduced the notion of *autonomic computing* around concepts such as *self-monitoring, self-optimization, self-provisioning,* and *self-healing*. Modern digital systems realize this ambition and are robustly operated because of their *self-monitoring* and *self-healing* capabilities.

highlighted the tension between the need to change (at an accelerating pace) and the need to control the impacts of those changes. This topic is covered in the book *Accelerate*, which we will discuss in Chapter 7 and which focuses on DevOps practice.[36] The authors have measured that the companies that are able to provide services with very high availability are those that have mastered high-frequency changes. The only way to achieve this is to automate as much as possible and to treat each change as seriously as possible. One of the first missions of the SRE team is, therefore, to lead the preparation of changes and the evaluation of their impacts in a transverse way.[37]

To properly manage an exponential IS, it is essential to understand it as a system. This is one of Google's key messages: modern IS are complex, widely distributed systems, and systems engineering is the key skill that the continuous learning system must develop for all participants.[38] This is precisely *the collective skill* that the SRE team must develop to better manage change. In particular, it is essential to measure, model, and predict the system's load capacity in relation to the demands made on it, which is called *capacity planning*. As the SRE book notes, good *capacity planning* reduces the probability of cascading failures. It contributes to *reliability engineering* to validate redundant designs of the N+X type to ensure that the resulting load when one part of the machines becomes unavailable is effectively supported by the remaining one. *Capacity planning* is strongly coupled with the choice of architecture and load balancing technologies.[39]

The third practice that I would like to highlight is what could be called antifragile operations to echo the beginning of this chapter. To develop IS antifragility, **the SRE approach suggests extracting maximum value**

---

[36] The book *Accelerate: The Science of Lean Software and DevOps: Building and Scaling High Performing Technology Organizations*, by Nicole Forsgreen, Jez Humble, and Gene Kim, studies the deployment of *lean software* and *DevOps* practices (Chapters 6 and 7 of this book) through the study of more than two thousand companies.

[37] We have seen in this chapter that API management is an essential dimension of modern systems engineering. There is a strong dependency between modular architecture and building resilience. API change management is therefore a critical aspect of change management for SRE teams: "*While the modularity that APIs offer may seem straightforward, it is not so apparent that the notion of modularity also extends to how changes to APIs are introduced. Just a single change to an API can force developers to rebuild their entire system and run the risk of introducing new bugs.*"

[38] This is precisely the approach of *lean manufacturing*. We will come back to this in Chapter 7 when we talk about the contributions of *lean* software.

[39] The book focuses on load balancing techniques because they play a critical role in quality of service: "*Avoiding overload is a goal of load balancing policies. But no matter how efficient your load balancing policy, eventually some part of your system will become overloaded. Gracefully handling overload conditions is fundamental to running a reliable serving system.*"

from previous incidents, through root cause analysis (*RCA*), and building skills and resilience through the continuous and regular practice of recovery testing. In particular, continuous testing of the ability to restore data from backups is essential. In my twenty years of production responsibility experience, I have experienced many crises, some of them difficult. I have learned two fundamental lessons. The first is that recovery never goes as planned. In the set of components that participate in the theoretical redundancy that ensures continuity, there is always an element that does not work properly. On the other hand, the commitment and competence of the production teams lead to finding workarounds, demonstrating a resilience that is as much biological as it is mechanical.[40] The second lesson is that data recovery always takes longer than expected and much longer than desired at the time of the crisis. That's why developing data engineering, and operations skills is a major goal of exponential IS. And the only way to achieve this is to practice recovery tests on a regular basis. The practice of *chaos engineering*, popularized by the Netflix teams, consists of regularly putting oneself in a crisis situation, simulating the loss of one or more servers, one or more network elements, or even a data center. One of the key lessons of the SRE book is that running a large-scale distributed system is a complex task, which requires the development of multiple systems engineering expertise and knowledge, which is acquired through experience, capitalization, and discipline.

Summary

1. The radical change in digital technology is that this "*refresh rate*" of technical systems is multiplied by at least one order of magnitude (4.1.1).
2. The exponential information system must make massive use of what is done outside (4.1.3).
3. The multimodal approach consists in defining a service architecture in zones, organized according to the required refresh rate (4.2.1).

[40] This topic of organic production, which echoes the modern approach to resilience (cf. Werner Volgels's words, "*everything breaks all the time*"), is addressed in the author's first book, as well as in the principles of *autonomic computing*.

4. What characterizes digital systems is the return of the source code. The component, through its source code, becomes its own model, its own specification (4.2.2).
5. One of the characteristics of modern digital systems is precisely their scalability, which is based on an event-based approach, a massive distribution of processing and tools for processing event flows (4.2.3).

1. The "intelligent" capabilities of the IS are both an adaptive mechanism and a tool for capitalizing on experience, since the intelligence of the system is a form of knowledge (4.2.4).
2. It is essential to mimic nature and to add to any iterative process a cleaning and reorganization process (4.3.1).
3. Reducing its technical debt decreases future costs and increases the situation potential (4.3.3).
4. Monitoring and automation work together and are inseparable (4.4.2).
5. The SRE approach proposes to extract maximum value from previous incidents, through root cause analysis, and to build skills and resilience through the continuous and regular practice of recovery testing (4.4.3).

Chapter 5

Artificial Intelligence and Machine Learning

5.1 Taking Advantage of Exponential Technologies

5.1.1 The Toolbox and Opportunities

Artificial intelligence (AI) is a branch of computer science that focuses on the programmatic reproduction of behaviors that can be described as intelligent because they are non-repetitive, adaptive in a complex way (i.e., with multiple interactions with the environment) and that represent a cognitive effort from the human point of view.[1] Machine learning (ML) is also a computer science discipline, inspired by mathematics, statistics, and biology, which is interested in inductive programming, that is learned from examples. In this chapter, we will look at these two exponential technologies, AI and ML, as essential tools for success in the digital world. I refer the reader to the report of the French Academy of Technologies[2] to further elaborate and explain these topics, for example, to understand the relative positioning: AI and ML have a strong intersection, but these two disciplines have existed independently of each other for many decades.

---

[1] This last part of the definition is subjective and explains the continuous shift in time. As soon as an adaptive behavior on a computer seems simple and normal to us, it ceases to be perceived as AI. I chose the term "reproduction" to capture the importance of human imitation in the inspiration of AI, but in some cases it is more like "production."

[2] The report "Renewal of Artificial Intelligence and Machine Learning" is available online at the Academy of Technology website (www.academie-technologies.fr/). To better understand the different AI families represented in the five "boxes" and their respective influences, read *The Master Algorithm*, by Peter Domingos.

DOI: 10.4324/9781003272816-7

AI is not an isolated technology; it is from a practical viewpoint for companies, a modality of software systems. This is the double justification for this chapter in this book: AI is necessary for exponential enterprises to succeed in their digital transformation, and it requires an exponential IS that is able to host and develop these capabilities continuously and rapidly.

I use the term "toolbox" to consider AI from the practitioner's point of view, produced by different computing disciplines. In the report of the Academy of Technologies, a typology is proposed that I will comment on here, organized along two axes that are two questions that must be asked before choosing a particular technology. The first one is to know if we are dealing with a problem or open question (the form of the solution is not known at the beginning) or a precise question, "closed" in the sense that we know the type of answer we expect (classifying a situation, translating a sentence, making a scheduling decision are examples of closed questions). The second question to ask is how much data we have to use ML methods. Some approaches are more efficient but require tens of thousands or even millions of examples. Depending on the answers to these questions, one can use different approaches that can be divided into five toolboxes:

- The first, adapted to specific questions with little data, includes symbolic AI techniques, such as rule engines and logic-based tools, the various algorithms from operations research, but also all the language processing tools. Note that these NLP (*natural language processing*) tools require large data sets for their development but their implementation for business problems can be performed on small domains. Although the term "expert system" has become obsolete, many industrial configuration and monitoring systems rely on rules and symbolic approaches such as constraint engines.
- The second group of approaches is better adapted to open questions when little data is available, combining simulation and general system optimization methods such as game theory, evolutionary techniques (such as genetic algorithms) in the form of populations of agents. These approaches have the advantage of producing their own data on which learning methods can be applied.[3] It is with this type of tool that we

[3] As an illustration, the GTES approach developed by the author is a combination of Monte-Carlo simulation, local optimization, and evolutionary game theory. Another example of this type of approach is the French company Cosmo Tech, which specializes in the study of open questions on complex systems by combining simulation and augmented intelligence.

can study complex systems such as population movements in a city, ecosystem disturbances linked to global warming, or the resilience of large networks.

- The third box is the one that is receiving the most attention today, that of deep neural network learning, called *deep learning*. *Deep learning* has made dramatic progress during the last ten years and is now the best approach for a large class of problems, defined by a very specific question and for which a large volume of examples is available. For example, convolutional neural networks are a class of layered architecture that allows to classify images and thus to recognize patterns with high accuracy. We will come back to this in the next section.
- The fourth type of approach is one that is applied to open-ended questions when a large volume of data is available. The semantic network approach, which is old in the AI world, showed its power in 2011 when IBM Watson won the *Jeopardy* final. The set of techniques of networks, ontologies, or knowledge representation and management allows the exploration of open questions on a large data set. A typical application is that of robot-writers able to produce a summary from a set of information. Their use—even if it remains marginal, in the world of legal case preparation, or in the specialized press, in particular for sports—is progressing and testifies to the progress made in ten years.[4]
- The last box includes the more classical[5] ML methods, which are less data-intensive but still require *training sets*. These approaches can be used to answer specific questions (prediction or categorization) or more open questions. These classical learning methods are at the heart of most industrial applications today, from predictive maintenance to fraud detection. Besides algorithms, the toolbox contains a set of techniques to build a model from data, from selection to synthetic variables production, through all kinds of filtering and renormalization.

AI is not a question for tomorrow: today's technologies are already bringing benefits and transformation opportunities to

---

[4] Progress in AI is considered to be linked to the explosion of computing power, the increase of available data, and the continuous development of algorithms (accelerated by the sharing of open source code). These arguments are valid for *deep learning*, but they also apply to other types of AI.

[5] Without being exhaustive, I will mention the following examples: regression (linear or logistic), Bayesian networks, decision tree construction methods (such as *random forest* or *gradient boosting, support-vector machines*), or time series analysis methods (ARMA, ARIMA, etc.).

the companies that use them. I will only cite a few examples in this book, but I will refer the reader to the bibliography for a more substantial overview of what the technology can do today.[6] These technologies are already applied during each of the steps of the value chain that we saw in the first part: research and development, manufacturing, supply chain, sales, and customer relationship management. Learning methods allow pattern detection, which is useful for preventive maintenance or quality assurance. Intelligent assistance techniques for knowledge management are applied both upstream (to assist R&D) and downstream (to assist customers and vendors). In particular, machine learning methods play a key role in the recommendation algorithms of the web giants (Amazon or Netflix for products, Google or Criteo for advertising). The classical methods of rule-based programming, coupled with natural language recognition and synthesis techniques, have found a second life in the form of robot process automation (agents capable of performing automated steps in a process) and conversational agents (chatbots).

5.1.2 The Deep Learning Revolution

Deep neural networks have allowed AI to emerge from several decades of quasi stagnation on basic recognition tasks, whether of images, texts, or sounds. The scientific community has had data sets to compare the performance of different algorithms since the 1980s. For thirty years, not only was progress very slow, but performance was significantly lower than that of a trained human. From 2010 to 2016, there has been a succession of results, especially in the field of image recognition: we went from 72% accuracy in object detection on an image to 97% in 2016, where human performance is around 95%. Similarly, the error rate on word recognition in speech analysis (ASR [*automatic speech recognition*]) has gone from 20% in 2010 to 7% in 2014. This has led to algorithms capable in 2016 of recognizing and sending text messages faster and with a better error rate than young "mobile keyboard champions." This *deep learning* revolution is highly impactful for two reasons. First, deep neural networks can be applied to a wide range of pattern or situation recognition problems, beyond perception, for example, in the world of finance for portfolio management

---

[6] I recommend starting with the following two books: *The Mathematical Corporation: Where Machine Intelligence and Human Ingenuity Achieve the Impossible*, by Angela Zutavern and Josh Sulliva, *Human+Machine: Reimagining Work in the Age of AI*, by Paul Daugherty and H. James Wilson.

or in *digital manufacturing* to diagnose situations of concern. Second, the new perception capabilities can be combined with other AI techniques, such as shown with AlphaGo, which mixes *deep learning* to evaluate positions with MCTS (*Monte-Carlo tree search*) exploration, a "first box" technique presented above. In his book *AI Superpower: China, Silicon Valley and the New World Order*, Kai-Fu Lee recounts the exceptional impact of AlphaGo's victory over champion Lee Seedol in 2016. He emphasizes the importance of Go in Chinese culture and how the game of Go has long been associated with human intelligence. This is why the machine's victory caused an exceptional shock and a wake-up call for the Chinese government, giving rise to a very ambitious program of AI development in China.

ML using neural networks is a very powerful approach, capable of approximating the solution functions of a very large number of problems, and goes far beyond the classic toolbox (what we have called the fifth box). The shape of the activation function of the neurons and the architecture of the layers allow the reproduction of non-linear behaviors and thus the learning of complex behaviors. On the other hand, to successfully train these networks on difficult problems, one needs a lot of machine power, a lot of qualified examples, and a fair amount of practical experience. The explosion of machine power is behind most of the breakthroughs, both as a consequence of Moore's law and because more optimized architectures, such as GPUs and "neuromorphic" chips,[7] have become widespread. In the sequence of spectacular progress in machine vision, the role of the ImageNet database is underlined by all experts;[8] this database of more than ten million images has been assembled and qualified by a large community of contributors who have patiently described the content of the images. Kai-Fu Lee makes massive access to data the primary condition for success and dominance over competitors in the application of AI: "*If you have a lot more data, an algorithm designed by a handful of normal-level AI engineers will generally perform better than what a world-class specialist would do with less data.*" Developing back-propagation learning from data samples on layers of neurons is complex and requires a good deal of experience, but fortunately, much of that experience has been encapsulated in various

[7] GPUs are the graphics processors of computers, simpler and more specialized than CPUs (the main chip). GPUs allow better parallelization and better performance for a given volume or consumption. For a few years now, especially on smartphones but also on servers (TPU), even more specialized chips have been appearing in neural network calculations, offering significant improvements in terms of performance/consumption ratio.

[8] Read for example the testimony of Yann Le Cun or Fei-Fei Li in *Architects of Intelligence*.

open-source libraries and different platforms opened widely by the web giants, such as Google's TensorFlow or Facebook's PyTorch. This allows a generalist engineer to learn and use these techniques on their favorite problems. The Academy's report gives examples that show how the openness of software tools makes it possible to apply *deep learning* to a very wide variety of problems in a way that is accessible to as many people as possible.

However, *deep learning* is not a panacea, and it does not replace other AI techniques.[9] As we said in the previous section, *deep learning* needs a lot of "labeled" data and a precise question to be answered. The data set is oriented by this question since the labels are the answers provided by humans according to the problem to be solved. If the question changes drastically, the entire data set must be requalified for learning. As Kai-Fu Lee puts it, "*To do deep learning, you need a massive amount of data appropriate to the problem, the right algorithm, a narrow domain and a concrete goal. If any of these conditions are not met, things don't work.*"

Moreover, deep networks represent "black box" algorithms, whose decisions we cannot explain. For some problems (placing an advertisement or recommending a shampoo), this is not prohibitive, but in other cases, it poses a problem of trust and ethics (prescribing a medical treatment or driving a car amongst pedestrians). Like all machine learning algorithms, *deep learning* is sensitive to biases in the data—we will come back to this subject later—but because the algorithm is a black box, it is difficult to notice these biases without doing a large number of tests, which are themselves complex to design. Finally, the availability of software tools should not mask the difficulty of development. Many criticisms are frequently made because the results are not necessarily reproducible. With the same data and the same toolboxes, not everyone reaches the same result. Experience plays a very important role, which explains the war for talent and the very high remuneration levels in this field.

5.1.3 Hybridization and Meta-Heuristics

AI is a rich set of methods that are most often used in a hybrid fashion. This means that one can combine methods from the five boxes we described

[9] It is important to understand the power of *deep learning* and not to underestimate the quantitative leap that these advances allow AI. To have a balanced judgment and also understand the deep limitations of this type of method, one can read *Rebooting AI*, by Gary Marcus.

in the first section. Examples of hybridization (combining two or more approaches) can be found in most spectacular success stories, whether it is AlphaGo, IBM Watson, or Todai Robot, the University of Tokyo's software that is capable of passing a college entrance exam.

The case of DeepMind is particularly interesting because the vision of its founder, Demis Hassabis, is precisely to build complex cognitive systems by assembling multiple methods.[10] This approach has given AlphaGo and AlphaZero (capable of learning Go and chess by playing only against oneself) and also AlphaFold, a software that applies deep learning to protein structure reconstruction, one of the most important scientific problems of the time, with major impacts to help design new drugs. AlphaFold is today the most powerful algorithm in this field[11] and another illustration of the use of *deep learning* as a component in a hybrid approach. In the book *Human + AI*, the authors give examples of enriching intelligent assistants with other AI techniques, from NLP tools to deep learning. The development of Google Duplex comes to mind here, but the authors detail the example of SparkCognition: "*a product called DeepArmor, which uses a combination of AI techniques including neural networks, heuristics, data science algorithms, and natural language processing methods to be able to detect previously unseen threats.*" Another very interesting form of hybridization is the combination of random exploration to generate data with AI. These "generative" approaches allow new areas of design to be explored. The machine is able to produce, select and then optimize new objects, whether they are designs—an approach that has been strongly emphasized by Autodesk—or processes.

There are many ways to use and combine the "elementary" algorithms of the toolbox. The notion of meta-heuristics describes "algorithms that parameterize and drive other algorithms." AI, like operations research, has produced multiple meta-heuristics for decades, which play a key role in building hybrid solutions. Without going into too much technical detail, I will describe some examples:

- *Reinforcement learning* is a very old technique in AI, based on a continuous improvement loop by selecting small incremental changes through a "reward" function. Libratus, the world champion poker player

[10] You should listen to *DeepMind: The Podcast*, presented by Hannah Fry. In particular, the eighth episode with the interview of Demis Hassabis, is very interesting to understand the SoS approach.

[11] Read, for example, the article "*AI protein-folding algorithms solve structures faster than ever*" on the Nature.com website, whose subtitle is "*Deep learning makes its mark on protein-structure prediction.*" AlphaFold is also the subject of one of the episodes of the DeepMind podcast.

developed at Carnegie-Mellon University, is a combination of classical statistical learning and *reinforcement learning*. In another way, *lean startup* product development is also reinforcement learning.

- Probabilistic methods (such as the Monte-Carlo approach) and their adaptation to massive communities of agents are essential for exploring search spaces, as the DeepMind examples show. The combination of generation and optimization has a place almost everywhere, including in the automation of the development of AI algorithms themselves. Many platforms offer "auto ML" functions—that is, the automation, through classical optimization (the first box) and probabilistic exploration techniques, of the parameter space of a machine learning algorithm.
- Evolutionary methods are another meta-heuristic from the world of AI and classical optimization, which make a large community of agents evolve according to laws that seek to reproduce natural selection (Darwin), the genetic mutation of species, or the search for an equilibrium (Nash) in game theory.
- The world of deep learning has also produced different meta-heuristics, such as *transfer learning*, which allows to reuse a "low layer" learning, obtained on a very large volume of generic data, on a new network that will be trained with a smaller number of examples specific to the problem we want to treat. The notion of adversarial network (GAN [*generative adversarial network*]) seeks to improve the robustness of deep networks (which are often defeated by a small variation) by building a pair of neural networks, the second one looking for counterexamples to the first one's training, in order to build by reinforcement a more robust global system. A last example of meta-heuristics is the reinjection of data from the calculation into the input stream, which is called recurrent networks. LSTM (*long short-term Memory*) networks are an application of this principle that gives excellent results in recognizing time series, such as speech streams.

The thing to remember from this section is that **one must have a broad view of AI and stay up-to-date with the state of the art both in terms of tools and composition methods**. The "deep learning brick" is one of the indispensable components today because of the spectacular progress of the last decade. On the other hand, composition with other approaches allows, for example, to mitigate the drawbacks of the "black box" approach if one combines a "white box" method of the "decision tree" type with deep learning. Mastering meta-heuristics allows one to play with deep learning like a Lego brick and to build more general systems. For example, when we want to detect very rare defects, there is not necessarily a sufficiently large database of examples to train a neural network to recognize them. A dual approach consists in training an *auto-encoder*, a network able to recognize and "compress" the normal situation (absence of defects) for which it is easy to have millions of examples and to train another network to decompress (reconstruct the original image, for example). This pair then allows the detection of a defect by the difference between the source image and the reconstructed image. This small example of mental gymnastics (learning from the complementary), successfully used in the sheet metal industry,[12] shows the importance of the practical mastery of AI tools.

5.1.4 Reinventing Processes and Products with Artificial Intelligence

AI is an opportunity to reinvent product development. For companies, this is undoubtedly the most important and revolutionary message. This is particularly clear in the field of R&D. I reproduce here a long quote from the book *Human + Machine*: "The *use of AI in the various stages of R&D—observation, hypothesis generation, experiment design, etc.—The use of AI in the various stages of R&D—observation, hypothesis generation, experiment design, etc.—produces remarkable gains at all levels, in a number of different fields. It is becoming possible to reproduce in a few months discoveries that took a decade, producing dramatic cost reductions.*" This message is disruptive in the sense that a company that does not heed this advice could see a weaker or less capable competitor catch up and reverse its product R&D lateness because its better use of AI allows this competitor to gain more business knowledge from the same experiments or customer feedback. This practice of experimentation is remarkably explained by Jeff Bezos, for whom companies that do not experiment and make the most of failures find themselves in very delicate positions where they are forced to make very risky "big bets." This is particularly the case in the area we mentioned in the first chapter, the smart coupling of *supply chain* and *demand management*. The *smart supply chain* needs real-time information about

[12] The *autoencoder* and *decoder* neural networks are trained on tens of thousands of defect-free sheets so that a sheet image is first compressed and then decompressed with excellent fidelity. Defects in the sheet metal "break" this mechanism and cause differences between the input and output images.

customer demands, and customers expect real-time order tracking. Giants such as Amazon or Alibaba are not just online supermarkets; they are above all *supply chain* champions that have accumulated a very fine knowledge of customer needs, precisely with the massive accumulation of data and the use of AI to process it.[13]

We find here the arguments of the book *Exponential Organizations* presented in the first part. Algorithmic competence (i.e., the ability to exploit the methods and tools of the "boxes" presented in the three previous sections) defines the potential of the company to exploit the opportunities in its environment. Companies that develop this competence can make spectacular progress on old and difficult problems. Salim Ismael cites the case of *All State*, which held a competition open to more than one hundred participants, who improved the performance of their internal algorithm, optimized over several decades, by 271%. The contest, with a $10,000 prize, earned the company tens of millions of dollars. The book *Exponential Organization* contains other examples in the medical, transportation, energy, and financial worlds. In transportation, UPS uses the full range of exponential technologies from capture to optimization to manage a fleet of fifty-five thousand trucks that were making—at the time the book was published—more than sixteen million deliveries a day, resulting in earnings of more than $2 billion.

AI is a learning loop with humans inside. This is, in my opinion, the most important idea of the book *Human + AI*. The role of the human (*embedded*: inside) is multiple; it is both to organize the learning of the machine, to participate in its learning, and to use the value produced by algorithms. Besides the cases of completely automated systems, the vast majority of intelligent systems are assistance systems and decision support systems. Just as for chess, the best agent to solve a problem or to drive a process is a centaur, the combination of man and machine—in chess, centaurs do better than programs, which do better than humans. The co-development of the centaur (of the human agent and intelligent assistant pair) is a formidable adventure in the reinvention of professions and a race to create new competitive advantages. The amplification loop

---

[13] On the evolution of the *supply chain* in the VUCA world described in the first part, read *Demand Driven Material Requirements Planning*, by C. Ptak and C. Smith. Smith, in which we find this quote: "*Product variety has risen dramatically. Supply chains have extended around the world driven by low-cost sourcing. Product complexity has risen. Outsourcing is more prevalent. Product life and development cycles have been reduced.*" This book explains remarkably well the necessary integration of hazards in management systems.

dimension induces first-mover advantages that are self-sustaining. The *embedded human* is also the one who helps to collect, classify, and qualify the data. The role of the human is fundamental here, as we have already underlined the importance of qualified data sets for developing algorithms.

5.2 Conditions of Implementation

5.2.1 The Data Engineering Process

In practice, an AI strategy for a company starts with a data strategy. The definition of a given strategy by the business actors requires reflection and ownership: we must ask ourselves what data is needed and why.[14] The first step in the application of AI is data collection, both the data that already exists and that needs to be circulated more freely—what is generally referred to as "de-silo-ing the data"—and thinking about the data that is produced but not collected, or not collected systematically and with sufficient frequency. There is a "chicken and egg" effect: you have to collect the data you need to investigate a problem, and what you can do with AI depends on the data available. The answer is necessarily a learning curve—a cycle, which we will come back to in the next section. **It is fundamental to think of data as a continuous cycle of collection: future data is more valuable than past data.** The reality of successful industrial projects does not reflect the metaphor "data is the new oil" but rather the creation of value from a constant flow. Data collection must be accompanied by the process of qualifying the data by producing *metadata* (labels that qualify the data). The creation of qualified data sets is the foundation of all the successes we have described here, most often by collection and qualification by business experts but also, on some problems, through data generation. The qualification phase is accompanied by a diagnosis of the quality of the data. Contrary to popular belief, we can do remarkable things and extract value from noisy or incomplete data, provided we are aware of the limitations of this data. The example of the FAA cited above illustrates a big success with

---

[14] On the subject of data strategy, read the previously mentioned book *The Digital Playbook*, which makes it one of the pillars of digital transformation: "*To create good data strategy, you must begin with an understanding of the four templates of data value creation, the new sources and analytic capabilities of big data, the role of causality in data-driven decision making, and the risks around data security and privacy.*"

partially incomplete data.[15] This assessment of data quality covers both the completeness and accuracy of the data collected but also possible biases in the collection process. As we will discuss later, it is essential to ensure that the data you collect are representative.

The second step is the creation of a learning platform by building a model that can be instantiated from collected data. While the *deep learning* approach is generally capable of absorbing large amounts of data and letting the algorithm decide what is useful, classical learning methods require the selection and construction of *feature data*, which are the data retained in the model. Once the model is built, the algorithms of the toolbox and the assembly or parameterization meta-heuristics must be selected for their implementation. A good rule of thumb, recommended by Silicon Valley experts, is to always start with a simple algorithm, such as regression or *k-mean* clustering, to have a point of comparison.

The third step in this data engineering process is to rigorously define the learning protocol. The learning protocol explains how to train the algorithm (most often, the combination of algorithms) from the qualified data to produce the best solution for the problem at hand, both in terms of accuracy and robustness. As the solution is produced and used in the form of a business application, this training protocol may be seen as a recipe for producing code from data.[16] The know-how is not expressed in the finished product but in the recipe and in the ingredients (the qualified data). The learning protocol is a mix of business expertise to define the right objectives that will bring value to the company and technical expertise to produce in a robust way (for example, by separating learning data from test data). The learning protocol captures the scientific rigor needed to produce useful applications and takes advantage of *data science*.

It is interesting to illustrate this point about data engineering by taking the example of conversational assistants, better known as *chatbots*. Today's *chatbots* have a simplistic way of working: a search for intentions based on the analysis of the dialogue, then the application of a script (rules, most often very simple) to find the action to apply or the answer to make. This approach only works well in a narrow domain (for example, assistance

---

[15] The fact that statistical methods of learning and classification work on incomplete data is not new. One of the first scientific works of the author in 1985 already dealt with the statistical analysis of highly incomplete archaeological data ("*A Method for the analysis of incomplete data and its application to monastic settlements in Italy*").

[16] This explains the somewhat simplistic aphorism "data is the new code" —read the report of the Academy of Technologies on Big Data: "Big Data: one paradigm shift can hide another."

in diagnosing a breakdown or on the procedure to follow following an incident) so that the intention capture (what the customer wants) is sufficiently precise.[17] Experts caution that today's platforms are not capable of capturing the semantics of user dialogues, but continued advances in NLP techniques, which are fueled by the use of *deep learning*[18] as a core technology, will progressively allow for a better understanding of intent, on larger perimeters, as long as companies have large volumes of dialogues to train the next generation of algorithms. It is, therefore, important to start using *chatbot* technology right away, with narrow perimeters and simple technologies, to capture dialogues and create the volumes of data that will enable the development of tomorrow's solutions. To caricature, a "mediocre" *chatbot* is a tool to produce dialogues that will drive the next generation of intelligent assistants. The co-development of systems and data is so important that we will devote the next section to it.

5.2.2 Build a Circular Learning Flow

While writing the report "*Big Data: One Paradigm Shift Can Hide Another*" for the Academy of Technology, we explored the engineering of advanced optimization solutions from companies like Criteo, Google (for AdSense), Amazon, or Netflix (for recommendation). In almost all cases, we are struck by two things. First, the algorithm used is not revolutionary; it is the engineering of the implementation on very large volumes of data that impresses (we often find "simple" logistic regressions on millions of parameters). Second, when these companies started, the performance of the algorithms was not very good; it was a laborious process of continuous improvement that produced the current performance. This is represented by Figure 5.1. Algorithms are only a "source" element; they must be integrated within a computer system. The algorithms are trained from existing data and then deployed, via applications, in the form of services that generate usage and new data that enrich the original data. The virtuous circle is set up: more data produces more relevance, more relevance leads to more usage, and more usage provides more data.

---

[17] *Chatbots* have suffered, like most new smart technologies, from over-enthusiasm followed by disillusionment. Yet when applied to a narrow domain, they work well and are appreciated by users.

[18] Read *Architects of AI* and *Rebooting AI*: deep learning is not the right technology—for now—to extract semantics from a dialogue, so hybrid approaches must be developed. But progress in the "lower layers" of perception/recognition will spread to the systems of systems of language and dialogue processing, such as the Google Duplex system.

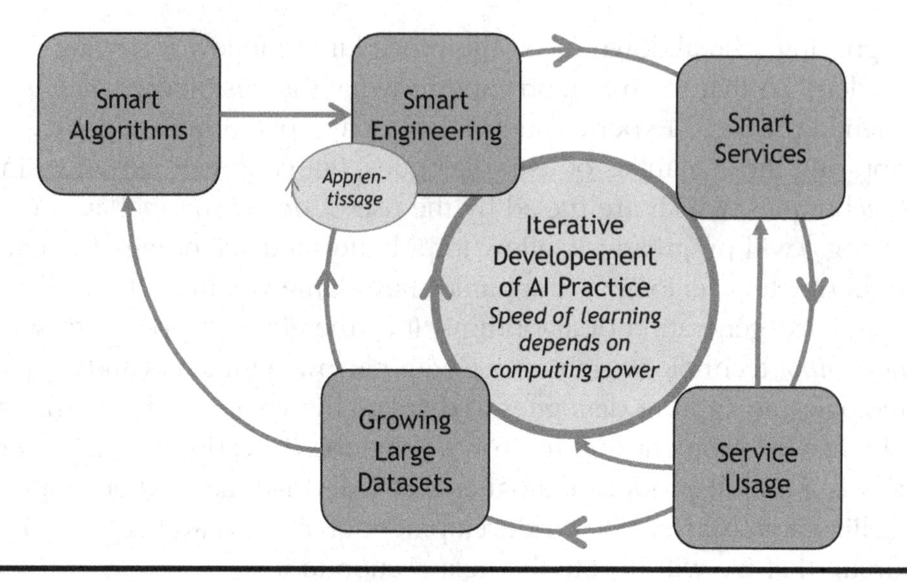

Figure 5.1 The virtuous circle of algorithm/data learning.

The implementation of AI-enhanced applications must be seen systemically as a loop. The virtuous circle in Figure 5.1 is not just about data and algorithms; it is also about the actors in the system—remember the earlier phrase "AI is a learning system with humans in it." There are two key roles for humans in this diagram. The first is to train the learning system and to develop the algorithms. As we saw in the first part, we do not find the right method right away; engineers gradually learn by trial and error what works and what doesn't. It is, therefore, important to be able to iterate quickly in order to learn faster. The second human role is that of the user. In the case of a B2C application, it is the customer of the service; in the case of a B2E application, it is the employee who uses the AI-enhanced application to do his job better—the operator in a factory, for example. Taking into account the user's learning is fundamental to create value with AI. In both roles, human skills must be developed to make the "human + machine" synergy work as well as possible. To summarize, there is a learning curve, and it takes time.[19]

The importance of stepping back to build the "big learning loop" in Figure 5.1 (as opposed to the small loop found in developing algorithms from data) comes from the fact that one is not simply trying to develop

[19] Read the book *Human + AI* mentioned above. The example of intelligent (because continuously adaptive) scheduling from Percolata in Japan illustrates the power of combining a systemic loop vision and machine optimization

an algorithm but an SoS. Human actors are elements of that system, but there is also—more often than not—a combination of AI subsystems that require some learning to perform a successful integration. To give this expression "SoS" a more concrete reality, I will take the example of home automation (i.e., the realization of a *smart home*). This example is both easy to understand and easy to transpose to other domains. A *smart home* is a living system: it perceives signals from its environment and produces events to be processed (it will thus use an event-oriented architecture, as indicated in the previous chapter).

To make decisions, the house must have intelligent perception (i.e., recognize images, sounds, situations). As we said above, these functions require the use of *deep learning* algorithms—as we can see with the generalization of intelligent cameras that include face or situation recognition functions. Some of the actions must be reflexes, executed instantly, and in an auditable way for security reasons. This leads to the use of more classical AI techniques, such as symbolic AI or the use of decision trees. To be intelligent, a house must have a memory and be able to learn[20] (i.e., to adapt to its occupants and not the other way around). Implementing the learning function of the house already requires a more complex assembly of elementary functions and meta-heuristics, such as reinforcement learning. Some of the actions that the house must perform are complex actions that require planning to execute. This requires both a knowledge representation effort to build an operational model of the house world and the use of classical AI algorithms or even specialized operations research algorithms. What characterizes intelligence, as Yann Le Cun points out, is not just reacting to the environment but anticipating it. A smart house must, therefore, have predictive capabilities, as well as a model of how its internal and external environment works. It must predict what time the occupants will come home from work, what time the boiler should run a bath, or which light paths should be turned on (to provide more comfort than just motion detection). This most often requires the use of the classic toolbox of machine learning, such as time series manipulation tools. Finally, the smart house must be able to implement the global learning loop, a form of systemic reinforcement learning, for which evolutionary algorithms

[20] I use this example here without going into technical details (which techniques to use) or systemic justifications (why multiple approaches are necessary). I refer you to the book *Rebooting AI* for an introduction to this topic. This example is illustrated in more detail in my blog post "*Event-Driven Architecture and Biomimicry.*"

are probably the best approach today.[21] The interest of this example is to show that, in order to obtain an "intelligent" behavior that is up to the expectations of the occupants, one is quickly led to integrate multiple capabilities of AI and to assemble them with a biomimetic architecture, which brings out different layers and different time scales in the processing of events.[22] As with a living being, this SoS approach is necessary for control, resilience, and security. Elementary functions must be handled with robust and certifiable mechanisms, while some cognitive functions may involve black boxes or partial and imperfect methods.

5.2.3 Data Lab Culture

The successful development of AI in a company requires a culture that favors experimentation, in line with what was said in the first part for digital transformation. The authors of *Human + Machine* propose the acronym MELDS (*mindset, experimentation, learning, data, skills*) to characterize the different components of this transformation. These different aspects are linked: the same attitude that encourages experimentation allows learning from data to develop skills. The culture of experimentation is necessary in the first place because we do not know in advance what will work as expected and create value. Experimentation is the most efficient strategy for exploring how much value can be extracted from the digital world (of data). Second, the culture of experimentation is linked to learning and skill development. As with most digital and exponential technologies, one must practice in order to learn, and one must learn to develop the skills to truly create value. The same book points out that companies advanced in this field of AI "*have recognized that this is not a classic investment since the value produced by this investment increases progressively over time by developing, consequently, the skills of the designers and users of these solutions.*"

AI development should not be specialized by domain or by role. Experimentation by cross-functional teams is a distributed strategy for

---

[21] From a technical point of view, this requires two things that are characteristics of complex systems: goal reification and the manipulation of heuristic valuation functions, which could be called emotions in anthropocentric terminology. Goal reification requires a more complex model and uses classical AI techniques. This allows us to take advantage of tools from logic to do planning. Optimizing evaluation heuristics via an evolutionary approach is similar to the evolution of species that shaped our reflexive and emotional system, which we inherit at birth before doing our own learning.

[22] The consequence of this proposition is that if one simply introduces elementary "intelligent" objects unable to communicate with each other to bring out a system with superior contextual intelligence, the contributions of home automation are often perceived as marginal and disappointing.

exploring value. The term "distributed" emphasizes that there are multiple application areas for AI and that each business unit must have the freedom to explore these opportunities.[23] The use of cross-functional teams, which we presented in Chapter 3, is necessary because the development of business intuition, the development of software tools, and the practice of learning algorithms develop in parallel, in the form of loops. **The data lab model seeks to capture three ideas: it is a place where different professions and skills work together, it is a place of experimentation, and it is a place of scientific discipline in the conduct of experiments.** The data lab is not a centralized structure but rather a network precisely because of the distribution of opportunities. The development of protocols for learning solutions, which we mentioned above, requires a great deal of rigor and care to build the assemblies of techniques, to parameterize them, and to verify that the results obtained are robust and significant.

This point is worth emphasizing: it is important to use *data science* not to develop what works but to understand what doesn't. No matter what solution and platform vendors say, assembling an AI platform that works robustly is as much an art as it is a science (which explains the debates about the difficulty of replicating the results described in papers, which itself justifies the emphasis on experience, and the insistence on experimentation). This extraordinary power of machines and these storage capacities that have allowed the progress of AI mentioned above are also the cause of many fragilities, such as *overfitting* or the appearance of *spurious correlations*.[24] The more powerful the machine and the more parameters are used, for many algorithms, the easier it is to extract "patterns" in the data, but in a non-robust way. The more data there is, the higher the probability of seeing correlations between "variables" (characteristic quantities associated with the data) that do not make sense from a business point of view. I will not go here into detail about all the difficulties that exist to obtain results that are statistically valid, relevant from a business point of view, and robust over time. I refer you to the books in the bibliography.[25]

---

[23] This idea is remarkably expressed by Gary Hamel in his book *The Future of Management*.

[24] *Overfitting* is the process of producing models that are overfitted to the initial data set at the expense of the robustness of the predictions. Chance correlations are statistical relationships that appear between unrelated quantities, such as the number of Nobel Prize winners and chocolate consumption (the web is full of amusing examples).

[25] The very interesting subject of data collection that minimizes bias (since bias will be found in the results if not identified) is particularly well exposed in Cathy O'Neil's book: *Weapons of Math Destruction*. Similarly, one must read Nassim Taleb to understand that the use of AI on stochastic problems is a risk amplifier, which was formidably illustrated by the *subprime* crisis in 2008. If we are not careful, the "intelligent" algorithm will most often produce an improvement in results, to the detriment of extreme cases for which it will prove catastrophic (in every sense of the word). In statistical terms, we gain on the mean but we lose in standard deviation (which means amplification of the risk).

The gradual and interlocking development of skills and value creation makes it necessary to follow an experience curve. The same advice is given by many experts:[26] "*start with simple solutions, introduce more sophisticated algorithms and meta-heuristics in a progressive way*" because simple methods work well most of the time and because the analysis of the first results makes it possible to understand where to put one's effort. The experience curve also applies to the search for external cooperation. The better one understands the problem to be solved, the more value one will derive from an academic collaboration, the use of a world-renowned expert, or more simply, the organization of a hackathon open to external teams. The general advice in the context of digital transformation to "know how to rely on external expertise" applies to the world of AI, but the value that the company derives from its openness depends on its own level of expertise, as well as the depth of analysis and preparation of the data. This principle of continuous progress based on reinforcement loops (see the previous section) is being developed in many ways. For example, the use of advanced visualization techniques is inseparable from the development of learning algorithms. Visualization feeds intuition; intuition and experimentation lead to new models, which enrich visualization. We can thus add a fourth characterization to this *data lab* principle: it is a place where we continuously look at data.

5.3 Impact on the Information System

5.3.1 Data Architecture

I will end this chapter by returning to the exponential IS and the capabilities that must be developed to take advantage of AI. Very logically, the first capability is the ability to collect, store, and process very large volumes of information. In particular, the *machine vision* revolution means that we must develop the ability to capture images and videos on a massive scale.[27] The spectacular progress in image quality and price (we are thinking here of

---

[26] Read the report of the French Academy of Technologies or the book *Human + Machine*: "*Don't be intimidated by the scale of the data that you encounter. Focus on simple AI challenges first and move on from here.*"

[27] I take here the example of video collection because it is the one that has the most impact in terms of storage capacity and consequently requires a proactive effort to make the systems evolve, but *deep learning* also works on audio signatures, and what will be said about image capture consequently applies to sound capture.

consumer products such as GoPro cameras) means that it is becoming easy to capture manufacturing or distribution processes. *Deep learning* algorithms are capable of recognizing defects or helping to optimize these processes, but a substantial history is required for learning. Therefore, we need to have the capabilities to store, manipulate, and enrich these images or videos to enable business experts to perform the data enrichment mentioned above. In the book *The Mathematical Corporation*, there is a very interesting example of using deep neural networks to estimate "ejection fraction"[28] from echocardiography videos. A medical department held a competition open to teams of external *data scientists* to find the best algorithm capable of learning to estimate this ejection fraction. This example is interesting for two reasons. First, the captures are only two-dimensional, and the goal is to estimate a volume. The fact that the "machine vision" approach can obtain excellent results without 3D modeling shows the power of "black box" approaches. Secondly, the winning team was composed of *data scientists* coming from the world of finance and without medical experience, but a considerable amount of work had been done by the medical teams beforehand to produce the qualified data (associating volumes and annotations to the images).

The data collection architecture must be open because it is often possible to considerably enrich the model on which the algorithms work by crossing the company's data with external data. We saw this in the first chapter when we talked about the DMP (*data management platform*), which makes it possible to cross-reference one's own browsing data with that of other sites visited by one's customers. Another example described above, that of Merck in *The Mathematical Corporation*, shows the interest in crossing production data (digital traces of vaccine manufacturing flows) and environmental data (outside temperature, pressure, hygrometry).

This ability to collect all available data sources in the company and to associate external data with it is based on the existence of a unique and shared business data model. The data model is the backbone of the IS architecture. It describes "business objects": the way in which the company's knowledge is described (in order to share a common semantic) and organized (the information content of the "objects" and the relationships that link them). There are different ways of modeling data, but what is important is to have a common and shared model, which is

---

[28] The ejection fraction (EF) is the percentage of blood ejection from a heart chamber during a heartbeat (Wikipedia).

essential to de-silo ISs and to ensure that data can circulate without losing digital continuity.[29] The requirement from the point of view of AI is to have an open model, which is applicable to the entire IS. The openness of the model (i.e., the ability to easily adapt to data enrichment) is essential to capture external data as well as to be able to track ongoing progress in terms of capture, which we described in Chapter 1. In the book *Reinventing the Product*, the authors note that "*the data models used by the majority of companies that make products are decades old . . . the reality is that data models are too siloed and need to be reinvented.*" Modernizing and unifying the business model is also necessary for the company to realize the full value of the API exposure strategy presented in the previous chapter: it's not enough to make data available with a REST API; it's also necessary for the information to be understood consistently by all consumers, based on the same shared model.

5.3.2 Data Infrastructure

The IS is, first and foremost, a data manipulation platform. I will not go into details here that go beyond the scope of the book, but I distinguish between the data architecture, which is a model of the system (the business model, the data distribution principles, the life cycle process, etc.), and the data infrastructure, which is the part of the system itself dedicated to data.[30] The data infrastructure covers the areas of capture, storage, sharing (with all the problems of competing accesses to the same data), movement (because response times are important, it is often necessary to duplicate and thus move data), and backup (as mentioned in Chapter 4, resilience requires taking into account the failures of the various components). Figure 5.2 briefly describes the different areas of the data infrastructure. The main evolution of

[29] All the components of the IS work with a data model, whether explicit or implicit. The challenge here is to have a global model that is shared throughout the enterprise and that enables data to be cross-referenced between the various subsystems, with the assurance that producers and consumers share the same meaning for the elements of information (what we call semantics). This does not necessarily mean that the data representation model is unique: in a multimodal architecture that evolves at different rates, the representations (the way the data is implemented) may evolve with some disorder, but the semantics, the meaning associated with the data, must be uniquely defined and shared. This is precisely what allows us to federate zones by guaranteeing the relevance of exchanges.

[30] For more details, read the author's first book *Urbanization, SOA and BPM* or the course "Theory and Practice of Information Systems" available online. Defining the life cycle, the owner of a business data and the "reference" (whether it is a dedicated technical system (the repository) or an operational system) are essential steps in data governance.

exponential ISs is the strong decoupling between storage and use, with the appearance over the last ten years of the *data lake* concept. The *data lake* replaces the principle of the data *warehouse* by focusing on the collection and keeping the data in its original format. *Data lakes* have emerged to meet the challenges of the data explosion presented in Chapter 1: more volume, more variety, and more need for velocity. The *data lake* is a simpler data warehouse so that it is more scalable and more flexible and can adapt more quickly to a new type of data. This means that the work of normalizing and transforming data into different formats is done by the data analysis platforms, which are the "consumers" of the *data lake*(s). Because the functional role is simplified, the *data lake* concept can be divided into several systems, and one can choose to use a federation of *data lakes* rather than a single system, depending on one's own constraints: security, data localization with respect to legal obligations, performance, and availability requirements.

Data lakes are fed from multiple sources, both internal and external, through the collection infrastructure. The collection infrastructure is the technical system that urbanizes (rationalizes, groups, and simplifies) the flows that transport the data from the source systems to places of use, such as the *data lake*. Here we find old concepts such as repositories, which are intermediation systems for sharing business data. The repository associated with a business data (a customer, a product, etc.) is the designated intermediary for any other system that needs to access a data, which protects and decouples the source systems. Urbanization through repositories is an old practice but one that remains relevant for organizing the data infrastructure of the exponential IS.

The second characteristic of the data infrastructure of the exponential IS is that it is built around change, as we pointed out in the previous chapter. In this universe of permanently changing and circulating data, data repositories give way to flows of events that materialize these changes. This is why we introduced the notion of event-based architecture in the previous chapter (EDA). In addition to the classic methods that work on "photos" of the situation contained in databases (such as the *data lake*), we are seeing the emergence of methods that analyze the "films" of changes. We often speak of cold processing (on data) and hot processing (on changes), and the exponential IS must be able to support both approaches.[31] In a rapidly changing digital world, the notion of "freshness"

---

[31] The term "lambda architecture" appeared a few years ago in the world of BI systems to refer to the coexistence of cold data processing systems and hot events, using data-stream-processing platforms, such as Kafka or Spark.

of data is very important and sometimes essential. This implies two things. First, the engineering of the data infrastructure must include constraints on data freshness, and it is, therefore, essential to control the performance of transfer, propagation, and synchronization. Second, part of the processing must be rethought in flow mode, deconstructing databases to replace the concept of persistent storage of a value by a continuous process of change propagation.[32] The consequence for the data infrastructure is that it does not only contain subsystems for data collection, storage, and processing but also a flow processing system that uses events to combine transport and processing, which we discussed when we talked about reactive systems in Chapter 4.

The third characteristic of this data infrastructure is that it is massively distributed for reasons of performance (reducing latency by bringing data to where it will be used and increasing bandwidth by using parallelism) and resiliency (using redundancy and separation to avoid the consequences of failures). What changes in modern massively distributed systems compared to classical ISs is the "CAP theorem," which states[33] that one cannot simultaneously obtain consistency (guaranteeing that the value that will be used locally as a copy of a business data is consistent with the source), high availability of the systems (the ability to read these values at any time), and resilience to events (disruption in the network) that would create a partition of the system. Since distribution and resilience are intrinsic characteristics of the digital world, inconsistency evolves with new data infrastructures. The classic consistency of the transactional/ACID model is being transformed into *eventual consistency* with operating modes that evolve accordingly. Consistency is no longer a global and universal property; it is expressed through business processes. To simplify, we can say that the notion of accuracy is transformed into data freshness and that the event flow approach makes it possible to

[32] This is what we call *event sourcing*: a deconstruction of the concept of database (knowing how to answer the question "What is the value of X?") in favor of direct processing of the flow of update events (knowing how to chain the consequences of the event "X went from 100 to 102 at such and such a time and at such and such a place"). This is not a universal solution, there are still cases that are better suited to storage to guarantee a "*single source of truth*" and transactional behavior, but the flow approach allows for both very high scalability and the coexistence of hot and cold processing.

[33] For more details on these concepts, from repositories to distribution constraints and resilience, see the author's first book.

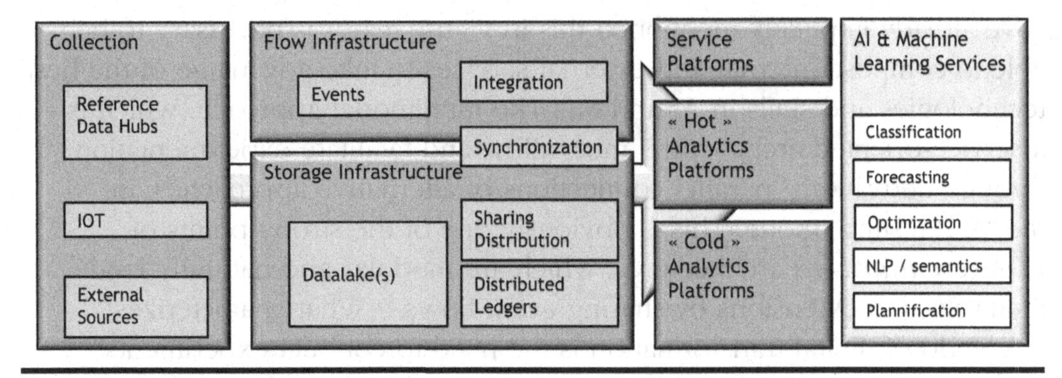

Figure 5.2 Data infrastructure.

circumvent the CAP theorem since the absence of storage eliminates the question of consistency.[34]

5.3.3 An Information System Designed for Experimentation

The IS participates directly in the culture of experimentation that we have previously emphasized. If the IS is not designed to encourage experimentation, it is done outside, and the integration of new solutions becomes a long and painful problem (especially since the value created by AI is important). **The exponential IS must be open and modern to easily absorb the continuous flow of software innovations.**[35] This characteristic is strongly linked to the frequent renewal requirements we mentioned in Chapter 4: the elements of the exponential IS must be renewed frequently not only to continuously adapt to the business requirements but also to be up-to-date in terms of technologies and versions with external software environments, in particular *open-source* strains, in order to facilitate import and integration.

The second requirement of the exponential IS is to have an open and recomposable architecture, based on APIs and a multimodal approach. We

[34] It is also worth noting that *distributed ledgers*, one of the underlying technologies of *blockchains*, have their place in the arsenal of solutions for distributing shared data repositories, with a long-term consistency guaranteed by consensus.

[35] A famous quote from Jensen Huang, CEO of NVIDIA, says that "software is eating the world, and AI will eat the software." The share of software that will incorporate AI approaches will grow rapidly, for example in automotive or healthcare. The notion of modernity is not absolute; it depends on the expected pace of evolution and the need to absorb technological innovations. Figure 4.1 illustrates an IS with varying degrees of modernity.

have already implicitly mentioned this in Figure 4.1: it is necessary to be able to compose internal and external services to take advantage of the best technologies and skills in AI and ML. The multimodal approach, which is a service-oriented architecture, must allow and facilitate experimentation through derivations, parallel connections of alternative approaches, in the "A/B testing" mode. This is obviously one of the strong points of EDA (*event-driven*) architectures, which are modular and naturally lend themselves to extensions by sharing event flows.[36] What characterizes the world of digital transformation is the need to conduct experiments in production on real data. This ability to experiment, under obvious constraints of cybersecurity, resilience, and high availability, is a distinctive feature of the digital systems of the web giants.

The exponential IS must provide its advanced users with the computational resources to accelerate their learning cycle. Recall the cycles described in Figure 5.1—the training cycle and the improvement cycle—they are both sensitive to the available computational power. The importance of having the right resources to do machine learning is one of the key ideas in the Academy of Technology report. Francis Bach, one of the world's leading experts in machine learning, explains that the "step" of a development cycle varies between a day and a week of computational time—depending on the patience of the teams—so access to very large computational power (to be concrete, thousands of GPU processors) significantly accelerates development since it reduces the number of iterations needed as a result. *Airbus Defense and Space* reports a similar experience using the power available on Google's *cloud*: a dramatic acceleration in the performance of *machine vision* algorithms. Demis Hassabis, when he joined Google with DeepMind, quoted access to very large computing power as the major reason for his choice. The same comment can be made about the global learning loop. Software velocity, both in the production of applications that are the vehicles of these new technologies and in the velocity of information processing, is a major factor in the competitiveness of companies in their digital transformation. **The success of services in the digital world is a race to learn, and access to the right computing and data processing infrastructures is a major factor in learning faster.**

---

[36] Here we find the "publish/subscribe" architectural pattern, which is at the heart of almost all modular systems, such as mobile operating systems.

Summary

1. AI is not an isolated technology; from a practical point of view for companies, it is a modality of software systems (5.1.1).
2. AI is not an issue for tomorrow: today's technologies are already bringing benefits and transformation opportunities to the companies that use them (5.1.1).
3. It is important to have a broad view of AI and to stay up-to-date with the state of the art in terms of both tools and compositional methods (5.1.3).
4. AI is a learning loop with humans inside (5.1.4).
5. It is critical to think of data as a continuous cycle of collection: future data is more valuable than past data (5.2.1).
6. The implementation of AI-enhanced applications should be viewed systemically as a loop (5.2.2).
7. The "data lab" model seeks to capture three ideas: it is a place where different professions and skills work together, it is a place of experimentation, and it is a place of scientific discipline in the conduct of experiments (5.2.3).
8. The ability to collect all the data sources in the company and to associate external data requires the existence of a single, shared business data model (5.3.1).
9. The exponential IS must be open and up-to-date to easily absorb the continuous flow of software innovations (5.3.3).
10. Developing successful services in the digital world is a race to learn continuously; access to the right infrastructure, both computing and data processing, is a major factor in learning faster (5.3.3).

Chapter 6

Governance, Architecture, and Situational Potential

A chapter that talks about IS governance and costs may come as a surprise in a book dedicated to digital transformation, ExOs, or AI. However, the success of digital transformation and the mastery of modern technological tools require stepping back and looking at the enterprise as a system. This chapter does not pretend to be exhaustive on the complex subject of governing the digital transformation. It will focus on three governance questions that are related to the theme of this book:

- There are systemic cultural and organizational preconditions to the successful implementation of the work methods described in this book from the *lean startup* approach to *lean* and agile software development methods.
- The digital capabilities of the enterprise form a complex system, which requires thinking in terms of situational awareness, transformation, and architecture.
- The IS is a common asset of the enterprise, built by generations of actors, which reflects its organization[1] and history. Digital transformation is not done in isolation; it requires interlocking with the sustainable development of the IS.

[1] See for example the famous Conway's law, which notes the similarity of architecture between systems and the organizations that build them.

DOI: 10.4324/9781003272816-8

6.1 Lean and Agile Governance

6.1.1 Agile Software Development

The purpose of this book is not to dive into development methods details, nor even to explain the *Agile Manifesto*[2] principles. Instead, I will summarize agile development with four ideas:

- Development is organized in an iterative way, in small batches called *sprints*, which are constrained in duration.
- The main objective is the satisfaction of the customer or user, measured frequently and enriched by collecting *feedbacks on a regular basis.*
- Development is led by cross-functional teams composed of both "business" and "technical" team members, which are autonomous and self-organize to produce the design, implementation, and architecture simultaneously.
- Teams work in sync and prefer face-to-face communication to share information and to collaborate—first, because the subjects are complex and written communication is costly and imperfect, and second, because the physical dimension of communication is essential to true synchronization.

There are several branches of agile practices, such as Scrum, which is one of the most popular. Agile practices have been enriched over time—for example, with visual management and team rituals such as *standup meetings.* Team rituals use boards and walls to foster communication. The placement in plain view of all relevant information makes it easy for everyone involved to understand the system at a glance. This helps self-directed teams to keep a good work rhythm and to facilitate greater fluidity of inter-team handovers.

Another way to characterize agile methods is to understand the shortcomings of traditional V-cycle (or *waterfall*) approaches when applied in complex and changing environments. To simplify, **waterfall processes have four problems, which are the "negatives" of the characteristics we want to achieve, and which we can use to measure and evaluate the software development process' efficiency: *rework*, TTM, non-deployed code, and waste of time**. The first problem is *rework*, which

[2] The *Agile Manifesto*, published in 2001, can be found at http://agilemanifesto.org/.

is sending work outputs back up the value stream to a previous process or process step to fix problems due to specification changes or misunderstood requirements. The second is "code delivered too late," TTM that is too long, which is an acute problem in the digital world where value changes rapidly over time. The third is code produced but not deployed, a common *lean* waste and is unfortunately very frequent in the world of large software development. The last problem is coordination and communication overhead which does not create value compared to development time and may be qualified as "*talking versus doing*." One of the principles of the *Agile Manifesto* reminds us that the main measure of progress is the amount of working software.

The agile approach is a natural response to the way the digital world evolves, as mentioned in the first chapter. Working in small batches (*sprints*) with a reprioritization of the *backlog* at the end of each sprint is a response to volatility. The fact that requirements are expressed using *user stories* makes them more future-proof since the team can adapt its effort and what it produces to uncertainties. We require *user stories* to be not too prescriptive on the "how" so that the team is autonomous enough. The iterative approach with frequent user *feedbacks* helps cope with complexity and ambiguity. However, the agile approach is not enough to properly deal with complexity. The agile approach has evolved over the last fifteen years by adding *lean software development principles*, which leads to a lean and agile practice.

6.1.2 Adding Lean Roots to Agile Practice

Lean software shifts from the project approach to the broader product development approach. The difference between the product approach, which is by definition a long-term and open approach, and the project approach, which is more "closed," is one of the important differences that Mary Poppendieck emphasizes. As the authors of *lean architecture*[3] point out, the agile approach is designed for change and "organic" complexity, while the *lean* approach is concerned with large-scale complexity and long-term system resilience. The product approach and *lean software development* practices provide a natural framework for thinking about capability development, continuous team training and skill development, or continuous elimination of technical debt.

[3] I will quote several times the book *Lean Architecture*, by James O. Coplien and Gertrud Bjørnvig, because it is one of the best references on the juxtaposition of *lean* and agile approaches.

From the beginning, the agile principles provided for reflective practice for continuous improvement: "*the team reflects at regular intervals on how to become more efficient.*" This ambition has been codified and amplified in the practice of Scrum retrospectives. But the *lean* approach goes much further with the practice of *kaizen*, team problem-solving. *Kaizen* is a tool for continuous improvement, but it is also a tool for developing systemic and collaborative skills. The use of tools such as the A3 (the problem analysis and follow-up tool popularized by Toyota), the practice of systematically searching for root causes, the rigorous organization of action plans, and their follow-up considerably enriches the agile practice.

Lean practice is rooted in a *system thinking* approach, with the objective of enabling the team to understand and master complex systems. The practice of visual management is common to all modern approaches, but where agile methods focus on the description of the work to be done and the orchestration of tasks, the *lean* approach uses walls and visual management to build a collective understanding of the system through the A3 documents of *kaizen as* well as the shared diagrams of the architecture and functioning of the system.[4]

Through my experience of the last ten years, four practices distinguish a lean and agile approach from the founding principles of the *Agile Manifesto.* They do not replace agile practices, such as Scrum, but are added to reinforce the transition from a project culture to a product culture. The first practice is the presence of the *voice of the customer* (VOC) on the development floor. The voice of the customer must be displayed on the walls, in multiple forms ranging from usage statistics, verbatims collected—during tests, demos, or satisfaction surveys—and the treatment of complaints and severe incidents. The second practice is the use of A3 charts for continuous improvement. The third practice is sharing architecture diagrams and flowcharts (e.g., production processes) among team members by posting them on the walls (which requires quite a few walls). The last practice, which we will return to in Chapter 7, is the application of the 5 Ss of lean[5] to the code produced by the team (i.e., the constant care of organization),

[4] For an introduction to systems thinking, read *Thinking in Systems*, by Donella Meadows; for a deeper look, I recommend *Business Dynamics: System Thinking and Modeling for a Complex World*, by John Sterman.

[5] The 5S are *seiri*, *seiton*, *seisō*, *seiketsu*, and *shitsuke*, which translate into English as *sort*, *set in order*, *shine*, *standardize*, and *sustain*. The 5S have been adapted to the context of software development, for example in the book by Mary and Tom Poppendieck.

standardization, tidying up (for example, by taking advantage of modern code sharing solutions such as *Git*), and reorganization (i.e., *refactoring*).

The connection between lean and agile has been popularized by the various "agile at scale" frameworks such as LeSS (*large-scale Scrum*), *disciplined agile*, or especially SAFe (*scaled agile framework*).[6] SAFe proposes a global framework that integrates agile, lean, DevOps, *lean startup*, and *system thinking*. Since the objective is above all the coordination and synchronization of teams, the lean vision is above all global and systemic, focusing on the concepts of *flow*, *value stream*, and WIP. This global vision is both complementary and compatible with the *lean software factory* approach that will be developed in Chapter 7 (which proposes a local vision of lean and agile integration, focusing on people and code). On the other hand, it is important to consider these *frameworks* as toolboxes and not as instructions or guides for developing an agile practice. They provide a vision, experience, and tools to organize the orchestration of multiple teams[7] but remain far from the software development experience (*software craftmanship*, which is inseparable from lean, is absent). The SAFe approach has been strongly criticized by some agilists such as Martin Fowler for this reason: SAFe should not be taken as the method to work in an agile way, precisely because it is a very structured method. On the contrary, because SAFe is about a global view, it comes with a very Greek[8] and voluntarist vision that is completely out of step with what we said in the first part. It is easy to see in the SAFe approach the "illusion of control" and the primacy of intention over user reality—for example, through the role of architects. SAFe's references to *lean UX* and *lean startup* are succinct and easily irrelevant to digital service development. In some ways, SAFe seeks to encapsulate the complexity of Chapter 3 of this book in a "*continuous exploration*" box that fits into the grander scheme of strategic execution.

---

[6] These *frameworks* deal with the issue of scaling: how to organize the work of many agile teams working on a common system (goal). I do not deal with this topic in this book; to address it, read *SAFe 4.5 Distilled: Applying the Scaled Agile Framework for Lean Enterprises*, by R. Knaster and D. Leffingwell. SAFe is the most popular and richest of the "agile at scale" frameworks. You can also read *An Executive's Guide to Disciplined Agile: Winning the Race to Business Agility*, by S. Ambler and M. Lines, or *Large-Scale Scrum: More with Less*, by C. Larman.

[7] My experience with the Bouygues Telecom "*box software factory*" is precisely a "*Scrum of Scrums*," and we deployed several tools, including the backmap (the combination of a backlog and a roadmap), which would be advantageously replaced today by a LeSS or SAFe approach. On the complex subject of scaling up, you can also read *Scaling Up Excellence: Getting to More Without Settling for Less*, by R. Sutton and H Rao.

[8] In the sense of François Jullien introduced in Chapter 2: when one tries to impose his will to the world instead of adapting to it.

This approach may work for building large technical systems, but it is less realistic for conducting your digital transformation.

6.1.3 The Systemic Conditions of Lean and Agile

The agile approach must be a shared mental model to function in the company. The agile mode of operation is based on shared values, convictions, and representations of the world. For example, the values of effectuation,[9] knowing how to do things with what you have ("bird in hand") or accepting the unexpected ("make lemonade"), are factors in the effectiveness of an agile team *if they are shared with the business stakeholders*; otherwise, they are elements of tension. While *lean* practices can be adapted on a small scale (down to the individual level) and bring some value even in an agile environment, the agile approach is a system, which relies on the collaboration between business and technical roles and which requires an alignment on the iterative approach, progress in small batches, frequent feedback, and so on. The agile approach is not a martingale that would isolate the stakeholders from the vagaries of digital development; it is a conviction that requires from all participants a real motivation and a strong commitment.

The lean and agile approach requires teams and team members to have room to maneuver (buffers) in order to collaborate. Yves Morieux points out, "*To cooperate is to put one's room for maneuver at the service of others.*"[10] The emphasis on *buffers is* a direct systemic consequence of the queuing theory. When agents have a working queue whose load is close to their processing capacity, their response time increases exponentially, and the hazards propagate in a spectacular way that is very difficult to control in the processing chains. **This is one of the core principles of lean: reducing the load (WIP) to increase flexibility and responsiveness**. The WIP constitutes a form of inertia, which pushes the overall system to persevere in its initial direction. Reducing the WIP of the system's actors increases their ability to listen, react, and help each other, which also reduces stress. All this is fundamental for lean and agile practices to work with full efficiency. For example, the autonomy of the team to practice its continuous improvement and to organize its *kaizens* supposes a sufficient flexibility of the load and the existence of *buffers*.

---

9 Cf. the introduction of Chapter 2 or the following blog post: www.linkedin.com/pulse/five-principles-effectuation-bertjan-broeksema/.

10 I discuss this topic in more depth in my previous book "*Processus et Enterprise 2.0*".

To effectively achieve the expected result, namely customer and user satisfaction, the team must be guaranteed regular and easy access to users. The effectiveness and satisfaction of a *lean* and agile team cannot be decreed; it is not the result of *top-down* control but the emergent and *bottom-up* result of collaboration and individual effectiveness. The team develops its product or service using user or customer satisfaction as a compass, which requires the ability to easily organize the "feedback loop" in the form of tests, demonstrations, or field surveys. This rule is more complex than it seems because many companies have Taylorized this feedback loop: those who talk to the customer, those who understand what the customer wants, those who specify the customer's needs, and those who implement. The lean and agile approach requires both a strong and autonomous *product owner* and regular access for the whole team to the voice of the customer. The larger the system, the more it becomes broken down into multiple teams, according to the rule that says that an agile *team* can be fed with two pizzas. Yet the larger the system, the more the voice of the customer is a critical alignment element.[11]

6.1.4 Governance that Favors the Lean and Agile Approach

In order to deploy lean and agile practices, the governance of the IS and its components must reconcile a short and long-term perspective. The short-term approach is necessary, as we have said so that the whole company is agile and continuously adapts its objectives according to the reactions of the environment. The long-term approach allows instilling a product culture to build the situational potential and to make the continuous efforts of reengineering and cleaning up the technical debt. Long-term thinking to build the product's situational potential (i.e., selecting and building capabilities over a long period of time) is what provides the true agility to react to opportunities (without knowing them precisely, which we explained in Chapter 2). If there is not enough situational potential in terms of capabilities *or skills*, no amount of agile methodology will make up for it. To effectively build this dual approach, to prevent the long-term approach from polluting the need for short-term attention, governance must focus on increasing the frequency of delivery—that is, reducing the time between

[11] Coordination between *squads* in agile *at scale* must not give in to the temptation to revert to a *top-down* orchestration, where each component operates in an agile manner within an overall framework that is no longer agile.

deployments of two versions of the product. Constantly striving to reduce the time between deployments is the equivalent of lean manufacturing's lead time reduction. It is a good practice that builds agility and forces a higher degree of automation.

The governance of the exponential IS must guarantee the true accountability of autonomous teams. One of the rules that seems essential to me for successful service development in the digital world is that each developer should have the right to have a *product owner* (the one who prioritizes and explains the *user story backlog*) capable of answering any question about an ambiguous formulation or a specification conflict within half a day. This means that the *product owner* can decide on her own and that she is not the representative of a committee of higher-level managers. **Easy and direct access to the "business" decision for the development team is a decisive condition for success and an important difference between small autonomous structures such as startups and some of the digital teams of large companies.** True empowerment is necessary to address the complexity of the challenges of the digital world; I quote Jurgen Appelo in *Management 3.0*: "*The real reason for empowerment is the ability to manage complex systems. Smart managers don't delegate to get beaming faces of satisfied employees. They delegate to prevent the entire system from crashing due to complexity.*" The more you increase the frequency of production, the more you increase the number of decisions to be made every day and the more essential it becomes to be able to make decisions locally within an autonomous team, without having to validate with managers who are both remote from the context (let's remember once again that the characteristic of a complex situation is that it is difficult to judge from the outside) and less available (and, therefore, less willing to participate in accelerating the frequency of decision-making).

IT systems governance is a witness to *customer-centricity* in the enterprise. Being customer-centric means recognizing that the customer is in control, that his or her opinions and behaviors determine the proper development of ISs capabilities. Since the customer is the "architect of his or her experience," the approach to exposing services and building external APIs must be driven by customer needs rather than by the vision of architects or the insights of executives. We've talked about the importance of software ecosystems; they are most often decided by customer usage. The company must package and deploy its value in the "digital places"—the software ecosystems—chosen by customers. As we pointed out in the first chapter, in the digital world, it is no longer the customer who comes to meet the company, but the company that must move to the customer's smartphone OS, to his preferred social network or online ordering solution, or to the intermediation platform of his choice. We saw in Chapter 3 that the analytical approach (understanding the customer through the analysis of digital traces) is not sufficient. You have to constantly talk to the customer. This is an essential element of corporate culture and an essential objective of digital transformation and its governance.

6.2 Which Architecture in an Uncertain World?

6.2.1 The Role of the Architect in an Agile Team

IS development requires the expertise and contribution of architects within agile teams. We have already mentioned the main reasons: to move from project mode to product mode, to build a global multimodal architecture, and to develop today the capabilities that will enable tomorrow's agility. In a lean and agile approach, development, design, and architecture are co-created by the team and evolve simultaneously—the focus on development does not invalidate the need for design or software architecture. It becomes an iterative process in which each dimension influences the others. The team's architect plays an essential role in the development of the product seen as a software object. She must "tell the story" of this product, just as the *user stories* tell the story of the services rendered by the product. One of the primary roles of a product architect is to facilitate communication, both within the team and between teams. Architecture tools are essentially abstractions—such as diagrams—to facilitate dialogue and understanding (communication in space, so to speak) and stories, narrative diagrams that capture intentions (to communicate in space and time, so future team members understand what their colleagues try to achieve). As James O. Coplien and Gertrud Bjørnvig note in *Lean Architecture for Agile Software Development*, the idea that agile development can do without documentation is a myth and stress that "*we want the documentation that packs the punch . . . Don't sweat the small stuff. Focus on what matters.*"

Within the product team, the architect is "the technical debt's advocate."[12] She must take on this role because she is in the best position to evaluate and control the increase in complexity (previously defined as the marginal cost of integration[13]) because she also has the global vision and knowledge of the interfaces with the rest of the system. In order to do this, we must ensure three things—that correspond to three time horizons, from large to small.

- First, some sprints should be primarily dedicated to refactoring and eliminating technical debt. This is when the action plans produced during the RCAs or retrospectives become priorities in the *backlog*.
- Second, to avoid accumulating technical debt, a certain amount of "bandwidth" must be preserved in each sprint for "non-functional requirements," which are essential in the digital domain (performance, robustness, security, etc.).
- Finally, and to make the link with the previous section, each sprint's load must be restricted to maintain what we have called the *lean buffer*: a margin of maneuver available to the team to work well and continuously improve the quality of the software product.

The chronological order of architects' influence on developers has changed. Applying *lean* principles, we shift from *push*—the architect specifies the technical design that the developer implements—to *pull*—the architect assists the developer in choosing her software architecture and integration *patterns*. The agile team's architect plays a key role in reviewing the team's code, which presupposes that she has an interest in and familiarity with code equal to or greater than architecture patterns and rules created by tools such as PowerPoint. The architect thus becomes a coach for developers, in addition to the *tech lead* role. We have to find a balance between simplicity and capacity building; *lean software* practice (for example, as proposed by Mary and Tom Poppendieck) recommends

---

[12] I use the word "advocate" because the prioritization of the *backlog* remains the responsibility of the *product owner*, and the whole team must feel ownership of its technical debt.

[13] Let us recall the essential idea here: from a practical point of view, complexity is the marginal cost of integration. Complexity is in fact what happens inside the system, but its visible manifestation is the extra cost when one has to modify or extend the system. For example, complexity can be measured as the ratio of the full cost of the change in the system to the cost of developing the new function as an isolated module.

in an uncertain world not anticipating future needs too much (*delay design decisions*).

To conclude, the architect plays an essential role in the deployment of the product culture, that of a system engineering coach. Each sprint is lived on a fast tempo and with a short-term horizon, but the product is there to last. Its purpose and operating modes endure over the course of the releases. The team must understand both the internal workings of its product and, above all, its integration into the overall system.[14] Here we find the importance of visual management (see Chapter 4), which is the heritage of *lean manufacturing* in the tradition of the *Toyota Way*. The team must develop a detailed understanding of the functioning of the systems and, above all, visualize this understanding using visual artifacts displayed on walls to develop a shared understanding.[15] This means that architecture in a lean and agile approach is not a discipline reserved for experts but a skill that all team members must possess at varying levels. The agile approach does not mean that everything must be rediscovered in the field by trial and error. The practice of *design reviews* advocated by Scrum works even better when led by an architect.

6.2.2 Architecture and Gardening

Gardening is a constant source of metaphors for emergence management because it is about influencing the development of consequences by acting on the root causes, as we saw with François Jullien in Chapter 2. *Refactoring* is remarkably similar to the maintenance of a vegetable garden. We must constantly eliminate bad shoots, remove excess production, and amend the soil (i.e., work on the skills and capacities of both the system and the team). From a software perspective, one must regularly eliminate dead code, reorganize to put duplicated code fragments back together (this is the original meaning of the term "refactoring"), and make code easier to evolve—and, therefore, more productive—by making it more readable and

---

[14] The vision of the architect presented here is close to *continuous architecture*, the approach of Pierre Pureur and Murdat Erder, presented for example in their article *"Evolving an Architecture Over Time: Think "Continuous Architecture" and "Minimum Viable Architecture."* This section on the role of the architect also marks a difference with the SAFe approach, which remains influenced by the tradition of systems control by architects.

[15] Not surprisingly, the main lesson of *"Site Reliability Engineering"* is that the quality of service of operations on distributed systems relies on a good understanding of systems engineering, which must be built and renewed continuously. The architect, therefore, plays an essential role in improving the quality of service.

elegant, from renaming to the use of *design patterns*.[16] This work is done at multiple scales and at different times time. Part of it is done within *sprints* (the time unit for producing and deploying a change), both by integrating the technical dimension into the *backlog* and by allowing the team to build a culture of software excellence. Another part is done by regularly creating sprints dedicated to the elimination of technical debt. The rest is based on the rapid renewal of software assets and the ability to remove applications and rewrite them based on new technologies and architecture principles. The longer the time scale, the more technical debt and *refactoring* can be addressed on a large scale, the one of the components' architecture of the system.

The art of gardening also shows how to reconcile the architectural ambition of orienting the plant's growth in a given direction while respecting the freedom and self-organization of a living plant by using stakes and forms. In the software world, ***Service-Oriented Architecture* plays the role of a stake, defining a form that the iterative process of agile development fills.**[17] A common practice is to use *design patterns* and *frameworks*. The *design pattern* is a set of principles materialized by services, while the *framework* is a richer set of objects and elementary services that can be completed by the user. The vast majority of *open-source* software and libraries are designed as *frameworks*. In their book, Coplien and Bjørnvig devote some of their attention to the DCI[18] (*data, context, interaction*) design pattern, the objective of which is to improve the readability of object-oriented code by separating different functional aspects and, above all, by separating parts of the code that change frequently (the *context*, which represents the *use cases*, from the *data*, which represents the knowledge of the domain in the form of business objects). We find here, on a small scale, the same principles as

[16] The reference book is *Refactoring*, by Martin Fowler. This book underlines two essential points that we have mentioned: the iterative development process naturally produces an increase in complexity that we must think about cleaning up (hence the garden metaphor) and the importance of this cleaning up is proportional to the change that we wish to make in the system.

[17] In this book, SOA is taken in the broad sense of an architecture strategy directed by service exposure. This encompasses various forms of service delivery, such as microservices that we shall later see.

[18] The DCI pattern is an evolution (complementary) of the MVC (*model, view, controller*) model found in most mobile applications and a large part of websites. The MVC model separates the business model, the visualization and the control of interactions. The DCI approach reifies (represents in the form of objects) the *use cases* in the "context" pane, which gives both a better readability (a greater abstraction of the code that represents the use cases) and, consequently, an easier way to modify these *use cases*.

the multimodal architecture. When a pre-existing framework is not used, a SOA must be built, which will serve as a *framework* (i.e., a "form" that guides development and is maintained as modifications are made by agile cycles). Coplien and Bjørnvig explain that the idea that the agile approach would make it possible to do without anticipating the architecture is just a myth! *Refactoring* is essential, but it does not correct everything or make up for the lack of backbone in the organization of services. That's why we must continue to involve architects from the very beginning of the creation of a new software product.

Another gardening technique that finds its counterpart in systems architecture is that of grafting, consisting of feeding a branch of one plant by the nourishing structure of another. Here we recognize the extension of one system by relying on the APIs, the change in nature corresponding to the multimodal approach: the nature of the two systems can be profoundly different. The interest of the graft metaphor compared to the more mundane electrical plug metaphor is that it carries two things: the richness of the flows between the two systems (and the need for accounting, especially of data models) and, above all, the systemic interaction between the graft and its host—two dynamic evolving systems that influence each other because of the new connection. The open API-based architecture cannot work without some understanding of what the grafted system expects from the first system (e.g., in terms of *capacity planning*, as mentioned in Chapter 4) and without monitoring the operation of the overall system.

6.2.3 Continuous Learning of Systems Engineering

Building dynamic and evolving systems in an uncertain, volatile, and unpredictable world does not make architecture any less important, quite the contrary, but it is a different architecture, more organic than mechanical. It is first and foremost an architecture for evolution and resilience, which we discussed in Chapter 4.[19] The multimodal architecture that we have described is a SOA that is built with the joint work of enterprise architects (the architects of the overall system, also called enterprise architects) and the architects of the products that make

[19] The idea that the main role of architecture is to better manage evolutions is beautifully expressed by Robert C. Martin in his previously mentioned book, *Clean Architecture: A Craftsman's Guide to Software Structure and Design*.

up the IS.[20] As previously pointed out, the multimodal service architecture is fractal: it describes an SoS, which can be decomposed on several levels of depth (not just two). The term "decoupling," which reflects the modularity and relative independence that one wishes to obtain between the subsystems, often leads to the use of the term "federation," as in the case of a *data lake* built by federating subsystems assigned to different business domains.

The subsystems are interconnected by interfaces (APIs); the teams are interconnected and collaborate on the overall system through a "collaborative grammar," for which the team architect is the guarantor. The grammar metaphor expresses the fact that this API catalog is both a set of nouns (the services) and *patterns* (the verbs). This grammar represents the "situational potential" discussed in Chapter 2 in terms of reusability—one of the key goals of a service architecture—and evolution. Coplien and Bjørnvig make this the most visible manifestation of the architect's role: "*The essence of lean in architecture is careful and insightful analysis that is materialized as APIs.*" It is, therefore, useful to highlight a third benefit of the API approach. We had talked about their role in opening up systems and their ability to implement decoupling—which creates an "expansion joint" within a multimodal architecture. Here we add the ability to implement architectural intent, to support reuse and evolution. In his famous memo,[21] Jeff Bezos requires that all Amazon teams expose the services of their software components and that all interactions between modules go through API calls. He insists that "*all service interfaces, without exception, be designed to be used by external developers.*" At the origin of this memo, there was not only the desire to expose Amazon as a platform (which is obvious after the fact) but also the desire to urbanize and control the complexity of an IS that had become too complex and too heavy.

In order for the IS to function harmoniously as a set of autonomous, modular, and evolving subsystems, it is necessary to progressively adopt a platform approach, either internal or external, depending on the position of

[20] It is not easy to characterize what the enterprise's IS is. Since "software is eating the world," there are many more software systems in a typical company than those managed by the IS/IT department. In this book, information system is taken in a broad sense, that includes service platforms or software systems embedded into the company's products.

[21] Jeff Bezos's 2002 memo on APIs was made famous by a blog post by Steve Yegge, easily found on the web as "*Stevey's Google Platform Rant.*" This post is worth reading, as it contains lessons learned by Amazon in deploying their service exposure approach, such as the need to have programmatic access to the service catalog or the importance of being able to measure and monitor call flows, to make one team's services robust to another team's use case misunderstandings.

the system in relation to the "edges" (cf. Chapter 2). This concept of platform is fundamental in the digital world, and we will return to it in Chapter 8. Each team that produces a component must behave—in the definition of its interfaces and the exposure, not to say the marketing, of its capabilities—like a *software vendor*, an internal software service provider. The architect plays an important role in helping the team to think of itself as a software vendor for its other colleagues. This transformation is congruent with the product approach in terms of version management, APIs, data model, testing, examples, training, and so on. **An API is more than a programming interface; it is also an intention that implies a common semantic between the producer and the consumer—hence the importance of the business data model—and an SLA that specifies the availability, the *throughput* and the response times (*latency*) that one can expect.** To summarize this section, we can say that the engineering of exponential IS develops continuously and is structured around a service architecture. This architecture is a backbone in terms of organization and a situational potential in terms of evolution. It is also an operational tool for controlling complexity and steering the functioning of systems, which requires appropriation by all the teams, with animation orchestrated by the network—or guild[22]—of team architects.

6.3 Sustainable Information Systems

6.3.1 Sustainable Development of the Information System

This book does not pretend to cover the complex topic of IS costs. However, to develop the principle of sustainable development of the exponential IS, it is necessary to talk about costs, both development costs and operating costs. Figure 6.1 represents the simplest possible life cycle model of a "software asset" (a set of lines of code, an application, a technical system, a platform, etc.). To avoid a complex debate about the measurement of an asset, we will simply use its acquisition cost here. The "NEW" flow in the figure represents the acquisition of new assets, which generate three families

[22] As mentioned earlier, Spotify's organizational model for coordinating multiple teams in agile mode is a reference that is widely described—for example, "*The Spotify model: agile at scale in a Swedish success story*," by David Machiels. Agile *squads* are grouped into tribes based on a business domain approach and organized in a matrix fashion with "guilds" and "chapters" to create communities of technical expertise.

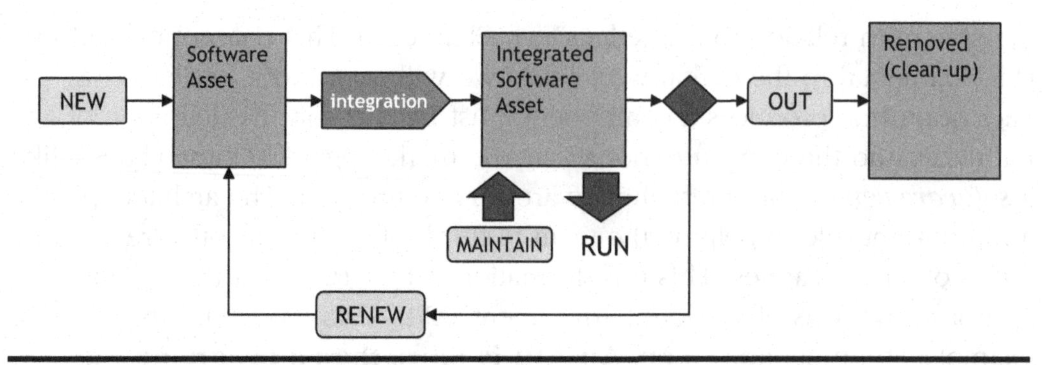

Figure 6.1 Software asset life cycle.

of costs, proportional to the acquisition costs: the integration cost (which depends on the complexity of the IS), the cost of operating the service rendered (the so-called run cost), and the maintenance cost—making the necessary evolutions on an ongoing basis so that the service is effectively rendered. The software asset ends its life cycle in two ways: either it is simply deleted, which induces an application cleanup cost, or it is replaced, which is represented here by the "RENEW" flow. This simplistic model illustrates two fundamental properties of the IS: it is a dynamic system—one could say a "living" system—characterized by input/output flows, and it is an accumulation system, whose behavior is mostly dictated by its history.

This preamble allows us to raise the question of the sustainable development of the IS. I define it, paraphrasing the Bruntland Commission's definition, as "**the ability of the IS to provide services that correspond to the company's present needs, without compromising the future ability to deliver services that will correspond to the needs of tomorrow**." This definition is important because the relevance of an IS development strategy, or any form of digital technical system, can only be assessed over time. It is easy to generate all kinds of technical debts, which are not always easy to understand and which will greatly reduce the system's ability to produce value in the future. The two aspects of this debt we will discuss here are complexity and aging of software assets. The purpose of sustainable development is to continuously improve a digital system so it continues to produce the expected services without adding unnecessary complexity or forgetting to renew its assets. In a digital world, this principle of sustainable development is fundamental because it is easy, as we have already noted, for today's agility to be obtained at the expense of tomorrow's agility.

If we assume that overall expenses are stable, for example, because the company is in an economic context of stable revenues, sustainable development consists of containing the increase in assets, and their associated costs, to what can be expected from productivity gains[23]. These productivity gains come mainly from two sources. In hardware, this is the consequence of Moore's law, which means that the cost of computers drops exponentially at constant capacity. This gain is accessible and significant as soon as we can take advantage of it, either by constant renewal (renewal allows access to new generations of computers) or by decoupling application/hosting, which is achieved, for instance, with a "cloud strategy."[24] As far as software and system operations are concerned, productivity gains come essentially from automation—this is the foundation of *autonomic computing*, discussed in Chapter 4. We will devote Chapter 7 to automation and the next two sections to controlling system complexity and software assets aging. Note that this approach consists of applying a "product approach" to the overall system (thinking in terms of life cycle, renewal, recurring costs, incremental development by release) as opposed to the "program approach" (the project approach in its global vision: a beginning, an end, and a goal-oriented effort). In an unpredictable world, thinking of IS as a product is the best way to avoid IT costs that slip continuously over the years.

6.3.2 Managing Complexity in a Sustainable Way

Complexity depends on both the number of objects and the number of relationships. The first imperative is, therefore, to control the size of the system, whether it is a global exponential IS or a dedicated digital system.[25] The metric does not matter—it depends on the domain and the level of maturity; one can measure the size of the functional perimeter, the financial weight invested (for example, the acquisition cost), or a census of the components (for example, the number of applications). What is important is to make this measurement consistently over time, from an asset perspective (the IS is an asset). The most

---

[23] It is worth noting, in the context of digital transformation, that IS spending may grow, relatively to the company turnover, because "*software is eating the world*": IS spendings are replacing other SG&A costs.

[24] To better understand the link between age (and therefore the renewal rate) and the beneficial effects of Moore's law, read *Information Technology for the Chief Executive*. The use of techniques that isolate applications from their hosting, such as *containers,* also allows to benefit from the continuous progress on hosting costs.

[25] This chapter applies equally to the IS as a whole or to a more specialized technical system. In the following I will refer to "system" in a general way.

important thing is to measure each year the flows of what comes in and what goes out (the two variables "NEW" and "OUT" in Figure 6.1). Experience shows that there is great value to shape IS governance in such a way that software assets' owners are also accountable for the overall size of the system and of the "in" and "out" flows—as opposed to assigning this responsibility to committees or processes. The concept is simple; implementing it is more challenging as it requires an application cleanup process to monitor and control the difference between incoming and outgoing flows.

Once this step has been completed, the real problem of controlling complexity appears, both in a global form, which is an enterprise architecture topic and in a local form specific to each component. We discussed a solution (global refactoring, replacement of components that are too old, urbanization, and service architecture) in the previous section; what interests us here is the governance that enables awareness. To borrow from an essential idea of Yves Morieux, we must project "*the shadow of complexity onto the future.*"[26] In my experience at Bouygues Telecom, we have used several approaches to reduce complexity. One approach proposed by OCTO consists in representing the main components with bubbles and links. The size of the bubbles represents the weight of the component, and their color represents the level of technical debt. The links help visualize the interdependence between systems and their components. The paradox is that the shadow of past complexity is very visible to business decision-makers: as we have said, complexity conditions operating and support costs and, above all, integration costs (see Figure 6.1). The usual complaint "in our company, it takes a million euros to do what is done for €200K elsewhere" is a visible manifestation of the accumulated complexity. **The challenge of good governance is to transform the frustration of complexity into simplification energy.** Good monitoring indicators in this governance process are those that make this "shadow of complexity" visible: **the ratio of the cost of support to the cost of run** (per component), **the average age** (we will come back to this), and **the cost of integration**. Integration cost is the practical indicator of complexity, defined as the ratio of the project cost of adding a new component or function to the acquisition cost (development cost, license cost, or rental cost for SaaS over five years).

---

[26] Read Yves Morieux's article "*Six Simple Rules for Overcoming Complexity,*" available on the BCG website. The fifth rule, "*extend the shadow of the future,*" is the essential rule of governance that I develop in this book: "*Have people experience the consequences that result from their behavior and decisions. Tighten feedback loops. Shorten the duration of projects. Enable people to see how their success is aided by contributing to the success of others.*"

The control of local complexity is exactly the same subject but on a smaller scale, that of the IS component. Governance is different since the team must play a more essential role in controlling complexity, which we have developed in the previous pages. The founding principle, which is one of the *lean* pillars, remains the same: complexity must be displayed (on walls), and invisible problems must be made visible (excessive complexity is a problem). We thus recommend using visual management to share with everyone (the whole team but also all stakeholders, in particular business and IT managers) the reality of the functioning of the global system. Once awareness has been achieved, reducing complexity is played out on multiple scales as presented in the previous section: permanent *refactoring*, *sprints* devoted to technical debt, and the renewal of components oriented by a service architecture. The practice of code reviews also plays an essential role in making complexity visible and revealing the shadow of the future, which is one of the essential benefits of the *open-source* approach. Finally, the rigorous measurement of usage that we indicated in Chapter 3 is an essential ally in avoiding unnecessary complexity. First, because it acts as a deterrent to avoid *feature creep* (the accumulation of superfluous functionalities that reassure both the client and the developer by concentrating on the technical act). But above all, measurement is a formidable tool for eliminating what is not useful, or very rarely useful, to the system's users.

6.3.3 Controlling the Age of Systems through Flows

We will end this chapter with an idea that is one of the common threads of this book: the **average age of systems must be reduced to improve the company's ability to adapt to its environment**. This is a functional issue since a more modern software system is better able to take into account digital needs that are constantly changing. But it is also a service quality and performance issue. Finally, it is a cost control issue. From a hardware point of view, it is a question of benefiting from the constant progress of technology (and this is broader than just Moore's law). This is also true for licensing costs, whose prices increase with age,[27] to the point

[27] The cost curve for components, software and hardware, is often likened to the shape of a bathtub because there is a phase of over-cost for very young components (both in development and in paying for novelty), then a phase of stability, followed by an increase that accelerates with obsolescence. This curve reflects economies of scale, and the fact that suppliers seek to avoid conserving too many resources for obsolete products.

of reaching dissuasive maintenance levels for obsolete components. Let's also note that the control of age and complexity are irremediably linked: aging induces an increase in complexity, and complexity reduces the ability to rejuvenate frequently.

The management of the system's age is essentially done by acting on the flows represented in Figure 6.1. The first step is to carefully measure the age of its software assets and to provide this data to stakeholders, in particular to those responsible for the IS components. In addition to the two NEW/OUT flows previously mentioned, the main topic becomes the renewal flow (RENEW). Without going into the details of the modeling in Figure 6.1, let's put forward a few simple elements that allow us to both better understand and obtain orders of magnitude. Clearly, if we want to achieve an average age of N years, in a stable world, we need a refresh every 2N years, which gives a refresh rate of (1/2N), which represents a significant allocation of the *build* budget—the portion of the IT budget allocated to projects, as opposed to the *run*, the portion allocated to operations. There is no ideal average age; it depends on the business domain and the desired agility. In a multimodal approach, it also depends on the position of the component in the system (see Chapter 4 and Figure 4.1). The "border" systems in contact with the environment must be renewed frequently to be able to integrate with the constraints and opportunities of the company's customers. On the contrary, "core" systems can—and often must—live longer and work well with older technologies.

The table in Figure 6.2 provides a simple illustration of the numbers that can be obtained by making simple assumptions. The cost of the run is directly related to the cost of acquisition. The figure that is often found in the literature is 15% of the acquisition cost.[28] The table is obtained in the following way: for each column, I propose a maximum target age according to the type of component, then I calculate the share of the *build* budget

---

[28] This figure is only an order of magnitude, even if it is frequently quoted. I refer you to the book *Information Technology for the Chief Executive: Value Analysis, Organization and Management*, in which I go into more detail on modeling IT costs and what can be found in *benchmarkings* and classic books. As far as maintenance costs are concerned, I use a ratio of 5% (of acquisition costs), which corresponds to the low range of what is found in the literature, but which corresponds here to my objective of illustrating the principle of management by flows (Table 6.2 is, therefore, conservative). It is a simplistic approach: on the one hand, the table does not take growth into account, and on the other hand, it overestimates the cost of renewal. But these two flaws compensate each other, and it gives an order of magnitude. What is important is to understand that as soon as B/R is smaller than the indicated target value, we start creating a debt.

	"edge" (front-office)	Service factory (middle-office)	Core domain (back-end)
Target max age	5 Years	10 years	15 years
Target (min Build / max Run) as % of total	62% / 38%	50%/50%	45%/55%

Figure 6.2 Budget *build* reserve by target age.

necessary for the maintenance part and for the new flow. This minimal budget is then translated into *run* costs, using the ratio between acquisition cost and run cost, in the form of two percentages that represent the *build* and *run* allocation of the overall budget. This table also illustrates that the target age varies by zone, and therefore, the "average age reduction" goal is not uniform.

Though the table is simple, it has two interests. First, it highlights the need to think about the age and balancing flows in a recursive way for the overall IS as well as for its components. Therefore, it is important to break down your operating costs and be able to attribute them to the different business areas and the different main components of the IS. It also underlines what we said in Chapter 4: the multimodal approach makes it possible to introduce different target ages for different components of the IS, but it does not allow parts of the IS to age indefinitely in order to build others. The second interest of the table is to underline that refreshment is a constraint! The values are not the *build/run* ratios to be expected, but the minimum values to be reserved for building one's IS in a sustainable way. In practice, it is also necessary to be able to add budget for the "NEW" flow, which is never absent. In most companies and their ISs, the observed ratios are lower. The natural consequence is twofold: loss of agility and lower quality of service. Indeed, the absence of the necessary budget causes two things: components are allowed to age to reach suboptimal ages (responsiveness and quality of operations) or operating costs are constrained (less resources also yield a drop in responsiveness which penalizes both agility and MTTR). In this situation, when the *build/run* ratio is too low, the solution is not to increase *build* expenses; it is to simplify the system in order to reduce the *run*. This is the essence of sustainable development: don't build an IS you can't afford to maintain.

Summary

1. Complexity produces four difficulties, which can be measured and used to evaluate the efficiency of the software development process: *rework*, TTM, non-deployed code, and wasted time (6.1.1).
2. Lean practice is rooted in a systemic approach (*system thinking*), with the objective of enabling the team to understand and master complex systems (6.1.2).
3. One of the key principles of *lean* practice is to reduce the workload (WIP) to increase flexibility and responsiveness (6.1.3).
4. Easy and direct access to the "business" decision for the development team is a decisive success condition and an important difference between small autonomous structures such as startups and some of the digital teams of large companies (6.1.4).
5. The development of the IS requires the expertise and contribution of architects, even within agile teams (6.2.1).
6. *Service-oriented architecture* (SOA) plays the role of "stake"; it defines a form that the iterative process of agile development fills (6.2.2).
7. An API is more than a programming interface, it is also an intention that assumes a common semantics between the producer and the consumer and an SLA that specifies the availability, capacity, and response times that can be expected (6.2.3).
8. Sustainable development describes the ability of the IS to provide services that correspond to the company's current needs without compromising the future ability to deliver services that meet the needs of tomorrow (6.3.1).
9. The challenge of good governance is to transform the frustration of complexity into the energy of simplification (6.3.2).
10. The average age of systems must be reduced to improve the company's ability to adapt to its environment (6.3.3).

SOFTWARE PLATFORMS AND SERVICE FACTORIES

Chapter 7: DevOps and Software Factories

Chapter 8: Putting Platforms at the Service of Digital Transformation

Chapter 7

DevOps and Software Factories

This chapter covers software development automation, continuous deployment, and software factory. The term "factory" may come as a surprise in the digital world, where the constraints of innovation and agility are often associated with practices that are freer and more creative than those of the industrial world. For the past ten years, I have been using the term "software factory" to emphasize two requirements that look paradoxical in the digital world: automated and disciplined/professional development process.[1]

In this chapter, we will discuss DevOps because it is today the dominant approach to CICD. Understanding how DevOps works is as important to a successful digital transformation as understanding the lean startup approach. Even if technology is just a tool, secondary to the main goal of building customer satisfaction through digital experiences, the best digital players have a high level of excellence in the practice of CICD, which is at the heart of the DevOps ambition.

[1] It would be more appropriate to speak of a *micro factory*, in the same sense as *micro brewery*, which is what we did in the introduction. The term "software factory" is often associated with the pooling and development of an external competence center. The micro software factory, even if it is based on a global infrastructure such as cloud computing, is a local structure, strongly coupled, and often co-located, with the business need.

DOI: 10.4324/9781003272816-10

7.1 Automate the Software Process

7.1.1 Automate for More Quality and Efficiency

The main idea of Chapter 2 was the need to automate software production to face the challenges of the digital world. Since "software is eating up the world," more and more software needs to be produced. Over time, there has been a steady improvement in software productivity (the time it takes to produce a function point is decreasing), but it is slow, and it is not keeping up with demand. The massive computerization of digital transformation requires the reuse and integration of software components, especially *open-source*[2] ones. One of the first objectives of software factories is to assemble and integrate software components to develop products in the most efficient way possible.

Automating the software product development process is necessary to enable companies to win the innovation race, to reduce TTM, and to better satisfy their customers by iterating at a faster pace the "continuous product discovery" cycle presented in Chapter 3. This is a key dimension of digital transformation: going faster means learning faster and being able to co-construct the products and services that customers need more quickly. Automation also contributes to improving service quality and reducing costs.[3] As we said in Chapter 4, human error is still a frequent root cause of production incidents. The more frequent the deployment and release processes are, the more repetition leads to careless errors if manual processes are kept. Moreover, manual processes require important documentation (operating procedures) that must be constantly updated in the constantly changing world of digital transformation.[4] The example of security policies (antivirus, firewall rules, authentication rules, etc.) perfectly illustrates the virtues of automation. When an intrusion is detected, it is most often necessary to react by modifying some of these policies and then

[2] The practice of *open source* is old, but it is the digital transformation that has produced an "in-draught" (opportunities for massive sharing). This has amplified the development of this practice and led to the rapid development of solutions for automating the integration and deployment *pipeline*.

[3] Here we have an interesting reinforcement loop: to update systems more regularly, it is necessary to reduce the *run* costs in order to be able to invest more in the *build* (see previous chapter). But the effective reduction of costs through automation is greatly facilitated with recent and up-to-date software stacks.

[4] These arguments are developed in the reference book *Continuous Integration and Continuous Delivery: Reliable Software Releases through Build, Test, and Deployment Automation*, by Jez Humble and Dave Farley, from which I draw for the description of CICD in the rest of this chapter.

deploying them as quickly as possible, without error. Automation is the only way to combine speed and accuracy.

The automation of software production is part of an industrial approach that begins with nomenclatures and inventories.[5] In the world of software factories, the founding tool for development automation processes is configuration management. In their book *Continuous Integration and Continuous Delivery*, Jezz Humble and David Farley write, "*Configuration management is the foundation of CICD. It is impossible to do continuous integration, automated deployment without it.*" A configuration management system—CMDB (*configuration management database*)—contains a description of the various hardware and software components that is precise enough to be able to build or rebuild the various software systems from the elementary components. The configuration management and the code and artifact repository are carefully versioned to ensure traceability of changes and, above all, to allow easy reverting to previous situations. **An essential property of an industrial software deployment process is to be able to guarantee the reproducibility of deployments, and this requires rigorous configuration management.**

7.1.2 Continuous Integration

The most important change in the last twenty years is the practice of continuous integration. In a traditional development cycle (called a V-cycle or waterfall process), code is produced from specifications, then unit tested, then integrated and tested as a whole system. A lot of time can pass between the start of development and the integration phase. All the code produced represents a complexity that accumulates with two resulting disadvantages: the integration phase becomes increasingly difficult when the complexity of the environment increases and the probability of having to go back and change the code because of a difficulty in the architecture of the overall system also increases (thus producing higher integration costs and more *rework*). **Continuous integration consists of performing this integration phase regularly and very frequently—for example, every day—so as not to let this "integration complexity debt" grow.** The fundamental change with respect to traditional development cycles is

[5] We could add to the aphorism "you can only optimize what you measure" another aphorism: "you can only manage what you identify." However, inventory management (from hardware configurations to software versions) is often in a state that is more of a craft than an industrial practice.

to have a working reference system (built and integrated, which is called a *build*) at all times and not to have more than a few hours of unintegrated development.[6]

Continuous integration is about maintaining a desirable state (built and integrated code) by taking small, traceable, reversible steps. In the words of Jezz Humble and David Farley, "*every change in the system must be traced and exposed to a feedback process as soon as possible.* This is a *lean* approach by nature: detect non-quality (failure to integrate a component change with the rest of the system) as early as possible. Each change produced by a team member becomes visible to all during a *check-in*[7] in the version management system. This ensures the traceability of changes and requires the necessary practice of team members to comment on their *commits* with clear and explicit messages. Continuous integration is, above all, a team practice that requires a high degree of commitment and discipline from the development team.[8] The famous rule of thumb "*don't check-in on a broken build*" (don't add code while the system is no longer integrated; i.e., while the integration is no longer working) is reminiscent of the Toyota *andon*. When the *build* no longer works, the whole team must stop producing new code and help to return to a state of integrity, even if it means using *versioning* to go back. The tradition says that you don't go home with a build that doesn't work.

The rigorous and regular practice of continuous integration requires automation. The practice and the various tools have been developed over the last twenty years, and today there are remarkable solutions to automate the *build*[9] process. Automation and the associated tools must offer three things: simplicity (the goal being to be able to do the entire *build* with a single command), speed (since the *build* will be done in a repetitive

[6] This makes integration a team responsibility, and it changes the way developers collaborate.

[7] The version management system makes it possible to retrieve (*check-out*) the state of a file associated with a given version and then to record (*check-in*, or *commit*, depending on the centralized or decentralized mode) a new state associated with a version.

[8] From a release management perspective, continuous integration is associated with what is called trunk development as opposed to branches. The same idea of wanting to avoid too much integration debt leads to avoiding branches (a copy of a system that is left to evolve in a different way for a certain period of time, either because you want to explore another approach or because you want to parallelize the development).

[9] There are a wide variety of continuous integration engines, such as Jenkins, GitLab, Bamboo, CircleCI, or TeamCity.

way—we can consider that what made the practice of continuous integration possible is the acceleration of compilation and link editing times thanks to the power of machines), and ease of reverting. It is not just the *commit* that needs to be automated but also the rollback. Modern tools make it possible to produce *builds* with readable and relatively elegant scripts (we are talking here about conciseness and degree of abstraction; cf. the remarks in Chapter 4 on the importance of *integration as code*). The scripts written with these tools are declarative: they describe the target state and let the tool decide on the best construction path (we find here the concept of idempotent script presented in Chapter 4).

7.1.3 Continuous Deployment

The term CICD covers the automation of the entire software product development and deployment process. We speak of a deployment pipeline for all the stages described in Figure 7.1. The beginning of the process is the production of code that leads to *commits*; we find continuous integration as the second stage,[10] then a stage of tests that are all the more frequent as they are automated, then deployment. The frequency of each stage decreases along the pipeline (by construction) and the manual test stages, such as UATs (*user acceptance tests*), are placed at the end of the process and executed with the same frequency as deployment. The figure shows the systems shared by all the stages of the deployment pipeline: source code management, configuration management (environment and application), and the repository of artifacts (the binaries and metadata produced by the various build processes).[11] The principle of a software factory is to build a reliable and reproducible process to execute this pipeline, automating as much as possible. The authors of CICD provide advice in the tradition of *lean manufacturing*: "**If the build pipeline is not working well, run it more frequently and highlight the difficulties.**"

---

[10] I agree with Jez Humble and David Farley; continuous integration is the central practice of CICD: "*If you were to choose just one of the practices in this book to implement on a development team, we would suggest that you choose Continuous Integration. Time and again we have seen it make a step change to the productivity of software development teams. . . . Implementing CI forces you to follow two other important practices: good configuration management and the creation and maintenance of an automated build and test process.*"

[11] The *artifact repository* is the "cache" of the *build and deploy* process; it is used to build items—such as binaries produced by compilation—only once.

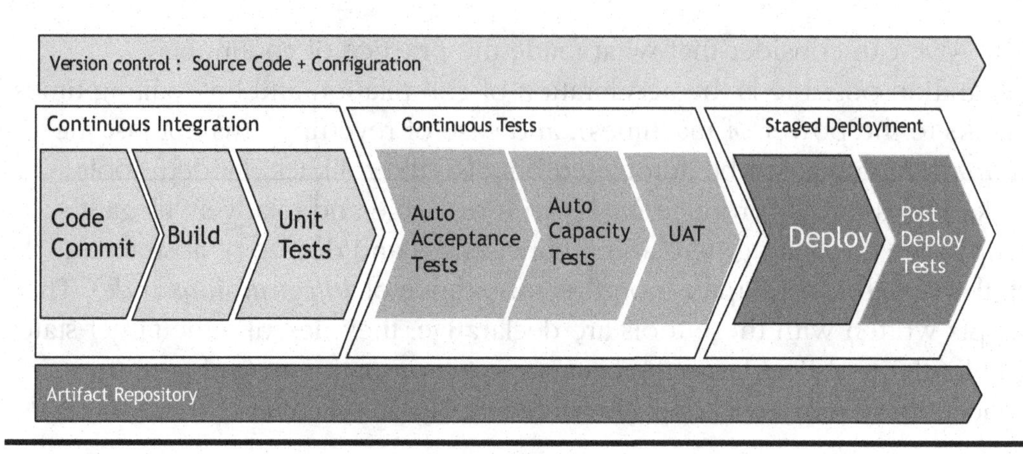

Figure 7.1 The continuous deployment pipeline.

The frequency of continuous deployment is high compared to conventional development cycles.[12] It is, by construction of the agile process, a multiple of the duration of the sprints (from 1 to 4 weeks in general), with the progressive objective of minimizing the quantity of changes to be put into production as we know how to deploy efficiently. Continuous delivery actually comes in two flavors, depending on the type of software asset: the software product may be released as a whole (after each sprint), or each subcomponent may be released independently, at a higher frequency. Automation is necessary to reconcile the high quality of the build and deployment process with the increased frequency. If we take a step back, we see that this is a trade-off: by increasing the frequency, we bring in local difficulty (that of executing a technical process without errors) to reduce the global difficulty of complexity (knowing how to predict the consequences of interactions in a complex system). If deployments are frequent, the difference between *releases* is small, which greatly reduces the risk associated with change in the overall system and makes it much easier to *roll back* if necessary.

Continuous deployment is as automated as possible; it is reversible and most often broken down into successive stages (*staged*) that allow risk to be

[12] The term "continuous deployment" does not mean that everything that is built is automatically deployed. As we'll see in the next section, some of the testing remains manual, and some of the deployment process is significantly more cumbersome than the "automated build" (generally speaking, but there are exceptions). In some cases, the release is separated from the activation of new *features*—which is what web companies do—and this allows for a decoupled release, at a pace that can be very frequent. But this requires a great deal of control over the quality of the software since some of the testing takes place after the release.

reduced and better controlled. Indeed, any change represents a risk—which testing will seek to reduce, which is the subject of the next section—and the residual risk produced by the software development pipeline materializes at the time of release. Continuous deployment uses the same tools as *build* and release for the different test phases. The same care must be taken to automate installation, de-installation, and reverting to a previous version (see Chapter 4). The "phased" deployment consists of breaking down the deployment so that it can be rolled back more quickly in the event of difficulties. The most common approach, called *blue-green deployment*, is to have two production environments, blue and green, which allow the new version to be installed on the blue environment while the green environment is active, and then to switch usage to the blue environment while keeping the green environment for a *rollback in* case of problems. The *canary deployment* approach is a form of A/B testing in which a few users test the new version before deploying it more widely to all users. This approach is appropriate when there are concerns about difficulties with real data from production environments that would not be apparent with data from test environments. If the possible difficulties are related to the volume, this approach can be refined in the form of progressive deployment, made famous by Facebook, in which the new version is deployed on increasingly large perimeters of users. In all cases, progressive deployments are accompanied by *post-deployment tests*, production tests whose purpose is to find out, before the users, if there is a problem.

7.1.4 Automate the Tests

The principle of continuous integration is to have a permanently integrated and viable system. A viable system is a "system that works," and what this phrase means precisely depends on the ability to automate the tests.[13] We can identify three groups of tests:

- Tests related to the continuous integration process, which are mainly **unit tests** that developers produce to ensure that their code works properly, and a (small) part of the UATs that can be automated. The tools that allow the simulation of user behavior (similar to the robots

[13] I quote Jez Humble and David Farley here: "*The shorted feedback loops are recreated through sets of automated tests that are run upon every change to the system. Such tests should run at all levels—from unit tests up to acceptance tests (both functional and non-functional).*"

used in RPA [*robot process automation*]) are constantly progressing, and it is now easy to test user interfaces automatically.

- The second group of tests includes **performance tests and acceptance tests** that will be performed manually before moving on to deployment. Performance tests are multiple: we find load tests, response time tests, and also availability and resistance to failures. We can also extend the technical tests to the field of security and operability (the ability of the system to be integrated into the monitoring and automated production follow-up tools). As shown in Figure 7.1 and explained in the book by Jez Humble and David Farley, some of these tests can be automated and, therefore, executed more regularly, and this before arriving in the UAT for deployment.
- The last group of tests contains the **tests associated with deployments**, those that will be run automatically during deployment, and the **post-deployment tests** that we mentioned earlier. The automatic deployment tests verify that each deployed component is "alive" and "working" (we often speak of *smoke tests*).

The development of unit tests plays a key role in continuous integration since they sanction the fact that the *build* works. Martin Fowler points out that the proper completion of unit tests is essential to the practice of *refactoring*, which we discussed in Chapter 4. The automated *build* and unit tests are the "safety net" that allows the developer to reorganize his code more quickly (always the same idea of frequent feedback and the simple, automated ability to go back). The importance of unit tests has produced the TDD (*test-driven development*) approach in which the developer builds his tests before producing his new code. TDD has its own virtues because it forces the developer to focus first on what is observable. Moreover, from the point of view of continuous integration, this approach guarantees good quality and coverage of unit tests.

The set of tests is a common asset of the team,[14] **which is built by continuous improvement.** The improvement here consists of extending the coverage of the tests, but above all of building the automated tests that can be placed "as far ahead as possible." This remark is at the heart of the test improvement strategy, such as the one we built a few years ago

---

[14] I quote Jez Humble and David Farley: "*High-quality software is only possible if testing becomes the responsibility of everybody involved in delivering software and is practiced right from the beginning of the project and throughout its life.*" The responsibility of testing is collective; it is shared with the developers.

in AXA's Digital Agency. As part of the regular retrospectives of the Scrum methodology, the team must analyze the most important bugs (defects) and ask itself when this defect could have been detected by a test: a unit test, an automatic acceptance test, a user acceptance test, a system test, a deployment test, and so on. This collective work of assigning defects to the phases of the development pipeline is particularly fruitful for increasing the team's maturity on its product. The objective is, of course, to reduce the rate of defects found in production, but this approach makes it possible to build several indicators of the relevance of the tests associated with the phases of the pipeline. This method takes up a very old, antifragile practice of growing the test base from incidents to avoid regressions that are always badly perceived by users.

7.2 DevOps

7.2.1 A Cross-Functional Team to Implement CICD

DevOps dates back about ten years and aims to implement the CICD approach presented in the previous section: according to Wikipedia, it is a set of practices whose objective is to reduce the time needed to put a change into production while ensuring high-quality software. *DevOps* is the contraction of *developers* and *operations*; it is an approach based on collaboration and sharing within a cross-functional team. There are actually four components to this approach: (1) the CICD ambition we just described, (2) mix *dev* and *ops* in the same team, (3) the ability to treat one's environment as a programmatically configurable object—what is called *infrastructure as code* (IaC) and will be the focus of the next section—and (4) the ambition for continuous progress, in the form of a cycle. Where the CICD pipeline is a sequence, which most often corresponds to a list of sprints, the common representation of DevOps is a ∞ (the symbol for infinity), which represents **a double-loop product approach: each release (*deployment*) is an opportunity to learn and make improvements in the next development cycle**.

If you search for DevOps on the web, you'll find a huge number of practices associated with implementing CICD.[15] What makes DevOps

[15] See for example the e-book *Five Foundational DevOps Practices*, co-published by Puppet and Splunk. These practices concern testing, deployment, and monitoring, using various CICD tools, such as configuration management and operations automation.

enrich the CICD ambition is the collaboration between the different roles in the team. Operations are enriched by development by systematically seeking as much automation as possible, from deployment to operations, from monitoring to incident handling (which we described in Chapter 4). Symmetrically, the *ops* vision is present from the development phases of the cycle to ensure both simpler and more robust deployment. The cycle approach (the "figure of 8" loop) is essential to nurture collaboration because what is deployed is used to learn and improve the next release. DevOps practice, as iterations progress, produces teams with cross-functional, T-shaped profiles,[16] with skills specific to each but also a versatility that allows, in the words of Coplien and Bjørnvig, to have *all hands on deck* when a difficulty needs to be solved, like a *commit* that refuses to build properly.[17]

This cross-functional practice is intended to address topics that will be critical when the software is in production, such as support or security, as early as possible. Many DevOps teams go so far as to integrate support roles into the cross-functional team or to make going through support a mandatory step in training developers on the system they are building. In the DevOps culture, there is a dual purpose to this rapprochement: taking calls and handling user requests is an excellent way to guarantee the customer orientation we mentioned in the first part. Symmetrically, for the support role to be effective and rewarding, software systems must include all the tools for easy diagnosis and repair (in other words, they must be operable). The integration of security constraints and best practices from the very beginning of development has given rise to the acronym "DevSecOps." We have already seen in the previous section that it is useful to bring security tests into the scope of automated CICD tests. The DevOps approach allows for collaborative dialogue between developers and security experts to achieve what is often called *security by design*.

---

[16] The T profile refers to the combination of a broad spectrum of skills (the horizontal bar of the T) in a shallow way, but allowing for collaboration with other team members, and a deep area of expertise on a specific domain (the vertical bar of the T; e.g., development, architecture, databases).

[17] I've been lucky enough to recruit developers who have previously worked with a true DevOps culture. They are often surprised at the Taylorization of roles that is retained in large organizations. In a DevOps team, anyone can play the role of support, test, deploy, and fix an incident in production.

7.2.2 Infrastructure as Code

The concept of IaC means that development, test, and deployment environments have programmatic interfaces (APIs) that allow developers to configure, obtain, and manage the computing resources (computation, network, and storage) they need.[18] The ambition of this IaC formula is that *hardware* resources can be manipulated with the same flexibility as software resources. This freedom has three consequences: the *shift left* for part of the *ops* tasks, the ability to go much further in automating the CICD pipeline, and the possibility of setting up elastic resource consumption.

The first virtue of an API for provisioning hardware resources is to save time. Self-provisioning by means of a portal or a script is in itself an optimization from a *lean point of view*: it eliminates a step and allows the need to be met more precisely. On the other hand, it requires greater competence on the requester's side: the developer must acquire some skills on the *ops* side since the famous "validation of the need" step is not required. This is precisely why you need both the tools (IaC) and the collaborative culture of DevOps teams.

Self-provisioning through a portal is a first step, but it remains a manual approach. In order to automate the *build* and provisioning of software products for testing and deployment, we need to move to the API approach, which allows us to build the available resources with scripts that are incorporated into the CICD pipeline tools. This automation step allows, as already mentioned, to gain not only in speed but above all in reproducibility and, therefore, in error reduction. It is, therefore, clear that IaC is also an essential skill for accelerating the frequency of the deployment pipeline.

The final benefit of IaC is the ability to continuously and programmatically change the number of resources allocated to a product or service as demand changes. This is known as elastic resource management, a term that came about with *cloud computing* (to truly program the cloud and not just use it as an external resource, you need IaC capabilities). This advantage is critical in the world of digital services and platforms, more than in the world of ISs. Using IaC, automation, and orchestration together, for example, by using the Kubernetes platform to configure and provision

[18] In this book, I will keep the discussion very general without going into more technical details. The virtualization of resources means that the IaC is materialized by intermediate objects from virtual machines to *containers*.

containers, enables highly resilient systems to be built, capable of adapting to large variations in load as well as the unavailability of resource providers.

7.2.3 Results of the Early Adopters

The DevOps approach is now practiced by many companies for several years. I highly recommend reading Nicol Forsgreen, Jez Humble, and Gene Kim's book *Accelerate: The Science of Lean Software and DevOps; Building and Scaling High-Performing Technology Organizations.* This book is the leading reference on the relationship between the performance of organizations in the digital world and their software development and deployment capabilities. It is the result of a quantitative and analytical approach based on the study of more than two thousand companies. As the subtitle of the book indicates, the authors' ambition is to propose a synthesis of the best practices of successful companies and to link the company's performance to the quality of the software production process. In this section, I give you a short summary of the main findings.

The DevOps approach is the common foundation for companies that excel at software development and deployment. DevOps emerged as a common practice among a small number of organizations that had the same problem of producing scalable and repeatable distributed systems that are secure, resilient, and able to scale at a rapid rate. DevOps has led to the formalization of continuous build, integration, and deployment processes: "*Continuous delivery is a set of capabilities that enable us to get changes of all kinds-features, configuration changes, bug fixes, experiments-into production or into the hands of users safely, quickly, and sustainably.*" These goals can only be achieved through close collaboration between all those involved in the various phases of the software build/delivery process. These CICD practices help to achieve the industrial consistency that is expected from a software factory. It is necessary to work relentlessly to eradicate the fear of deployment: "*The fear and anxiety that engineers and technical staff feel when they push code into production can tell us a lot about a team's software delivery performance. We call this deployment pain, and it is important to measure because it highlights the friction.*" In a resolutely *lean* approach, this, of course, means accelerating the pace of deployments. We also find the recommendations from the previous pages on building resilient systems that facilitate the work of development and operations: "*In order to reduce deployment pain, we should: Build systems that are designed to be deployed easily into multiple environments, can detect and tolerate failures in their* *environments, and can have various components of the system updated independently; Ensure that the state of production systems can be reproduced (with the exception of production data) in an automated fashion from information in version control; Build intelligence into the application and the platform so that the deployment process can be as simple as possible."*

Effective organizations are, first and foremost, learning organizations. Digital performance starts with human capital: "*People are at the heart of every technology transformation. With market pressures to deliver technology and solutions ever faster, the importance of hiring, retaining, and engaging our workforce is greater than ever.*" The exponential pace of technological change means that the issue of continuous employee learning must be addressed. This leads irrevocably to the principle of the learning organization, in a digital world where learning means doing: "*Our analysis is clear: in today's fast-moving and competitive world, the best thing you can do for your products, your company, and your people is to institute a culture of experimentation and learning, and invest in the technical and management capabilities that enable it.*" This objective of continuous progress is reflected in the organization, but above all in the culture and daily practice, with a strong borrowing from the lean approaches and Deming's legacy: "*This practice of rapid exchange of learning, enabling the frontline teams to learn about strategic priorities and the leaders to learn about customer experience from frontline team customer interaction, is a form of strategy deployment (Lean practitioners use the term Hoshin Kanri). It creates, at all levels, a continuous, rapid feedback cycle of learning, testing, validating, and adjusting, also known as PDCA.*"

Performance and resilience rhyme in a complex world. Resiliency is one of the original goals of the DevOps movement. Because modern digital systems are complex—frequency and richness of change and complexity of user interactions—failures are also complex. Preventing and dealing with errors is, therefore, a practice that requires training. It is thus not surprising to find recommendations for frequent *disaster recovery* plan validation exercises: "*Use disaster recovery testing exercises to build relationships . . . Create a training budget and advocating for it internally. Emphasize how much the organization values a climate of learning by putting resources behind formal education opportunities.*"[19] Resilience is also achieved by promoting automation and continuous proactive monitoring. We find the recommendations of the *Google Site Reliability Engineering* book mentioned in Chapter 4: "*Make monitoring a priority. Refine your infrastructure and*

[19] My reference on this topic is Klaus Schmidt's book, *High Availability and Disaster Recovery*.

application monitoring system, and make sure you're collecting information on the right services and putting that information to good use . . . Practices like proactive monitoring and test and deployment automation all automate menial tasks and require people to make decisions based on a feedback loop."

7.3 Lean Software Factory

7.3.1 The Metaphor of the Lean Software Factory

The concept of *lean software factory* is the result of an evolution of a progressive absorption of different influences of software methods, on an agile development structure. The first step was to move from a generic agile practice influenced by the *Agile Manifesto* and the principles of XP (*extreme programming*) to the Scrum practice. Scrum brings many rituals to facilitate the collaborative work of the team, a reinforced practice of visual management and a structuring of the roles, in particular that of the *scrum master*. The next step was, in early 2010, to adopt a CICD ambition, starting with the practice of continuous integration.

In the context of the development of Bouygues Telecom's set-top box software, the practice of integration, testing, and continuous deployment was a fundamental milestone, both from a business point of view—the ability to develop innovative solutions—and from a technical point of view. The important requirement of implementing CICD quickly led us to a DevOps approach (adding the dimension of continuous improvement by iterative product cycle and cross-functional collaboration mentioned in the previous section). This *lean* root of DevOps led us to look for other sources of inspiration from the side of *lean software development*, in particular on the use of kanban (to limit intermediate inventories and waiting phases) and the intensification of continuous improvement with the practice of kaizen. Figure 7.2 represents my vision of the *lean software factory* in 2012.

I will now come back to the *lean* dimension of software development, which gives its name to *lean software factory*. I was influenced by three books:

- *The Art of Lean Software Development*, by Curt Hibb
- *Implementing Lean Software Development*, by Mary and Tom Poppendieck
- *Lean from the Trenches: Managing Large-Scale Projects with Kanban*, by Henrick Kniberg

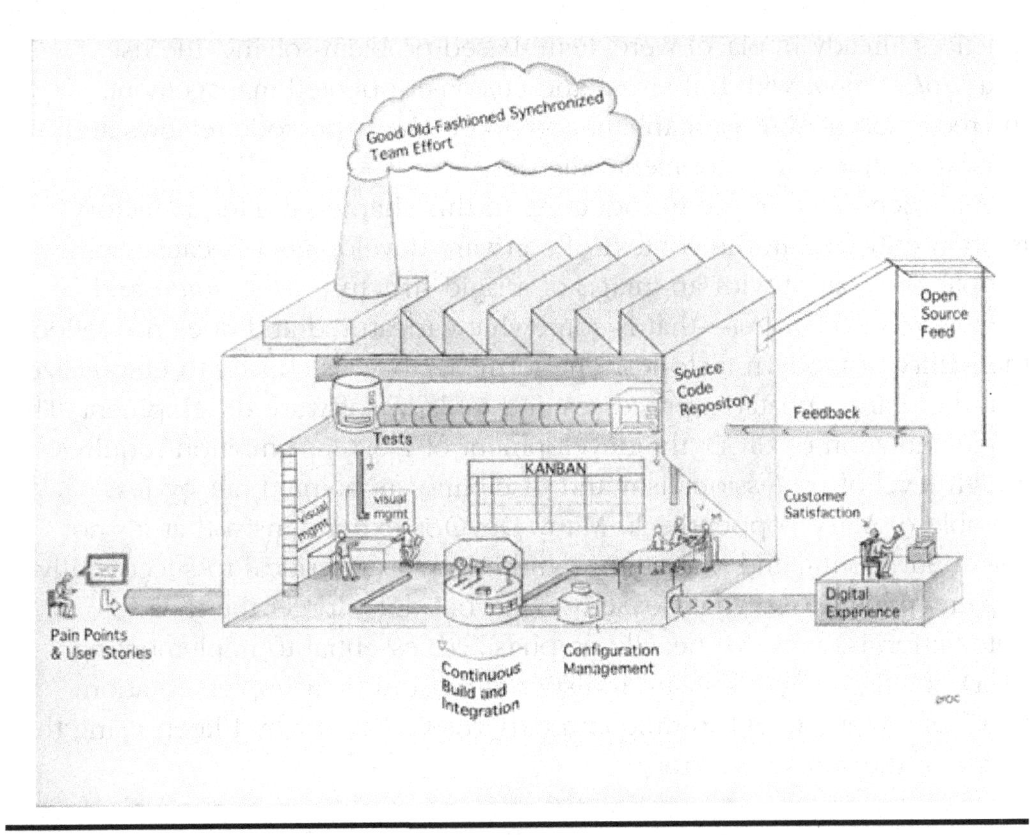

Figure 7.2 ***Lean software factory*** **(2012 vision).**

The first book lays the foundations of a tool-based development process (*source code management, scripted build, automated testing, continuous integration*) which was a precursor to the CICD approach described in Section 7.1. This book also insists, quite logically, on the participation of users in development, which we saw in Chapter 3.

Mary and Tom Poppendieck's book focuses on the transition from project to product culture, on the elimination of waste in the *lean* tradition, on the global systemic vision, and on the importance of collective learning. The *lean* approach enriches the agile practice with the concept of (development) standards and practices such as 5S (working better by tidying up your work tool, which applies perfectly to software).

The third book focuses on the importance of kanban. It also details the use of Toyota's A3 to support *kaizen*. When introducing *lean software* at Bouygues Telecom in 2011, the four priorities (in addition to the Scrum practices already in place) were: team-based problem-solving, the use of a *project room* with full visual and customer-oriented management, the reduction of WIP via kanban, and an emphasis on code reviews and standardization of development practices.[20]

As I mentioned in the introduction to this chapter, the term "factory" is often criticized in the context of software development because some people associate it with an image of a rigid structure—*top-down* and *command and control*—that is somewhat caricatured and does not reflect the reality of modern factories. The term "factory" is chosen to emphasize that there are repeatable processes and tools in software development. The implementation of CICD, the development of DevOps ambition requires a high level of professionalism and discipline, as pointed out by Jez Humble or Mary Poppendieck. Many DevOps experts insist that it's not just about tooling and that culture and mindset are critical to successfully implementing CICD. That's exactly right, but don't forget the tools. Automation is, as we've heavily emphasized, essential to implementing CICD practices. The tools are indispensable, and their implementation requires an investment in time and expertise. This is why I keep using the image of the software factory.

7.3.2 The Twelve Principles of Lean Software Factory

The drawing in the previous figure reflects the essence of the ambition formulated in 2011. Since then, the lean software factory concept has progressed; in 2014 I summarized it by twelve principles at the Lean Summit conference in Lyon. I deliver here a summarized version because we have already seen most of these concepts in the previous chapters.

1. **Work is distributed and organized around autonomous cross-functional teams**. The T profiles mean that the team is autonomous because it has the necessary skills to build its product in an excellent way but also that it develops a form of versatility that allows strong cooperation and involvement of all to solve problems.
2. **Teams work synchronously, around a common and shared representation of time**. Priority is given to face-to-face communication,

[20] For more details, I refer you to the "*Lean Software Factory*" presentation I gave in 2013 at the European Lean IT Summit. The slides and the video are available online.

from daily stand-ups to pair collaboration.[21] The common time is the client's time; it is a factor of commitment and collective energy, the orchestration of the cooperation is visible (on the walls) and shared.

3. **The voice of the customer is present on the development floor**, development is organized around *user stories*, and the team mobilizes the talents and skills of designers. Customer satisfaction is the common obsession and the foundation of an approach that seeks quality from the first line of code.
4. **Development and progress are built iteratively, in small steps**. The "small steps" approach reduces the difficulty inherent in complexity and allows an adaptive approach to its environment.
5. **You have to take care of your code, share it, and make it shareable and, therefore, as readable as possible**. The "lean software factory" approach is relevant in the digital world, where code changes very often. The code review increases the quality of the code and reduces the cost of modifications (changes) and maintenance.
6. **Walls must be used to take advantage of the power of visual management**. The use of digital tools is an excellent practice because digitization allows for easy memory and search, and it is essential as soon as teams are geographically distributed, but the wall is a "radiator" of information that allows stigmergy.[22] Visual management is used to make visible the complexity and difficulties that are "hidden" in the code.
7. **Each team member produces what the others need at the right time without accumulating and producing delays**. The team visualizes the flow of sequences and drives it in a pull mode while minimizing work in progress. The team continuously develops its capacity model through continuous improvement to avoid overloads.
8. **All the construction, testing, and deployment processes are instrumented** to allow complete reproducibility of the development stages, the ability to go back, and the most advanced automation possible.
9. **The team works in continuous integration mode and rebuilds its product daily**. The team is aware of the accumulation of technical

[21] The importance of synchronicity in a complex environment is essential. Read, for example, *The Joy of Work*, by Bruce Daysley, or *How Google Works*, by Eric Schmidt and Jonathan Rosenberg. Work that is simply done asynchronously tends to become commoditized in marketplaces, waiting to be processed by robots one day (asynchrony is a mark of simplicity, the ability to specify what needs to be done).

[22] Stigmergy is a form of communication through place or space (indirect coordination through traces left in space). Communication between ants by pheromone deposition is an emblematic example of stigmergy.

debt produced by iterative approaches and reserves the necessary time for refactoring.

10. **The key is to "catch what doesn't work" as early as possible so you can get it right faster.** Test development is part of product development, and the team is constantly working on automating and executing tests as early as possible in the development process.
11. **The team deploys successive versions of its product at a regular and sustained pace** to foster continuous innovation and strengthen the team's technical skills.
12. **Problem-solving is done in teams** in a collaborative way and serves to develop transversal and systemic skills (understanding the product we build as a system and integrate into the global system).

7.3.3 A Lean Factory for Learning

The twelve principles of the previous section are a synthesis in which we find the principles of the *Agile Manifesto*, the additions specific to XP, those specific to the Scrum approach, and the import of three practices that are particularly emphasized in the *lean software* approach. I will briefly review these three practices which, in my opinion, represent the contribution of *lean thinking*[23] to software development. This is not to say that these practices do not exist in agile approaches, such as Scrum, but to emphasize that *lean* practice goes further in terms of both methods and objectives.

- The use of kanban, in the form of cards (Post-it) that serve to materialize a flow of tasks, has become relatively common in agile practices and has even become the name of a practice.[24] The associated visual management is more specific than the classic categories (*backlog, plan, do, done*) because it materializes the different

---

[23] Many of the ideas in this section can be found in the previously mentioned book *Accelerate*. It proposes twenty-four practices that are validated by their correlation with the performance of the companies that practice them. The authors explain the *lean* concepts from the *Toyota Way* and their scientific interpretation in a queue management context. Here is an example: "*Once utilization gets above a certain level, there is no spare capacity (or "slack") to absorb unplanned work, changes to the plan, or improvement work. This results in longer lead times to complete work.*" The main elements of *lean* that apply to software are as follows: the WIP limit, visual management, implementation (production) feedback, and lean change approval processes. Various more detailed examples of implementation in companies such as ING highlight the practice of visual management, for performance analysis, strategic alignment and problem-solving using Toyota-inspired A3s.

[24] Read for example the article by Max Rehkopf, "*Kanban vs. Scrum*," on the Atlassian website.

roles specific to the team's process, and it allows to visualize the flow of tasks. The first objective is to avoid the accumulation of pending tasks (limiting the WIP) and then to progressively switch to "pull" transitions, within the team but especially between teams. Because the lean software factory team cultivates versatility, this shared display of the flow allows the team to see how best to use each person's talents, depending on the current load.

- The practice of *kaizen* in a team is fundamental in the *lean* approach. It is more than a method of problem-solving; it is also a practice of collaboration as well as a tool to constantly enrich the learning of the team on its system and to continuously improve the visual management that is used to manage this system. **Working together on the same problem forces one to build a common vocabulary and develop a better understanding of the other team members' points of view.** Problem-solving uses two main tools: the five whys (the search for the root causes, a practice that is more difficult than it seems) and the famous A3, which is used to establish the diagnosis following the search for the causes, to build and assign the action plan and especially to follow it up. The practice of development in complex environments such as the world of digital services shows that it is difficult to know why things are getting better and that the absence of an A3 for monitoring improvements makes it very difficult to capitalize on and, therefore, to make long-term progress. The real success of *kaizen* is not in having solved a problem but in having enabled the team to collectively understand what made the problem possible and to have changed skills and practices in such a way that the possibility of a similar problem occurring is greatly diminished.
- The *lean software* approach implies a particular attention and care for the code, in order to optimize the operations (adding, maintenance, refactoring, cleaning, fault finding, etc.) in the long term. The 5S concept in *lean software development* translates into the following five practices: *sort*: reduce the code base, eliminate dead code, refactor; *systematize*: organize into modules, packages and projects, apply code standards and so on; *shine*: pass quality tests, clean up what is not readable, practice code reviews, improve test coverage rates, and so on; *standardize*: continuously improve the team's standards and ensure that they are respected, in a double loop of capitalizing on good practices and eliminating bad ones; and *sustain*: write all these steps into rituals

and make them part of the team's development culture. More generally, one of the *lean* principles is to make the invisible waste of the development process visible. This applies to the process made visible by kanban and to the code itself.

What these three *lean* manufacturing-inspired practices have in common is that they provide the team with tools for continuous learning, for constantly developing its business expertise (*mastery* in the sense of Daniel Pink). As we saw in Chapter 3, there is a double learning loop. The product develops thanks to user feedback, but users also progressively develop their own learning of the product. This is why design skills are essential, both to learn from the observation of uses but also to build an experience that takes the user's learning into account.

Just as products and users influence each other, the team and the product strengthen each other. The more the team develops its skills, both the technical skills of each individual and the collective skill of integrating all the elements into a single product, the better that product becomes and the more value it provides to users. But conversely, the more the team develops the product, the more it develops its skills. The application of the three *lean* practices is intended to accelerate this skill development, but it happens anyway. On the other hand, each of these loops works with a delay, and the combination of the two loops adds up to delays. This is why it is difficult to succeed with your first digital product from a "cold" start and iterations, and the accumulation of experience is necessary to succeed more quickly (i.e., to iterate more rapidly towards user satisfaction). Here we find the opposition detailed in Chapter 2 between the long time it takes to build skills and the necessarily short time it takes to develop and adapt a product to its users.[25]

7.3.4 Software Craftmanship

Among the four principles chosen in 2011 to create a *lean software factory* at Bouygues Telecom is "love of code." Loving code means loving both your own code and that of others. The objective of this care for the code is, on the one hand, to produce better, more elegant code, but above

[25] The difficulty comes from the fact that the customer's non-satisfaction is visible, whereas the improvement of skills is not easily visible. I have seen several times projects stopped when the team's competence had finally reached the desirable level (the digital world is a demanding one, the competition is severe). Trusting a team that is just starting out on a new digital project is no substitute for experience.

all to develop interest and pride, which are necessary for code sharing. Code sharing is organized in many ways. It starts with the practice of *peer programming*, which is one of the specificities of XP,[26] one of the agile development families. It continues with the practice of code reviews, which is a fundamental tool for a software factory. The code review is used to increase quality (in particular error detection), reduce technical debt, improve maintainability, and facilitate evolutions. Code reviews have always been a good practice, but they are now indispensable for code that must change continuously. From my point of view, **digital transformation reintroduces the need for code reviews**. Code sharing is also done by publishing one's code in *open-source* form if the component is intended to be shared, but also in fragment form in the many community tools.[27] The love of code means producing code that you want to share with your team members as well as with the members of your community. It also means having the desire to look at and read other people's code because the efficiency and productivity required by digital transformation require knowing how to reuse the code of others. Finally, sharing code as widely as possible is the best way to increase quality—both because *more eyeballs find more bugs* and because the programmer's pride leads him to better develop code that will be shared with his peers.

The reference to the love of code is a way to highlight the emotional and affective dimension of programming. Programming well is an art and a science.[28] The *software craftmanship* movement is beyond the scope of this book, but it is important to mention it for two reasons. First, its ambitions[29] are perfectly aligned with those described in this book—the manifesto insists on the quality of software, its ability to evolve well over time. Second,

---

[26] I won't describe XP in this book, but it has been one of my main sources of inspiration for the last twenty years (and therefore implicitly present in the *lean software factory* principles). I refer you to the excellent book by Rich Sheridan, *Joy, Inc.*, which describes in detail the approach and benefits of XP for his company Menlo. Note that *peer programming* is similar to a continuous code review.

[27] For example, being a mobile app developer today means being part of several communities and continuously using code fragment sharing tools, such as the famous StackOverflow.

[28] One of the fundamental works of programming, due to the genius Donald Knuth, is titled "*The Art of Computer Programming*." This monumental work spans fifty years and perfectly illustrates the duality between science and practice in software development. To better understand this affective dimension of programming, read *Decoder les Developers*, by Benjamin Tainturier and Emmanuelle Duez, who point out that developing necessarily combines designing and executing. Separating these two stages of creation has little relevance outside the Taylorian factory.

[29] One can start by reading the manifesto on the http://manifesto.softwarecraftsmanship.org website, to understand the importance of practice, *well-crafted software*, and communities (with a reference to the guilds found in Spotify's agile model).

it would be easy to see an opposition between the uniformity of software factories and the individualization of crafts. However, similar to the world of industry, it is necessary to combine the use of methods with craftmanship. *Lean manufacturing* reconciles the two around the concept of standard. The standard belongs to the team and is constantly evolving. It is a way of capitalizing on and sharing experience, of making practice something noble. **Developing programming standards—or refactoring standards[30]—is both necessary to encourage *code reviews* and *peer programming* and useful to let the team organize its continuous training, alone or within a guild of programmers who share a technical or functional domain.**

If we talk about loving your code, it is because there is an implicit aesthetic. Without getting into a discussion that is beyond the scope of this book, we can say that beautiful code is used, readable, and elegant. Usage is a simple and obvious metric of the digital world. Like *PageRank*, Google's original algorithm for identifying the most relevant pages, the best demonstration of value of a piece of code is the number of developers who use it.[31] Readable code—in the basic sense that it can be read and understood easily—is code that facilitates sharing, from code review to reuse. Code standards play an important role in standardizing readability rules.

The notion of elegant code is more subjective, yet it is also linked to business interests, and the goal of elegance is found everywhere in *open-source* communities. Elegance combines minimalism, readability of intent, and virality of design.[32] Minimalism consists in producing its effect with minimal effort. The intent is readable if the code is its own documentation and requires (almost) no comments. The term "virality" translates the fact that a programmer, after seeing an elegant fragment of code, will remember to reuse some elements (a form of iteration, functional nesting, use of

---

[30] Cf. the book *Refactoring*, by Martin Fowler previously cited.

[31] This utilitarian dimension of aesthetics is Darwinian: a code that is reused is alive, a code that is used only once is about to become a dead code.

[32] To illustrate what readability of intent is, we can cite *domain-driven design (DDD)*, which is a layered object architecture based on a business domain representation. This approach aims to create a stable foundation (which evolves less quickly) associated with the domain. DDD uses the concept of *bounded context* (associated with the domain), which allows the modularization of the definition of business objects. Here is what Eric Evans, the father of DDD, says: "*In those younger days we were advised to build a unified model of the entire business, but DDD recognizes that we've learned that total unification of the domain model for a large system will not be feasible or cost-effective.*"

objects, etc.) one day. I emphasize these three traits of elegance, despite their subjective side, because they have a direct positive impact on the cost of development. In other words, teams and guilds should be allowed to define their own standards of elegance, but the elegance of the code produced by a software factory should be encouraged.

7.3.5 From Customer to Code and from Code to Customer

The subtitle of this book is borrowed from a 2015 presentation at the XEBICON conference. Figure 7.3 is the detailed version of the figure presented in the introduction, which depicts two major processes that are intimately related in the form of two arrows. The first arrow goes from the customer to the code and the second from the code to the customer. The first arrow represents the digital product discovery process, according to the lean startup approach we presented in Chapter 3. The second arrow represents the ability to build and deploy software products to their users.

This figure expresses three ideas. The first, developed extensively in this book, is that companies must master these two processes perfectly to succeed in their digital transformation. The second idea is that these are not arrows representing processes but loops that must be iterated, with high frequency, because excellence in the digital world is obtained at the price of perseverance and numerous iterations. To go fast, you have to be excellent. The third idea is that the two dimensions of product discovery and delivery must be unified, for a given product, around a common team. The term "team" is to be taken in a broad sense; it is not a single, co-located *squad*. The *design thinking* and prototyping stages can be done relatively independently. On the other hand, it is the same team that builds the MVP (minimum viable product) and then develops and brings the final product to life. The significant point is that the *lean software factory* is an asset of the product design/development team, which must participate in the entire process of defining and building the product. We find here the principle of effectuation, which requires that we take into account what we have to invent a new solution. Effectuation here is a feedback loop from the bottom (development) to the top (design). There is, therefore, a double feedback loop that must influence the innovation process: the customer feedback loop—what the customer thinks of what is proposed to him—and the feedback loop of the reality of the team software capabilities. Effectuation precisely reflects that the digital strategy is rooted in digital capabilities. There is no point—even if you listen carefully to your customers in an exemplary *lean startup* process—in designing products for which you do not have the necessary digital skills.

To conclude this chapter, I want to emphasize the idea that, even if there are several processes and different steps, the work must be organized around a common product and team.[33] The same people should be involved in both arrows, allowing the two iterative loops to run synchronously and without loss of context when moving from one to the other. For example, operations skills are needed to design successful products, just as designer skills apply to the entire digital experience building life cycle. This point only applies when you reach a certain size, and it makes sense, especially for large companies. Indeed, in a small structure like a startup, the proximity between the two arrows of design and construction and deployment of products is obtained naturally. It is only when the organization grows that Taylorization appears and that teams are separated according to the stages in the development cycle.

This "integrated double arrow" approach is thus opposed to the ever-present temptation to separate the two dimensions of innovation and integration/deployment, either within the company or even more so by outsourcing one of these two dimensions.

Learning, which is ongoing and vital in the digital domain, is a transaction cost in the Coase sense. To achieve success in a digital product, both dimensions must learn from each other, and this represents a cost, in time and resources, that is reduced by the unified team approach shown in Figure 7.3. The practice of continuous learning has a cost and represents a risk. If this were not the case, the *marketplace* model of expertise would have already triumphed. This does not mean that innovation is done autonomously and without external input. It means that the place where value is created is the place where learning takes place. To borrow an aphorism from Nassim Taleb's book *Skin in the Game*, "*no pain, no gain*": companies cannot outsource their learning, especially their learning of their digital environment. This is an extension of Coase's theory of the firm: the firm allows the costs of learning to be internalized (in addition to other transaction costs).

---

[33] Some of the ideas in this section can be found in the book *Lean Enterprise*, where we find this quote: "*Finally, taking a scientific approach to customer and product development requires intensive collaboration between product, design, and technical people throughout the life cycle of every product. This is a big cultural change for many enterprises where technical staff do not generally contribute to the overall design process.*"

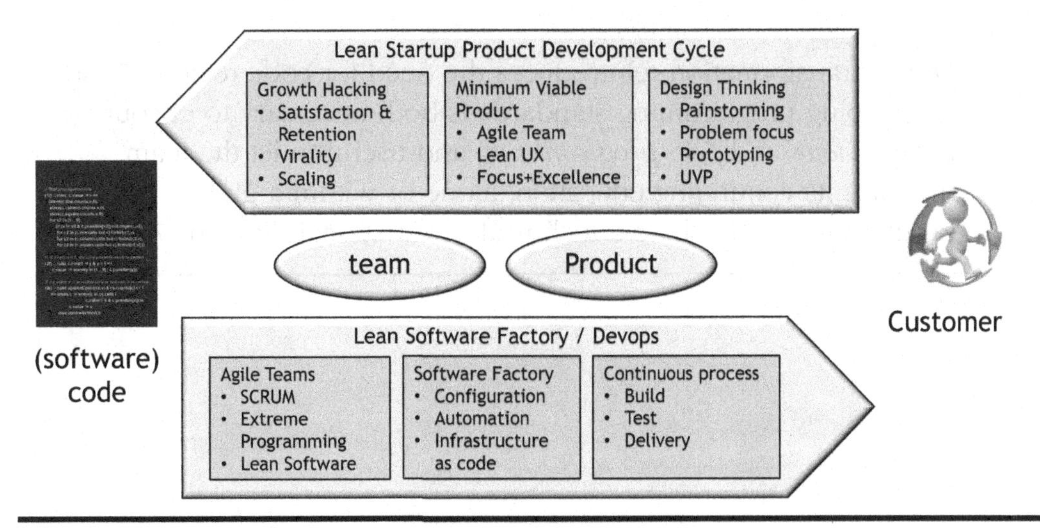

Figure 7.3 From client to code and from code to client.

Summary

1. An essential property of an industrial software deployment process is to be able to guarantee the reproducibility of the deployments, and this requires rigorous configuration management (7.1.1).
2. Continuous integration consists of performing the integration phase regularly and very frequently so as not to let the "integration complexity debt" grow (7.1.2).
3. If the construction pipeline is not working well, run it more frequently and highlight the difficulties (7.1.3).
4. The set of tests is a common asset of the team, which is built by continuous improvement (7.1.4).
5. DevOps is a product approach in which each *deployment* is an opportunity to learn and make improvements in the next development cycle (7.2.1).
6. The DevOps approach is the common foundation for companies that excel in software development and deployment (7.2.3).
7. Effective digital organizations are primarily learning organizations (7.2.3).
8. Working together on the same problem forces one to build a common vocabulary and develop a better understanding of the views of other team members (7.3.3).

9. Digital transformation reintroduces the need for code review (7.3.4).
10. Developing programming standards is both necessary to encourage *code reviews* and *peer programming* and useful to let the team organize its continuing education, alone or within a guild of programmers who share a technical or functional domain (7.3.4).

Chapter 8

Putting Platforms at the Service of Digital Transformation

This final chapter provides a short introduction to the concept of platforms, which play an important role in the field of digital services. Platforms are based on network effects, and their power is such that they are unavoidable in the digital transformation landscape. First, one must know how to identify and use the dominant platforms in their digital ecosystem. Second, there are multiple benefits to building your own digital systems as platforms. Thinking in terms of platforms means thinking in terms of customers, seeking to provide them with a richer offer because it is built by a community that goes beyond the company's own talents. It is also a way of thinking about the company in an open way, giving it a digital frontier that facilitates collaboration with an ecosystem of partners.

8.1 The Platform Approach

8.1.1 Which Platforms for the Digital Domain?

The word "platform" has become a *buzzword* in digital transformation, both to describe systems and business models. In *The Age of the Platform*, Phil Simon describes a platform as a "*powerful, value-creating ecosystem that adapts and grows quickly and easily, incorporating new features, new*

DOI: 10.4324/9781003272816-11

users or customers, and new partners." The key themes of this book, which date backs to 2011 but remains relevant, are **flexibility** (to adapt to rapidly changing customer demands), **scalability**, and **user satisfaction**. However, the notion of a platform exists in many contexts in the software world. Without being exhaustive, here are different examples that are all relevant in the digital world:

- The concept of platform in the software world is related to architecture and the desire to make modular and better reuse. In a layered architecture,[1] the platform proposes an implementation of the lower layers while letting the users build the upper layers. iOS as a platform—Apple's mobile operating system—is a good example of this approach.
- Similarly, the concept of product platform in industry is also an approach to product architecture that allows for modularity and reuse. Specifically, the term "platform" in the automotive or aerospace industry means that the modular architecture supports a combination of aggressive standardization while allowing for a wide variety of uses (e.g., having a large number of different car models that share the maximum number of common elements).
- A "distribution platform" is a tool for concentration (of resources) and standardization (of interfaces). It is a common and essential concept in the world of physical distribution, such as logistics platforms.
- The notion of exchange platform has the same fundamentals, at the service of a community of use. The platform is the combination of a place (virtual or physical) and a common interaction protocol.
- The intermediation platform is a special case of an interaction platform that serves as an intermediary between two or more communities, which use the platform to find each other and to interact. There has been a real explosion of such platforms in the digital world, but it is a very old model, that of marketplaces.

The digital world is particularly interesting because it uses the concept of platform from multiple angles. We can easily identify three aspects, each of which refers to the different meanings of the word "platform" from the previous section. The system aspect uses the platform concept to organize and build an object. The objectives are efficiency and reusability.

---

[1] Layered architecture is a decomposition by level of abstraction, in which each layer encapsulates the levels of detail of lower layers.

The functional aspect sees the platform as a tool for exchange and communication. The nature of digital activities (dematerialized) means that exchanges/communications are pervasive. Finally, the economic aspect sees the platform as a business model that delivers value from a community and its exchanges. Therefore, in the digital world, the overuse of the word platform is perfectly legitimate but may easily lead to some form of confusion.

In this chapter, we will look at digital platforms from two angles. First, we will consider the platform as an intermediation tool that serves to federate a community. This is the most important angle from a business viewpoint because the platform multiplies the value the company can offer to its customers. When we talk about digital platforms, we are most often referring to the power of the network intermediation model. It is this power of platforms and their associated ecosystems that have led us to write several times in this book **that one of the first steps in a digital strategy is to understand the ecosystems the enterprise belongs to and the existing platforms it must rely on.**[2]

The third section of this chapter will then deal with the platform as a mutualization tool to produce a service factory (i.e., a system approach to build as efficiently as possible changing services from a stable and reusable product platform).

8.1.2 The Network Effect of Platforms

A platform relies on one or more communities of users, developers, content providers, and so on. We often speak of the "sides" of a platform. **The network effect is a non-linear amplification of the value produced by the platform that increases faster than the size of its communities**. For a two-sided platform with providers on one side and consumers on the other (Airbnb, for example), the more providers there are, the more likely consumers are to find what they are looking for, and the more consumers there are, the more interesting it is for a provider to participate in this platform. Even for a platform with only one "side" (e.g., a community of developers who use the services of that platform), the fixed/variable cost

[2] On the importance of ecosystems associated with platforms, the book *The Digital Playbook*—which makes platforms one of the *building blocks* of a digital strategy—notes that the Web giants all collaborate with their competitors' platforms: *"But, in fact, all five are deeply enmeshed with each other, cooperating and linking their products and services. Apple devices have long run Google as their default search engine. Facebook is the most popular app on everyone's mobile devices."*

savings create a pooling effect, which favors platforms that attract the largest communities.

The virtuous effects can be of the first order (more suppliers; thus, more value), but they can have multiple reinforcements. In the case of social networks, getting more participants increases both the probability of finding your friends and the interest in the best content proposed by automatic curation.[3] In the case of the Uber platform, the size (of the driver community) reduces both passenger waiting and driver *downtime* and increases efficiency for both communities. This is a good example of reinforcement since better efficiency lowers prices and creates more demand, which then leads to the virtuous circle, "more demand attracts more drivers, and thus better coverage."[4] Mobile application development ecosystems provide another classic example of this network effect; more users motivate more developers, who offer more applications that make the smartphone more interesting. In the case of digital platforms, the platform can contribute to its own growth by using *growth hacking* methods, which we saw in Chapter 3, to develop "virality" (another term associated with the network effect). This is what drives application developers to include shareable experience elements so that the user community takes an active role in its growth.

In many cases, the advantages of the network effect of the largest platform are such that monopolies are created. The authors of *The Platform Revolution* explain that "*multiple scale effects appear in the demand economy around social networks, demand aggregation or application developments that make the largest networks bring more value to their users.*" This often leads to monopoly—*the winner takes all*, also known as *the Matthew effect*—which condemns platforms to a race for size. This is what we see in all areas of digital platforms, with a consequent race for funding and investment. It is also what accentuates their disruptive side. The investments to grow a platform are not marginal; they are not calculated with a short-term return on investment (ROI). They correspond to a bet on the strategic value that the platform can develop once it has acquired this monopolistic

---

[3] Curation is the art of selecting, arranging and proposing content. The greater the volume of content, the more essential the role of curation. Andrew McAffee and Erik Brynjolfsson's book, *Machine, Platform, Crowd: Harnessing Our Digital Future*, makes the link between the changes in the digital world described in the first part and the role of platforms (see Chapter 7 in particular).

[4] This example is from the book *The Platform Revolution: How Networked Markets Are Transforming the Economy and How to Make Them Work for* You, by Geoffrey G. Parker, Marshall W. Van Alstyne, and Sangeet Paul Choudary, which I will use several times in this section.

situation. This irruption of a new way of thinking about investments—because of network effects—affects all sectors of activity.[5]

8.1.3 Platform and Communities

Because the fate of a platform is directly linked to that of its community, all the experts cited in the bibliography agree that **a successful platform strategy depends first and foremost on building a satisfied community, which leads to cultivating user feedback loops**. In *The Platform Revolution*, we find the concept of CFLL: "*platforms are more successful than product production pipelines because they use digital tools and data to create feedback loops with user communities.*" For Phil Simon, creating a platform is about creating a community of passionate users. These users participate in the quality of the platform and help improve the level of content, products, or services offered on a continuous basis, using the power of collective intelligence. Platform marketing starts from the customers or users by listening—we find the *pull marketing* approach rather than a classic *push* communication strategy.

One of the consequences of creating value through network effect is that the platform model is necessarily very fragile at the beginning. As long as the critical mass is not reached, for the community or communities, the value perceived by the users is low. The metaphor of a rocket is often used to describe the business model of a platform with several stages. Only the last stage is viable (has reached profitability by network effect) when "the speed to orbit is reached" (which here represents the size of the community). It is necessary to develop the lower rocket stages, which allow the community to be built with additional advantages. The first stage often consists of acquiring valuable content and giving it away for free to attract the first users. This is why a platform strategy requires investment, especially if it is a two-sided transaction platform (see next section). If the business model includes charging participants, it is advisable to wait until a certain size is reached before doing so.

The approach used to build a platform is open and collaborative, which is a good way to attract talent. Examples abound, from Apple's opening of iOS to developers to the launch of Facebook Platform in 2007, that attest to

[5] Another quote from the same book: "*So platforms are eating the world. The disruption they are driving is reaching businesses one industry at a time and is likely to hit practically all information-intensive industries at some point.*"

the value of attracting an open community of developers. This is obvious for very large platforms that attract hundreds of thousands or even millions of developers,[6] but it is also true for smaller platforms, such as the *open-source* communities associated with some software tools. For a company to decide to open up its platform to external developers, it must be able to build a value proposition for these developers. The company must, therefore, put itself in their shoes—remembering that a platform that is just starting out is often risky and/or uninteresting from the developer's point of view—and above all to listen to them in order to co-build this external community. On the other hand, this approach attracts both new talent and a diversity of points of view, which is a strong value creation accelerator,[7] particularly because the diversity of talent allows us to explore the diversity of user needs. We find here a fundamental idea from the first part: the most successful digital systems are able to aggregate value produced outside the company.

8.2 The Power of Platforms

8.2.1 Innovation Platforms

In this section, I will borrow the distinction between innovation platform and transaction platform from the book *The Business of Platforms: Strategy in the Age of Digital Competition, Innovation, and Power*, by Michael A. Cusumano, Annabelle Gawer, and David B. Yoffie. The authors propose the term *platform innovation* when a player organizes and makes available a number of resources to attract a community. Conversely, *transaction platforms* connect two or more communities by playing an intermediation role. About a hundred cases have been analyzed and broken down into these two categories, whose intersection is not empty: some platforms, described as hybrids, combine both approaches. Building an innovation

---

[6] By design (and because of the network effects discussed above), there are very few mega-platforms that can attract a very large number of developers. To fit into this category, a platform's "rocket" approach must be able to rely on very large "boosters." The example of Microsoft, which has not been able to establish itself in the world of mobile OSes, attests to the difficulty.

[7] *The Platform Revolution* book offers many examples to better understand what makes platforms successful or to learn from the mistakes of famous precedents. For example, Chris DeWolfe, one of the founders of Myspace, explains why he should have tried to attract a community of developers: "*We tried to create every feature in the world and said, 'O.K., we can do it, why should we [open up to] let a third party do it?' We should have picked 5 to 10 key features that we totally focused on and let other people innovate on everything else.*"

platform is necessarily ambitious; it is about providing a community with resources and a space for sharing: "*Innovation platforms create value mainly by facilitating the development of complementary products and services.*"[8] The book gives many examples like iOS and Android, GE Predix, Force.com, AWS or Azure, WeChat, and IBM Watson. The software world is full of such platforms, from operating systems to *open-source* software. For an innovation platform to work, what is made available to the community, be it software, services, or data, must be both attractive and competitive.[9]

The concept of innovation platform is an important brick in a digital transformation strategy because it is a relevant model when the company wants to expose its digital capabilities to the outside world. **Platform thinking is a demanding approach, but it ensures more flexibility, adaptation to external ecosystems, and in the end, a greater value creation**. A platform is a complex system that continuously adapts to its environment, with differentiated speeds on the core and the borders. Platforms do not avoid the contradiction inherent in any IS that must both change rapidly to adapt to its environment and provide the wealth of services expected by users, which leads to the need to reconcile complexity and agility. The authors of *The Business of Platforms* suggest modulating the speed of evolution: "*We need to find a way to achieve a balance, changing the core of the platform more slowly, while allowing for faster adaptations at the periphery.*" Change is done in small steps, in a way that is transparent to the community and making sure that the team uses and validates the very elements they propose externally—the old advice "*eat your own dogfood*" is particularly relevant in the digital world. Change never stops, as innovation is a necessary condition for the sustainable development of the platform: "*As the platform matures and produces a sustainable business model through the size of the community, the ongoing challenge of user retention and growth requires the platform to continue to innovate.*" Building a team and a structure that allows for this continuous adaptation of the platform to its environment is a breakthrough in terms of management, which brings us back to Chapter 2.

[8] This concept is not necessarily a digital concept, there are many older examples: "*Mattel, for instance, introduced the Barbie doll in 1959. Over the years, the company faced competition on many fronts, but it evolved the Barbie product into an innovation platform.*"

[9] The authors of *The Platform Revolution* talk about an inversion similar to what we wrote in Chapter 2: "*Platforms invert the firm. Because the bulk of a platform's value is created by its community of users, the platform business must shift its focus from internal activities to external activities. In the process, the firm inverts-it turns inside out, with functions from marketing to information technology.*"

The role of trust and fairness is fundamental to developing communities. Platforms, as soon as they are open, have a societal responsibility, which requires anticipating possible problems before they are faced with mistrust from customers or investigation from regulators.[10] This ethical stance is intended to preserve the trust capital that is essential for the proper functioning of platforms. All platforms need this trust because they act as intermediaries between actors and resources, which often have no prior relationship. The notion of *fairness* is fundamental for each side of the platform to develop harmoniously. Unfortunately, it is easy to formulate rules for the internal functioning of the platform that have negative effects that are not necessarily visible. The book *The Business of Platforms* gives several examples applied to Uber that show that this question of equity of access to the platform must be asked repeatedly. The importance of the business model in the success of a platform should be stressed. The value distribution equation is part of the core of the platform. In the case of Uber, the remarkable idea is to have integrated customer satisfaction, measured by the double driver-passenger *rating*, into the algorithm that distributes tasks: the higher the rating of a driver, the more rides Uber offers him. The fixed point of this evolutionary system systematically favors customer satisfaction and mechanically eliminates participants with poor scores, whether they are customers or drivers.

8.2.2 Transaction Platforms

Transaction platforms differ from the previous ones because the units of value—provided to users—are contributed by one of the "sides" and not by the platform owner. Famous examples in this category include Uber, Airbnb, Upwork, LinkedIn, Alibaba, Facebook, Amazon (marketplace), Lending Club, or Trip Advisor. The notion of *sides* is essential; it is the different communities associated with different roles: service providers, consumers, advertising providers, content or advice providers, and so on. A transaction platform aims, as its name suggests, to create value by increasing the number of transactions, by facilitating *matchmaking*, by reducing the "friction" of transactions—i.e., the effort to complete a transaction—by offering complementary products and services or by monetizing digital

[10] In the same book, we read the following: "*we believe that platforms should pre-emptively self-regulate and reduce the likelihood that governments will intervene and alter the playing field in ways that are not good for them, ecosystem partners, or consumers.*"

traffic, for example with advertising. Remembering that one of the definitions of design is "to increase enjoyment and reduce friction," it is not surprising that experience design (*UX design*) plays a fundamental role in the success of platforms. The most classic type of transaction platform is the two-sided platform, such as Uber, which connects service providers and customers, but it is interesting to look more broadly and identify other "sides," actors that complement the transaction by adding additional value to the customer (precisely what Uber does for example with Uber Eats). The "complements" can participate in the notoriety (media and other social networks), facilitate the transaction (providing information and content), or enrich the service.

Network effects are particularly powerful, as we have said, for transaction platforms. One of the keys to success is to solve the "chicken and egg" problem—in other words, how to bootstrap the platform to reach critical mass on all sides. The problem with all platforms in their infancy is that the value derived from the communities is not yet developed. This is obvious in the case of two-sided platforms: there is little reason for sellers to join if there are few customers and little reason for customers to use the platform as long as the supply is low. As mentioned above, there are multiple approaches to this first stage of bootstrapping: buying the first participants (sellers), offering the services for free, finding other communities to bootstrap by combining the platform's services with other established services. Intermediation platforms provide spectacular returns on investment when successful, and they are often found in the digital strategies of companies. However, there are three difficult hurdles to overcome: as for innovation platforms, you need an excellent mastery of software development, you need the means and the patience to build the seed phase, and most importantly, you need a real intimacy with the communities you want to acquire, to build "frictionless" experiences of using the platform, for all the roles and not only the users.

Platform developers have two obsessions: to grow so that network effects multiply their value and to do so faster than their competitors because of the "winner takes all" effect. These two obsessions force transaction platforms to make significant and risky investments. In addition, they must protect the virtuous network effect and combat the *multi-homing* that occurs when a customer or supplier uses multiple similar platforms. Dominant platforms can protect themselves by rewarding loyalty on one side of intermediation or the other, by absorbing the most differentiating uses of their competitors, and when that is not enough by acquiring those competitors, which is what Mark Zuckerberg did, for example, when he acquired Instagram in 2012.

8.2.3 Platforms and Artificial Intelligence

Intelligent filtering is one of the core competencies of platforms; therefore, the development of AI fuels the growth of platforms. Filtering here refers to the algorithm that matches users with content, whether it be services, products, or other users. The relevance of a platform depends on its filtering qualities, and all the more so as the platform grows. This filtering is both an act of selection (*curation*) and proposition (*matching*), two dimensions that allow algorithms to be used for both search and recommendation. As the authors of *The Business of Platforms* point out, when curation is effective, users can more easily find products and services that correspond to their needs among an extremely abundant offer containing mainly things that do not concern them. For example, the quality of filtering is essential for social networking platforms. It is the algorithms that choose the thread of messages to be presented to each user, among a very large flow—including sponsored messages—with a strong risk that the lack of relevance reduces the interest of the platform.

The emergence of digital platforms over the last twenty years is clearly the most visible part of the digital transformation from an economic point of view. It is the consequence of the digital revolution discussed in the first part but also the application of new development technologies discussed in the rest of this book, from AI algorithms to (software) data processing platforms and continuous development and deployment methods. To dominate their sector, intermediation platforms must offer both the most choice by ensuring the growth of its community and offer the state of the art in terms of search and *matching* so that the abundance of supply is indeed an advantage. As we saw in Chapter 5, size is a double advantage since having more data allows for the development of better algorithms, but platforms nevertheless run the risk of disruption by players who propose better algorithms or are able to offer a better experience design. It is not by chance that the big American players in the platform field are all among the biggest investors in AI.[11]

Successful "platform" companies are almost always sources of inspiration for companies that want to succeed in their digital transformation because

[11] See the report of the French Academy of Technologies on Artificial Intelligence.

they are excellent in the three dimensions we just described. They are indeed models to be imitated, which is all the easier since most of them participate in the dissemination of their know-how through *open-source* tools. On the other hand, in a symmetrical way, one must understand the level of excellence required from a software engineering point of view, from algorithms to deployment, to succeed in a platform strategy and, in particular, a transaction platform approach.

8.3 Building Stable Platforms to Deliver Changing Services

8.3.1 The "Product Platform" Approach in the Digital Context

The concepts of innovation platform and intermediation platform are primarily business models. We will now discuss the concept of product platform, which is a modular principle of system organization. The product platform is a way of producing different objects with a great deal of variation while keeping a maximum of standard parts or components. In aeronautics, the performance of a platform is measured by multiplying two factors, the number of products that can be produced and the percentage of common parts. In the world of digital services, it is a question of organizing software platforms to produce the greatest possible variety of services while pooling as many common components as possible. There is also a dynamic dimension since the efficiency of the mutualization implies that the common components are as stable as possible—in industry, it would be a matter of maximizing the lifespan of the common parts—while the digital services are intended to be renewed frequently. The product platform is not an intermediation platform, but it has commonalities with innovation platforms because there is a community of platform users, those who produce products and services from the components and tools provided by the platform team.

The instantiation of a platform into a product is a combination of selection, parameterization, and reassembly of modular components. An industry product platform is a product factory, just as a software platform is a service factory. In the software world, there are three architectural "meta-principles" that enable this service factory:

- The "layered" architecture, which we saw a little earlier, in which the platform provides the services of the lower abstraction layers and lets the developers build the "high" (or "external") layer. The advantage of

a layered approach is that the bottom services are much more stable.[12] What determines the quality of a layered approach is the relevance of the functional analysis and, therefore, the knowledge of the business domain.
- The "Lego box" component library, which allows new services to be built by reassembling components. This approach works with different assembly techniques, from continuous integration of software components to API calls decoupled integration. If the components have their own execution resources and are assembled through API, we get a microservices architecture. In this case, what is critical to success is the definition of stable interfaces, which requires a good dynamic understanding of how the platform will evolve.
- Metadata-driven components, which are another way of separating what is stable (the behavior engine) from what is easily modifiable (the behavior, which is described by the metadata). This approach is quite old, it was popularized by software packages a few decades ago, but it has been revived by turning metadata into *scripts* and components into *interpreters* of a DSL (*domain-specific language*). For this third model, the success of the product platform depends directly on the software skills of the team.

These three approaches are independent and can be easily combined; for example, one can build a layered architecture that relies on microservices.

Like the innovation platforms mentioned in the previous section, product platforms must be scalable and constantly adapt to the needs of the user community. This is why the team that builds the platform plays a fundamental role. We can even say that it is **not possible to succeed in a digital platform project without having assembled the right team,**[13] **which has both the technical competence and the experience of dialogue with the user community**. If we take a step back, there is a real symbiosis between the technical system and the team that builds it, which we explained in Chapter 6 with the multiple learning loops. This is why we

---

[12] On the other hand, the complexity of the digital domain often conflicts with encapsulation (hiding the functioning of the lower layers) and leads to a preference for "vertical" integrations. This does not necessarily invalidate a layered approach (levels of abstraction exist) but leads to "transparent" approaches where the source code of all layers remains available.

[13] In one of my previous jobs, I had forbidden myself to participate in meetings where digital platforms were discussed, on PowerPoint, without having identified the team. You can't buy a platform strategy from the outside.

can also speak of a "centaur"—as we did for AI—that is, the combination of a software system and a team in a collaborative and learning approach. It is this collaboration between the technical system and the team that gives flexibility and produces the emergence of the overall system. The platform allows for continuous innovation on production flows and systems, which justifies the importance and popularity of DevOps approaches that we will highlight at the end of the chapter. This "system + team" synergy is also explained by the fact that the platform is a tool for work and collaboration. The platform as a system supports the cooperation of multiple talents: *data scientists*, developers, designers, system engineers, digital marketers (for example, for *growth hacking*), or *product managers*.

8.3.2 Platforms, Architecture, and Emergence

The architecture of platforms must be the object of constant attention to promote modularity. Given the need for platforms to be flexible in order to continuously adapt to their environment, the authors of *The Platform Revolution* insist, "*Modularity is a strategy for organizing complex products and processes in an efficient manner. A modular system is composed of units (or modules) that can be designed independently but can work together as a system. Designers achieve this modularity by partitioning information into design rules that are visible to all and parameters that can be encapsulated, i.e., hidden.*" Building a modular architecture is not a simple thing, it is clearly an art more than a science, which requires experience.[14] Even if there are no systematic and efficient methods, many tools, such as the DSM (*design structure matrix*), can help to identify the modular sub-blocks. The practice of refactoring, which we mentioned in Chapter 4, is doubly essential—on the one hand, because any iterative approach produces waste and accumulation, and on the other hand, because the experience and feedback of users can be used to bring out a modular architecture that was not visible at the outset. The product platform is not simply a service factory; it is also a factory—one could say a laboratory—that serves to bring out an architecture, just as the MVP of the *lean startup* serves to bring out a business model.

[14] Two things can be learned from the various accounts of Amazon's "services, APIs and platform" approach—including the previously mentioned post from Steve Yegge: Amazon's platform approach is the result of Jeff Bezos's vision of a SOA, and success is the result of a long implementation experience: "*Over the next couple of years, Amazon transformed internally into a service-oriented architecture. . . . Overall it's the right thing because SOA-driven design enables Platforms.*

A product platform in the digital world delivers valuable components that are integrated by users to form services. Integration by API call is not the only approach, but it is clearly the one that dominates the digital software world for reasons of flexibility, speed of implementation, and above all, ease of upgrading. Here we find the reasons discussed in Chapter 4: an API-based integration is both dynamic and decoupled. A modern digital platform allows users to do everything by API call: provide the service, consume the service, and monitor and terminate the service. Such a platform is, in fact, an exchange platform, and its success depends on the quality of the interfaces (ease of discovering the APIs, experimenting, understanding the underlying model, and investigating error cases).[15] William Hurley writes, "*Most people don't understand the importance of open APIs. They think it's a technical feature, but that's only part of the story. Yes, APIs accelerate development and integration, . . . it's not just about code, but more importantly about community management.*"

Building a platform is about managing emergence: in the words of Kevin Kelly, "*a platform is grown, not designed.*" Over the past ten years, I have come across many companies that have unsuccessfully applied a proactive approach to building a platform by following a strategic plan. The role of the community and usage is so important in the development of a platform that it is pointless to try to predict everything. Growth follows usage by reinforcement. We can make the same reference here to the metaphor of muscles, which grow by self-repairing the fibers broken by effort. A digital platform is built by solidifying the most used services. It is also clear that, while there are best practices, building a community is an art of emergent gardening. The authors of *The Platform Revolution* write, "*One of the greatest assets any platform—indeed, any business—can have is a dedicated community,*" and give the example of the development of the iPhone AppStore, which followed a story of exceptional growth that was not part of Steve Jobs's original plans. To allow the community to emerge, some form of control must be relinquished.

Striving for simplicity, being focused on customer satisfaction, and knowing how to use the right software tools are essential to platform success. Simplicity is a fundamental characteristic for two reasons, because it translates to the customer experience (in the broadest

[15] Here we find the concept of *frictionless*, as highlighted by the authors of *The Platform Revolution*: "*Frictionless entry is the ability of users to quickly and easily join a platform and begin participating in the value creation that the platform facilitates. Frictionless entry is a key factor in enabling a platform to grow rapidly.*"

sense, for all sides of the platform) and reduces friction and because simplicity is necessary to maintain scalability and agility. One of the biggest lessons from the web giants is that only simple systems are truly scalable. The authors of *The Business of Platform* show that the lack of simplicity is often found in failed platforms: "*Some companies are too ambitious and have tried to connect too many sides, too early in their development cycle, to their platform. The result has been a platform that is too complex, unable to grow in a scalable way.*" Customer experience and user satisfaction are critical to the success of platforms. The same authors attribute an important role to customer satisfaction in Amazon's success—with the famous one-click shopping—and Taobao's victory over eBay in China. Technology plays a key role in platform relevance, as we saw in the previous section when we discussed filtering. The ability to make recommendations is a competitive advantage whose value increases with the size of the platform; for example, it is estimated that 40% of Amazon's sales come from the recommendation engine. The mastery of technology is also manifested in the ability to implement CICD processes. For example, in the browser war, Chrome was able to quickly produce seventeen releases (in 2012), double what Microsoft and Firefox had done in the same time frame.

8.3.3 Platforms and Software Factories

Successful development of a product platform requires that the development team take care of its developer users with professional attention as a software vendor.[16] It needs to facilitate usage—for example of APIs—as we said above by simplifying discovery and integration, it needs to renew its services frequently while maintaining longer backward compatibility, in order to decouple the rates of evolution, and above all, it needs users to be aware of and understand the evolution of the platform's services. The quality of service, in particular availability, must also be higher than that which the platform's users seek for their own service. Here we find a rule specific to infrastructures or to the "foundations" of an architecture: common services must be built with a higher level of quality requirement than the customer services they support. The challenge for digital platforms is to combine the

[16] We have already discussed this idea in Chapter 6. One can even say that even more care is needed to achieve co-construction with users, especially since the value of the platform increases over time, but starts slowly.

support of innovation through frequent renewal with an industrial quality of service.

As Mirco Hering points out, meeting all the requirements we have just detailed for a set of microservices, or even just for the catalog of APIs that must be managed like their own software products, requires a great deal of rigor in execution, which in turn requires a high degree of automation.[17] In other words, **the platform approach requires excellence in DevOps practice, a strong command of integration, and continuous deployment**. This is one of the reasons *cloud* hosting is a very good solution for building a digital platform. In addition to obvious reasons such as scalability of resources or network connectivity—hosting in the cloud allows you to benefit from the infrastructure of your host, which is often superior to that of your company in terms of performance and security—development in the *cloud* facilitates the implementation of the CICD/DevOps approach. Tools and communities of practice are readily available, and the ability to control resources via APIs (IaC) is generally superior to the company's own environments.

In theory, the platform approach can be applied anywhere, whether it is an information system or technical or service systems, as long as there is a community of users. In practice, we have just stated a certain number of constraints that make the platform approach work better at the enterprise's border. Figure 8.1 repeats a number of observations made in this book, which show that the frontier is better suited to implement CICD approaches to satisfy high rates of change on more granular and autonomous services. This is a general observation, with multiple exceptions. For example, test automation is actually easier in the core because the rate of change is lower and because user interfaces—which are more difficult to test in an automated way—are more developed on the "edges" of the IS. Nevertheless, the edge of the IS is the place where we find the most platform approaches, both because the edge is the place of exchange with external communities (a good reason to think about a platform) and because the degree of interdependence and integration of services is less there.

This figure also helps to understand why the microservices approach is not universal. The principle of this approach is to take advantage of the spectacular drop in hardware costs (computing and storage) to demutualize

[17] Read *DevOps for the Modern Enterprise: Winning Practices to Transform Legacy IT Organizations*. This book contains a very interesting chapter on the different *delivery models*, from *containers* to the *cloud*.

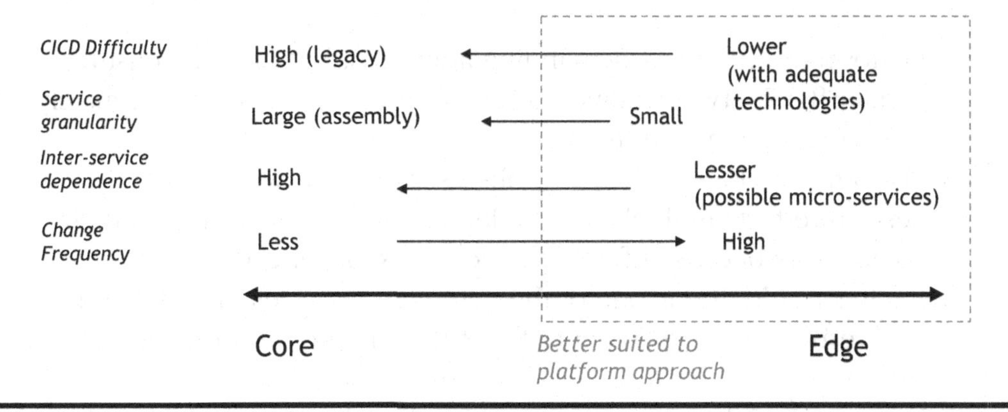

Figure 8.1 The platform approach within the IS.

services (to make them independent). The microservices approach allows to materialize a SOA by gaining flexibility and agility at the expense of costs and simplicity of operations. To compensate for this negative aspect, the automation of a software factory approach is necessary.

As a subsystem of the IS, a digital platform is a service factory, a technological solution for managing a very high rate of change (i.e., producing constantly changing services from more stable modular elements). Just like in the automotive industry, the platform approach allows to reconcile the economies of standardization with the flexibility of parameterization and recomposing. The architecture of a modern digital platform is designed to make the most of available technologies to offer scalability, robustness, and performance (low latency). It also allows for the adaptation to external technological requirements of simplicity and modernity of protocols and exchanges.

Summary

1. One of the first steps of a digital strategy is to understand the ecosystems to which one belongs and the existing platforms on which the company must rely (8.1.1).
2. The network effect is a non-linear amplification of the value produced by the platform that increases faster than the size of its communities (8.1.2).
3. A successful platform strategy starts with building a satisfied community, which leads to cultivating user feedback loops (8.1.3).

4. Platform thinking is a demanding approach, but one that ensures greater flexibility, adaptation to external ecosystems, and ultimately greater value creation (8.2.1).
5. Platform developers have two obsessions: to grow so that network effects multiply their value and to do so faster than their competitors because of the "*winner takes all*" effect (8.2.1).
6. Intelligent filtering is one of the core competencies of platforms; as a result, the development of AI fuels the growth of platforms (8.2.2).
7. It is not possible to have a successful digital platform project without assembling the right team, which has both the technical competence and the experience of engaging with the user community (8.3.1).
8. To be successful with your platform, it is essential to strive for simplicity, be focused on customer satisfaction, and know how to use the right software tools (8.3.2).
9. The platform approach requires excellence in DevOps practice, a very strong command of integration, and continuous deployment (8.3.3).

Conclusion

1. The Necessary Success of Digital Transformation

In the introduction, I tried to explain this book's ambition by outlining three questions readers may have about their digital transformation. My goal was to provide a set of keys to deciphering the challenges of execution. I'll begin this conclusion by asking the dual question: why did I think it worthwhile to write this book from the author's perspective and not the reader's? I believe that the success of digital transformation is vital for the competitiveness of companies, as expressed in many books from the bibliography, starting with *Designed for Digital*. This success is not a strategic option; in the long run, it is a necessity. I am convinced, on a more personal level, that the successful digital transformation of large companies, especially French ones, is a major challenge for our countries and our society. I will illustrate this somewhat grandiloquent statement with three points.

The success of this transformation is a competitive challenge for any large company, but French companies suffer from cultural disadvantages. We have already encountered them implicitly in the course of this book, but I will highlight four of them more explicitly here:

- French culture and its managerial education system put too much weight on conceptualization. We are, to use the metaphor borrowed from François Julien in Chapter 2, particularly "Greek" and very little "Chinese." Consequently, our mental model is particularly favorable to the Taylorist vision that separates thinking from doing. I started my management career in a world that classified responsibilities in a four-box matrix: design vs. execution, business vs. technical.

DOI: 10.4324/9781003272816-12

The transformation described in this book opposes these separations. Thinking and doing become inseparable.

- Our French culture of power and the role of the leader, which resembles that of other countries with high *power distance index*, puts a heavy symbolic significance on the role of chief/manager;[1] thus, it does not encourage the empowerment of teams. Networked organizational models, such as those advocated in ExOs, are not easy for countries such as France.
- A consequence of the first point is that we need to understand before we act, which the COVID-19 crisis demonstrated, because this is what we are taught at school or in our families since we are very young. The world of digital transformation, which is a world of emergence, requires, on the contrary, acting to understand. We find here, of course, the concepts of effectuation, as opposed to the rational need for a well-conceptualized plan. Wanting to have a good understanding before acting is a handicap on a constantly changing playing field, where first-mover advantages are consolidated by network effects and the capitalization of knowledge acquired through experimentation.
- The French management culture has not yet integrated the specificity of software development and its ecosystems. More often than not, the software domain inspires French managers with frustration (because the successes of software companies emerge from nowhere, while internal difficulties seem both inevitable and inexplicable[2]) and a lack of interest in a "technical thing" that is seen as a graceless mechanic. Leading digital companies have, dramatically, a much greater interest in and respect for the software domain and associated skills.[3]

My second observation, shared by many authors, is that the organizational transformation described in this book is necessary to

---

[1] One must read Philippe d'Iribiane's book, *La logique de l'honneur*, to understand the specificities of the French management model compared to, for example, the more contractual North American model. There is a clear parallel with Gert Hofstede and his PDI (*power distance index*) model, which also shows the particular role of the leader in the culture of French companies; see, for example, *Cultures and Organizations, Software of the Mind.*

[2] The idea that IT projects are too expensive, always late, and deliver unreliable results is frequently expressed. I refer you to my book *Information Technology for the Chief Executive* for an in-depth analysis, the two important points are that this common state of IT projects (proven) is neither surprising nor inevitable. The challenge of a *software-friendly* management culture is to understand why (complexity and technical debt being the key words, once again).

[3] This is beautifully illustrated in Ram Charan's new book, *Rethinking Competitive Advantage: New Rules for the Digital Age.*

increase or restore employee satisfaction, motivation, and engagement.[4] Like the world of customers, the world of employees has become highly digital. The company's employees thus expect to benefit from this transformation both inside and outside the company.[5] At a deeper level, the organizational modes—and new ways of working—described in this book, and in particular in Chapter 2, are essential to obtain employee engagement. I refer you to Yves Morieux's analysis: in a complex environment, if this complexity is installed in the company's processes without changing the modes of governance and work methods, disengagement is bound to occur. Digital transformation must "start from the ground up," in particular from employees in contact with customers. The emphasis in this book on execution capabilities and excellence in execution also contributes to employee satisfaction. Keeping employees engaged requires that the ambition of the digital strategy is within the reach of the company and perceived as such. The effort to develop digital skills and know-how is doubly essential; it must be highlighted and evaluated regularly—first, because it enables the success of the digital transformation from a business point of view, but also because it creates the conditions for buy-in from a human point of view.

More generally, successful digital transformation and the development of associated software capabilities are essential to enable companies to participate in the creation of tomorrow's world. The world we live in is rapidly changing before our eyes through the deployment of digital technologies. Every company, every country, and every citizen have a legitimate ambition to participate in this transformation, to help shape it according to their values and interests. The future of exponential technologies is not written; it belongs to us. To participate in the creation of tomorrow's world, in particular to develop new uses for AI and ML, we must be able to act and have the skills that make our actions relevant and meaningful. To take up one of the arguments of the French Academy of Technologies report, theoretical skills on algorithms are useless if the company does not have the necessary software know-how presented

[4] I will be brief here because this thesis is mainly the subject of my previous book, *Process and Enterprise 2.0*. The previously quoted book of Ram Charan is also a good place to dive deeper into customer satisfaction and digital employees' expectations.

[5] As James Heskett notes in his book *The Value Profit Chain: Treat Employee Like Customers and Customers Like Employees*, there is a symmetry of attention to be provided: what was said in Chapter 1 about customer expectations in the digital world also applies to the company's employees.

in this book.[6] For example, Europe in general and France in particular dream of imposing their ethical vision of the development of exponential technologies, while the digital services and products used by all are manufactured (in their vast majority) elsewhere. There is little interest in developing an ethical vision of AI if one is not able to participate in the Darwinian adventure of implementation.[7]

2. The Main Things to Remember

The time to close this book is approaching. I congratulate the reader for having made it this far because the ambition to obtain a systemic vision of digital transformation execution has produced a necessarily dense book, which is more a working guide than an essay. If we take a step back, this book describes three transformations:

- The company must become truly *customer-centric*, from observation to listening to co-development. The revolution of the 21st-century digital era is that customer orientation is much more necessary—the arguments were recalled in Chapter 1: era of abundance of supply, pace of change in usage, complexity of experiences, power of communities, and so on—and much easier, using digital tools and communities.
- It also needs to become an excellent software company, from creation to assembly (integration of its own elements but especially those of others) and *delivery*. Excellence is the combination of agility, speed (reducing the *lead time* from customer to product), and quality, both in terms of quality of experience and quality of service.
- The company must adapt its organization to become a network of autonomous teams. This network is organized around a single, common goal, but each team is empowered to act according to its local context

[6] It is interesting to compare the rich Cédric Villani report on AI with the book *AI Superpowers*, by Kai-Fu Lee, mentioned in Chapter 5. Despite its length, the report hardly speaks from the point of view of companies, at most a sectoral analysis is proposed at the end of the two hundred pages. There is no reference to the software dimension either, the Villani report focusing on algorithms and uses. In contrast to this very "Greek" report, Kai-Fu Lee's book insists on *software engineering* skills and on the importance of entrepreneurial motivation to explore value creation opportunities, as opposed to a planning approach.

[7] This was expressed by Antoine Petit, president of the CNRS, during the *AI for Humanity* summit: "*We must be careful that France does not become a specialist in artificial intelligence ethics when the United States and China are doing business.*"

quickly and by constantly learning from the environment. The structure of the network reduces the time it takes for information to spread, and its orientation from the outside increases the ability to listen and adapt.

This book does not pretend to be a digital transformation manual. The subject is too vast because the digital transformation of each company is intimately linked to the nature of its business, and I do not have the competence to do so. The bibliography is a good place to start to explore this topic. This book, as was said in the introduction, focuses on three dimensions of digital transformation, highlighted in *Designed for Digital*, which correspond to the implementation of three capabilities. The first, which is the subject of the first transformation mentioned above, corresponds to the *building block* of the **lean startup**. In my opinion, this is **the first element that every company must master in order to successfully complete its digital transformation**. The presentation of Chapter 3 is oriented by my own experience in large companies, but it is a synthesis of the main reference books in the field.

The next two elements are respectively **the exponential IS model** and the **software factory model for building platforms**. The first element responds to the *operational backbone* capability described in the introduction, the second element to this capability to build digital platforms. These two elements are jointly indispensable for the successful software transformation described above. The concept of exponential IS, developed in the second part, is a contribution specific to this book, which reflects my experience as a CIO over the last twenty years. On the other hand, the *lean software factory* approach in the third part is a synthesis of reference models, from CICD to DevOps and *lean software development.* Some people will criticize me for the overly technical developments on these software capabilities, for a book that is intended for general managers, but this is precisely a way to contribute to the development of *software-friendly* management culture.

The last *building block* of this book is the organization model of the company and the working methods, inspired by the ExO[8] approach. As explained throughout the book, this is the necessary condition for developing the three capabilities. The interest of the book, and what makes

[8] I used Salim Ismail's book as a reference on this topic, but the vision proposed in Chapter 2, Enterprise 3.0, is a synthetic vision that brings together multiple convergent works, from *The Future of Work*, by Gary Hamel, to *Reinventing Organization*, by Frédéric Laloux.

it original, is the global analysis, drawn from my own experience in the field of the interdependence between these four elements. This is also expressed in the double arrow that gives the book its subtitle: from customer to code, from code to customer.[9]

3. The Necessary Change in Our Companies' Culture

To conclude, I will highlight the necessary transformation of the corporate culture that accompanies digital transformation by restating some of the salient points that were developed in the previous chapters. Let's start by recalling why this culture change is necessary:

- Organizing in networks of autonomous teams requires a different vision of the role of management and corporate strategy (see Chapter 2). Transforming the systems is not enough; we must transform the mental models—the attitudes and behaviors that make the organization work.
- The "*outside to inside*" dimension, which we have discussed throughout the book, is based on the corporate culture, whether it is a question of listening to customers or to the technological and software ecosystems.
- Digital transformation can only be achieved through the talents of employees. The war for talent, whether it is recruitment, development, or retention, is first and foremost a cultural issue. In a world where competence is applied and developed from experience, the main recruitment tool is the co-option of talent (as opposed to diploma hunting and delegation to external hunting firms).

To simply summarize the main features of this culture change, I propose the following four points:

- The first cultural change is the transition from the Greek model to the Chinese model. **You have to let go to accept uncertainty without predictions**. I have used the mental model of effectuation extensively, as it seems to me to be both well adapted to the VUCA environment in general and to the requirements of the digital world in particular.

[9] We find this idea of interdependence of capabilities expressed in the digital principle, which states that the right teams for the development of innovative solutions combine three skills: digital marketing, experience design, and software development.

It is a powerful tool to help transform the mental model of managers because it is concrete and action-oriented. It is also essential to banish the culture of fear from the company.[10] The role of experimentation is fundamental, as emphasized throughout the book, both to explore and to learn by doing.

- It is **necessary to take customer orientation seriously,** which translates into a continuous search for dialogues (conversations) with these customers. The company culture must be open to design (from careful observation to optimizing experiences) and constantly seek to eliminate cognitive biases by anchoring decisions in facts. The digital world favors the capture of data; the digital customer orientation is *data-driven*. Customer orientation is, therefore, multifaceted and relies on a variety of skills. The book started with the first two chapters on the need to listen and dialogue. This attitude is a change that needs to be combined with the previous one: what complicates client orientation is precisely being too sure of yourself and relying too much on forecasts. We mentioned the importance of design in Chapter 3. The consequence is that companies must hire designers, whose role in cross-functional teams is essential because their training gives them different behaviors than their colleagues. Only when these two areas of expertise (listening and design) are mastered can we exploit the characteristic of the digital world, which is to produce an abundance of digital traces of use in order to use all the power of data to serve the experiences of customers.
- **Technology appreciation, and in particular software technology, must be integrated into the company's culture.** The company that wishes to develop and retain "digital talent" must be a place that recognizes practice, excellence, and technical beauty. This is why we referred to *software craftmanship* in Chapter 7. Curiosity and constant openness to the world must be developed and encouraged for all employees. What the second part of the book has shown is that software development and the IS are complex systems. Appreciating software technology and ISs integration requires learning about this complexity. This is the main message of SRE: to provide service excellence in the digital world, one must appreciate the complexity of the distributed systems on which these services rely.

---

[10] This is a key message of the great management books, but here I am thinking in particular of Jim Collins's *From Good to Great*.

- **The company's culture must be oriented toward continuous individual and collective learning.** This learning is based on the freedom given to all to experiment, without fear of failure, but with a concern for capitalization. Here we find the first point: the only attitude that allows us to be serene in the face of uncertainty is that of continuous learning—which is precisely an antifragile posture. This ambition of permanent and continuous learning must become a value, a behavioral practice (a habit), and a corporate strategy. Continuous learning is necessary to enable homeostasis: adaptation to a constantly changing digital environment. This learning is also necessary for each of the company's employees to provide them with antifragile stability in an uncertain environment.

Bibliography

Algan Y., Cahuc P., Zylbeberg A., *La fabrique de la défiance.* Albin Michel, 2012.
Amabile T., Kramer S., *The Progress Principle: Using Small Wins to Ignite Joy, Engagement, and Creativity at Work.* Harvard Business Review Press, 2011.
Ambler S. W., Lines M., *An Executive's Guide to Disciplined Agile: Winning the Race to Business Agility.* CreateSpace Independent Publishing Platform, 2017.
Appelo J., *Management 3.0: Leading Agile Developers, Developing Agile Leaders.* Addison-Wesley Professional, 2011.
Ballé M. & F., *The Lean Manager.* Lean Enterprise Institute, 2009.
Barabási A.-L., *Linked: The New Science of Networks.* Perseus Books, 2002.
Blank S., *The Four Steps to the Epiphany.* K&S Ranch, 2013.
Bossidy L., Charan R. *Execution: The Discipline of Getting Things Done.* Crown Business, 2002.
Caseau Y., *Urbanisation, SOA et BPM,* 3rd edition. Dunod, 2006.
Caseau Y., *Information Technology for the Chief Executive: Value Analysis, Organization and Management.* Author House, 2008.
Caseau Y., *Processus et Entreprise 2.0: Innover par la Collaboration et le Lean Management.* Dunod, 2011.
Charan R., *Rethinking Competitive Advantage: New Rules for the Digital Age.* Currency, 2021
Christensen C. M., Anthony S. D., Roth E. A., *Seeing What's Next: Using the Theories of Innovation to Predict Industry Change.* Harvard Business School Press, 2004.
Christensen C., Dillon K., Hall T., Duncan D., *Competing Against Luck: The Story of Innovation and Customer Choice.* Harper Business, 2016.
Colin N., Verdier H., *The Age of the Multitude: Entrepreneurship and Governance after the Digital Revolution.* Dunod, 2015.
Collins J., *From Good to Great.* Collins, 2001.
Cusumano M., Gawer A, Yoffie D., *The Business of Platforms: Strategy in the Age of Digital Competition, Innovation, and Power.* Harper Business, 2019.
Daisley B., *The Joy of Work: 30 Ways to Fix Your Work Culture and Fall in Love with Your Job Again.* Random House Business Books, 2018.

Daugherty P, Wilson H. J., *Human + Machine: Reimagining Work in the Age of AI.* Harvard Business Review Press, 2018.

Davenport T., Beck J., *The Attention Economy: Understanding the New Currency of Business.* Harvard Business School Press, 2001.

Deutschman A., *Change or Die: The Three Keys to Change at Work and in Life.* Harper Business, 2007.

D'Iribarne P., *The Logic of Honor—Corporate Management and National Traditions.* Welcome Rain Publishers, 2003.

Domingos P. *The Master Algorithm: How the Quest for the Ultimate Learning Machine Will Remake Our World.* Seuil, 1993.

Dupuy F., *Sociologie du changement.* Dunod, 2004.

Dupuy F., *La Fatigue des élites.* Seuil, 2005.

Ellis S., Brown M., *Hacking Growth: How Today's Fastest-Growing Companies Drive Breakout Success.* Dunod, 2011.

Ford M., *Architects of Intelligence: The Truth about AI from the People Building it.* Packt Publishing, 2018.

Forsgreen N., Humble J., Kim G., *Accelerate: Building and Scaling High Performing Technology Organizations.* IT Revolution Press, 2018.

Fournier-Morel X., Grojean P., Plouin G., Rognon C., *SOA—Le guide de l'architecte d'un SI agile.* Dunod, 2011.

Fowler M., *Refactoring: Improving the Design of Existing Code.* Addison-Wesley Professionals, 2018.

Friedman T., *The World Is Flat.* Farrar, Straus and Giroux, 2006.

Furr N., Dyer J., *The Innovator's Method: Bringing the Lean Start-up into Your Organization.* Harvard Business Review Press, 2014.

Gothelf J., Seiden J., *Lean UX—Applying Lean Principles to improve User Experience.* O'Reilly, 2011.

Hamel G., *The Future of Management.* Harvard Business School Press, 2007.

Hamel G., *What Matters Now: How to Win in a World of Relentless Change, Ferocious Competition, and Unstoppable Innovation.* Jossey-Bass, 2012.

Harry M., Schroeder R., *Six Sigma: The Breakthrough Management Strategy Revolutionizing the World's Top Corporations.* Currency, 2000.

Hering M., *DevOps for the Modern Enterprise: Winning Practices to Transform Legacy IT Organizations.* IT Revolution Press, 2018.

Heskett J., Earl Sasser W. Jr, Schlessinger L., The *Value Profit Chain.* The Free Press, 2003.

Hibbs C., Jewett S., Sullivan M., *The Art of Lean Software Development.* O'Reilly, 2009.

Hoftede G., Hoftede G. J., Minkov M., *Cultures and Organizations, Software of the Mind.* McGraw-Hill Education, 2010.

Humble J., Farley D., *Continuous Delivery: Reliable Software Releases through Build, Test, and Deployment Automation.* Addison-Wesley Professional, 2011.

Humble J., Molesky J., O'Reilly B., *Lean Enterprise: How High-Performance Organizations Innovate at Scale.* O'Reilly, Lean series, 2015.

Ismail S., *Exponential Organizations: Why New Organizations Are Ten Times Better, Faster, and Cheaper Than Yours (and what to do about it)*. Diversion Books, 2014.

Julien F., *A Treatise on Efficacy: Between Western and Chinese Thinking*. University of Hawaii Press, 2004.

Kahneman D., *Thinking, Fast and Slow*. Farrar, Straus and Giroux, 2013.

Kawasaki G., *The Art of the Start 2.0: The Time-Tested, Battle-Hardened Guide for Anyone Starting Anything*. Portfolio, 2015.

Kelly K., *Out of Control: The New Biology of Machines, Social Systems and the Economic World*. Perseus Books, 1995.

Knaster R., Leffingwell D., *SAFe 4.5 Distilled: Applying the Scaled Agile Framework for Lean Enterprises*. Addison-Wesley Professional, 2018.

Kniberg H., *Lean from the Trenches: Managing Large-Scale Projects with Kanban*. Pragmatic Bookshelf, 2011.

Kotter J., *Leading Change*. Harvard Business Review Press, 2012.

Laloux F., *Reinventing Organizations: A Guide to Creating Organizations Inspired by the Next Stage in Human Consciousness*. Nelson Parker, 2014.

Larman C., *Large-Scale Scrum: More with Less*. Addison-Wesley, 2016.

Lee Kai-Fu, *AI Super-Powers: China, Silicon Valley and the New World Order*. Houghton Mifflin Harcourt, 2018.

Levine R., Locke C., Searls D., Weinberger D., *The Cluetrain Manifesto*, 10th anniversary edition, Basic Books, 2009.

Liker J. K., *The Toyota Way*. Mc Graw Hill, 2004.

Marcus G., Davis E., *Rebooting AI: Building Artificial Intelligence We Can Trust*. Pantheon, 2019.

Martin R. C., *Clean Architecture: A Craftsman's Guide to Software Structure and Design*. Prentice Hall, 2017.

Maurya A., *Running Lean: Iterate from Plan A to a Plan That Works*. O'Reilly Media, 2012.

McAfee A., Brynjolfsson E., *Machine, Platform, Crowd: Harnessing Our Digital Future*. Norton & Company, 2018.

McChrystal S., *Teams of Teams, New Rules of Engagement for a Complex World*. Portfolio, 2015.

Meadows D. *Thinking in Systems: A Primer*. Chelsea Green Publishing, 2008.

Morris L., *Managing the Evolving Corporation*. Van Nostrand Reinhold, 1995.

Murphy N. R., Beyer B., et al, *Site Reliability Engineering: How Google Runs Production Systems*. O'Reilly Media, 2016.

O'Neil C., *Weapons of Math Destruction: How Big Data Increases Inequality and Threatens Democracy*. Broadway Books, 2017.

Owens T., Fernandez O., *The Lean Enterprise: How Corporations Can Innovate Like Startups*. Wiley, 2014.

Parker G., Van Alstyne M., Choudary S., *Platform Revolution: How Networked Markets Are Transforming the Economy and How to Make them Work for You*. Norton and Company, 2017.

Peppers D., Rogers M., *Extreme Trust: Turning Proactive Honesty and Flawless Execution into Long-Term Profits*. Portfolio, 2016.

Pink D., *Drive: The Surprising Truth About What Motivates Us*. Riverhead Books, 2009.

Poppiendick M. & T., *Implementing Lean Software Development: From Concept to Cash*. Addison Wesley, 2007.

Prahalad C. K., Ramaswamy V., *The Future of Competition: Co-Creating Unique Value with Customers*. Harvard Business School Press, 2004.

Ptak C., Smith C., *Demand Driven Material Requirements Planning*. Industrial Press, 2016.

Reinertsen D., *The Principles of Product Development Flow: Second Generation Lean Product Development*. Celeritas Publishing, 2009.

Ries E., *The Lean Startup: How Today's Entrepreneur Use Continuous Innovation to Create Radically Successful Businesses*. Currency, 2011.

Rogers D. L., *The Digital Transformation Playbook: Rethink Your Business for the Digital Age*. Columbia Business School Publishing, 2016.

Ross J. W., Beath C. M., Mocker M., *Designed for Digital: How to Architect Your Business for Sustained Success*. The MIT Press, 2019.

Rossman J. R., Duerden M., *Designing Experiences*. Columbia Business School Publishing, 2019.

Schaeffer E., Sovie D., *Reinventing the Product: How to Transform Your Business and Create Value in the Digital Age*. Kogan Page, 2019.

Schmidt E., Rosenberg J., *How Google Works*. Grand Central Publishing, 2017.

Schmidt K., *High Availability and Disaster Recovery: Concepts, Design, Implementation*. Springer, 2006.

Schulte W. R., Chandy K. M., *Event Processing: Designing IT Systems for Agile Companies*. McGraw-Hill, 2009.

Schwartz B., *The Paradox of Choice: Why More is Less*. Harper Collins, 2005.

Searls D., *The Intention Economy: When Customers Take Charge*. Harvard Business Review Press, 2012.

Senge P., *The Fifth Discipline*. Currency Doubleday, 1995.

Servan-Schreiber E., *Super Collective—The New Power of Our Intelligences*. Fayard, 2018.

Sheridan R., *Joy, Inc.: How We Built a Workplace People Love*. Portfolio, 2015.

Shirky C., *Here Comes Everybody: The Power of Organizing Without Organization*. The Penguin Press, 2008.

Silberzahn P., *Effectuation—Les principes de l'entreprenariat pour tous*. Pearson, 2014.

Silberzahn P., *Bienvenue en incertitude—Principes d'action pour un monde de surprises*. Diateino, 2021.

Silberzahn P., Rousset B., *Stratégie Modèle Mental: Cracker enfin le code des organisations pour les remettre en mouvement*. Dateino, 2019.

Simon P., *The Age of the Platform: How Amazon, Apple, Facebook, and Google Have Redefined Business*. Motion Publishing, 2011.

Sterman J., *Business Dynamics: System Thinking and Modelling for a Complex World.* Irvin McGraw Hill, 2000.

Sullivan J., Zutavern A., *The Mathematical Corporation: Where Machine Intelligence and Human Ingenuity Achieve the Impossible.* Public Affairs, 2017.

Surowiescki J., *The Wisdom of Crowds.* Anchor Books, 2004.

Sutton R., Rao H., *Scaling Up Excellence: Getting to More Without Settling for Less.* Currency, 2014.

Tainturier B., Duez E., *Decoder les developpeurs.* Eyrolles, 2017.

Taleb N., *Fooled by Randomness.* Random House, 2005.

Taleb N., *Antifragile: Things That Gain from Disorder.* Random House, 2014.

Tinelli M., *Le marketing synchronisé: Changer radicalement pour s'adapter au consommateur de l'ère numérique.* Editions d'Organisation, 2012.

Index

A

A3 PDCA tools, 81
AARRR (acquisition, activation, retention, referral, revenue) metrics, 75–77
A/B testing, 76, 87, 134, 167
Acatech, 22–23, 25–26
Accelerate: The Science of Lean Software and DevOps; Building and Scaling High-Performing Technology Organizations (Forsgreen, Humble, and Kim), 172
accelerating change, 30–31
acceptance tests, 168–169
advanced visualization methods, 25–26, 128
affordable loss, 50–51, 59, 64
agile at scale frameworks, 141, 143, 151
agile, lean and
  approach, 143–145
  software development, 138–139
  systemic conditions of, 142–143
Agile Manifesto, 138–140, 174, 178
aha moments, 77, 79
AI, *see* artificial intelligence (AI)
anticipation and agility
  cultivating innovation, 37–38
  customer orientation as compass, 38–39
  short time and long time, 36–37
  situational potential and anticipation, 34–36
antifragile/antifragility, 43
  concept, 51
  information system, 89–91
  operations, 108–109
  systems, 44–45
APIs, *see* application programming interfaces (APIs)
application programming interfaces (APIs), 88–89, 92–93, 133–134, 144, 149–150, 171, 201–202
  exposure strategy, 130
  integration by, 200
  microservices and internal, 93
architects/architecture
  continuous learning of systems engineering, 149–151
  and gardening, 147–149
  multimodal, 148–149
  platforms, 199–201
  role of architect in agile team, 145–147
artificial intelligence (AI), 7, 61
  application of, 121
  experimentation by cross-functional teams, 126–127
  learning loop, 120
  toolbox to, 112
Art of War, The (Tzu), 35–36
asset perspective, 153–154
auto-encoder, 119
automation, 97–98, 153, 164, 166, 170
  deployment tests, 168–169
  and monitoring, 105–107
  of production, 21–22
autonomic computing, 107, 109, 153
autonomous teams, networks of, 41–43
autonomy, 20, 41, 50
AXA's Digital Agency, 67, 80, 168–169

B

B2B (business-to-business) market, 13, 30
B2C (business-to-consumer) 30
BetaCodex group, 42
bimodal approach, 91–92
Black Swan, The (Taleb), 46
blue-green deployment, 167
budget, 156–157
build and deploy process, 165
business models, 50–51, 187–189
  canvas, 60–61
  of platform, 191
Business of Platforms, The: Strategy in the Age of Digital Competition, Innovation, and Power, 192, 194, 196

C

CAP theorem, 132–133
CCI, *see* customer-centricity index (CCI)
CFLL, *see* customer feedback learning loop (CFLL)
change management, 107
  for digital transformation, 47–48
  motivation and commitment, 49–51
  resistance to change, 48–49
Change or Die: The Three Keys to Change at Work and in Life (Deutschman), 48
chaos engineering, 109
chatbots, 122–123
China/Chinese
  military strategy, 36
  strategic vision, 34–35
Cialdini's six principles, 75
CICD, *see* continuous integration and deployment/delivery (CICD)
cloud computing, 171
co-creation
  with customers, 51
  principle of, 10
code, 95
  quality, 102
  reviews, 155
  sharing, 181
  standards, 182
community
  of ambassadors, 32–33
  of developers, 191–192
  growth of, 196
  platforms and, 191–192, 197
complex event processing, 98
complexity, 23–24, 153
complex systems, 99, 137, 140, 144, 193, 211
  holomorphism principle of, 43–44
  theory of, 34, 43
computer-aided design (CAD), 15
configuration management database (CMDB), 163
containers, 171–172
content strategy, 5–6
continuous delivery, 166
continuous deployment, 165–167
continuous improvement, 52, 61, 105, 107, 123, 142, 168
  kaizen, 140
  reflective practice for, 140
continuous integration, 163–165, 177–178
continuous integration and deployment/delivery (CICD), 165
continuous learning, 45–47, 108, 149–151
continuous product discovery, 16–17, 162
corporate culture, 3, 46, 145, 210
craftmanship
  software, 180–183, 211
CRM, *see* customer relationship management (CRM)
culture change
  for digital transformation, 47–48
  motivation and commitment, 49–51
  resistance to change, 48–49
customer
  experience, 8–10, 201
  feedback, 33
  journeys, 6, 74
customer-centricity index (CCI), 39, 144
customer feedback learning loop (CFLL), 80–81
customer relationship management (CRM), 5, 114
cyber-attacks, 27
cybersecurity, 27, 90–91, 134

D

data
  architecture, 128–130
  engineering process, 121–122
  lab principle, 128
  lake, 131
  modeling, 129
  science, 122, 127
data infrastructure, 130–133
data management platforms (DMPs), 7, 129
deep learning, 11–12, 113, 115–116, 118–119, 122–123
  algorithms, 125, 129
  revolution, 114–116
DeepMind, 117–118
demand management, 22, 119–120
design, 63–64, 68–69
  patterns, 148
  thinking, 6–7, 67–68, 70, 72–73, 183
Design for Digital: How to Architect Your Business for Sustained Success, xix
development, 138, 169
DevOps, 73, 161, *see also* software process
  infrastructure as code, 171–172
  results of early adopters, 172–174
DevSecOps, 170
digital continuity, 15, 130
digital homeostasis, 29
digital innovation, 58
digital manufacturing, 114–115
  maturity model for, 22–23
digital marketing, growth hacking and, 80
digital platforms, 93, 190, 203
digital products, 14–16, 183
digital strategy, 85
digital transformation, 48, 85, 162, 181, 187, 196, *see also* antifragile/antifragility; information system (IS); platform
  ambitions of, 21–23, 85
  continuous product discovery, 16–17
  conversations and content strategy, 5–6
  definition of, 3
  digital products and digital production, 14–16
digital twins, 18
  optimize with, 26–27
disaster recovery plan validation, 173
disruption, 89
DMPs, *see* data management platforms (DMPs)
domain-driven design (DDD), 182
domain-specific language (DSL), 198
DSL, *see* domain-specific language (DSL)

E

economy of intention, 7
ecosystem, 11–13, 206, *see also* digital ecosystem
effectuation, 183, 206
elegant code, notion of, 180, 182
emotional design, 74–75
error budget, 105
event-driven architecture, 96
evolutionary methods, 118ExO, *see* exponential organization (ExO)
experience design, 6–7, 74
experimentation, 93
  importance of, 41, 86–87
  information system designed for, 133–134
exponential information systems
  antifragile information system, 89–91
  continuous flow of technologies, 88–89
  IT for exponential organization, 86–87
exponential organization (ExO), 40–41, 87
Exponential Organizations, 40, 52, 120
exponential technologies
  deep learning revolution, 114–116
  hybridization and meta-heuristics, 116–119

F

Facebook, 14, 36, 191–192
federation, 150
feedbacks, 10–11, 69, 72, 138–139, 143
flexibility, 21, 26, 65, 103, 142, 188, 199–200
Francois Jullien, 34
France/French
  Academy of Technologies, 111
  culture of power, 205–206
  management culture, 206
frequency of delivery, 143–144

G

gardening
  architecture and, 147–149
Gartner curve, 19
Google, 14, 36
governance, 137–145, 154–155
GPUs, 115, 134
Greek model of thinking, 58
"grown, not designed" principle, 90
growth hacking, 63–64, 67–68, 75–77, 79
  AARRR metrics and data-driven steering, 75–77
  and digital marketing, 80
growth models, 76–77

H

homeostasis, *see also* anticipation and agility; culture change; digital homeostasis
  principle of, 88
  scalable organizations adapted to continuous change, 41–47
hook model, 80
hybridization, 116–119

I

IBM, 57–58, 107, 117, 193
IDEAS (interface, dashboards, experimentation, autonomy, social technologies), 41, 87
information system (IS)
  data architecture, 128–130
  data infrastructure, 130–133
  exponential, 87–88, 97, 131–134
  management of, 102
  reactive systems, 96–97
infrastructure as code (IaC), 169, 171–172
innovation
  accounting, 62, 77
  platforms, 192–193, 198
  thesis, 60
integration
  as code, 95
  patterns, 146
  technologies, 88–89
Internet, 3, 11
Internet of things (IoT), 3, 19, 25
intrinsic motivation, 49–50
IS, *see* information system (IS)
IT
  for exponential organization, 86–87
  management, 101
  systems governance, 144

K

kaizen, 61, 140, 142, 175–176, 179
kanban, 174–176, 178, 180
knowledge engineering, 17–19
Kubernetes platform, 171–172

L

large-scale Scrum (LeSS), 141
latency, 13–14, 132, 151, 203
"layered" architecture, 197
lean and agile
  approach, 143–145, 173
  software development, 138–139
  systemic conditions of, 142–143
lean canvas, 60–61
lean manufacturing, 61, 165, 182
lean software, 139, 175–176
  approach, 178–179
  development, 139, 174, 179
  practice, 146–147
lean software factory, 174–175, 180
  from customer to code and from code to customer, 183–185
  software craftmanship, 180–183
lean startup, 55, 137, 199, *see also* growth hacking; innovation; knowledge creation process
  design thinking, 69–71
  implementation of, 55
  Minimum Viable Product (MVO), 72–73
Lean Startup, The (Ries), 17
learning, 183

algorithms, 127
loops, 80, 120
licensing costs, 155–156
LinkedIn, 64

M

machine learning (ML), 7, 111, *see also* artificial intelligence (AI); exponential technologies; information system (IS)
machine vision revolution, 128
maintenance costs, 156
marketing, platform, 191
marketplace model, 183
massively transformative purpose (MTP), 40
Matthew effect, 190
mental models, 50
metadata, 121, 198
meta-heuristics, 116–119
microservices, 202–203
Microsoft, 201
minimum viable product (MVP), 63–64, 66–67, 73, 76, 199
ML, *see* machine learning (ML)
mobile application development ecosystems, 190
monitoring and automation 105–107Moore's law, 11, 31, 115, 153
motivation, 49–51
multimodal architecture, 91–94, 150
MVP, *see* minimum viable product (MVP)
mean time between failures (MTBF), 107
mean time to repair (MTTR), 107

N

natural language processing (NLP)
Netflix, 36
network effect, 195
networks
of autonomous teams, 41–43
neural, 113, 118
organization, 42
NLP, *see* natural language processing (NLP)
non-regression tests, 100

O

onboarding process, 76
opensource, 101, 162, 182, 192
operations, 170
organizational theories, 41–42

P

pain points, 70–71
peer programming, 181–182
performance, 203
and resilience, 173–174
tests, 168
"phased" deployment, 167
pipeline, 165–166
plan-do-check-act (PDCA), 63
plan-do-measure-learn cycle, 75
platform, 171, 202
and artificial intelligence, 196
business model of, 191
and communities, 191–192
concept of, 151, 187–189
network effect of, 189–191
PMF, *see* product market fit (PMF)
pretotyping, 63–64
product, 11–13
anthropologist, 69
approach, 153
culture, 175
development, 16–17, 119
owner, 143–144
platform, 188, 197–201
product life-cycle management (PLM), 15
product market fit (PMF), 64, 77–78

Q

quality, 162–163
assessment of, 121–122
automation and monitoring, 105–107
and efficiency, 162–163
of service, 14, 104–109
site reliability engineering, 104–105
SRE practices, 107–109

R

reactive systems, 96–97
refactoring, 99, 103–104, 147–149, 155
reinforcement learning, 117–118
resilience and quality of service, 97, 104
resiliency, 104
resistance to change, 48–49
return on investment (ROI), 190
revenue metrics, 76
rework, 138–139
roadmap, notion of, 37
robot process automation (RPA), 168
root cause analysis (RCA), 109

S

scalability, 188, 201, 203
SCALE approach, 41, 87
scaled agile framework (SAFe), 141
Scrum, 138, 140
security
  by design, 170
  developers and, 170
  field of, 168
self-organized communities, 32–33
self-provisioning, 171
service level agreement (SLA), 105, 151
service-oriented architecture (SOA), 149
shift left, 171
simplicity, 164–165, 200–201, 203
site reliability engineering (SRE), 104–105
  approach, 105
  practices, 107–109
situational awareness, 39
situational potential, 150
skills, 143
  and resources, 87
  time of development of, 37
smart home, 125
smartphone, 20–21, 30–31
smart supply chain, 119–120
smoke tests, 57
social networking platforms, 196
software
  age, 154
  automation, 23
  build/delivery process, 172
  craftmanship, 180–183, 211
  culture, 52
  ecosystems, 144–145
  factory, 161, 165
  product development process, 162, 165
software assets, 152, 156
  life cycle, 151–152
  management tools, 101
software process
  automating tests, 167–169
  continuous deployment, 165–167
  continuous integration, 163–165
  deployment pipeline, 165
  quality and efficiency, 162–163
Spotify, 33, 36
sprints, 138, 155
spurious correlations, 127
squad, 183
SRE, *see* site reliability engineering (SRE)
standup meetings, 138
storytelling, 74
strategy, 4–5, 33, 47
  deployment, form of, 173
  referent of, 48
supply chain, 119–120
sustainable development, 151–152, 157
sustainable information systems, 151
  age of systems through flows, 155–157
  development of information system, 151–153
  managing complexity in sustainable way, 153–155
synchronicity/synchronization, 7–8, 132, 177
system of systems (SoS), 15
systems
  co-development of, 123
  engineering, continuous learning of, 149–151
  models, 187–188
  thinking, 140–141
system-to-system interfaces, 87

T

Taylorization, 57, 183
teams work, 138

technical debt, 102–103, 146
management, 99
technical stacks, 88
technological innovations, continuous flow of, 88
Tesla, 16
test-driven development (TDD) approach, 168
test improvement strategy, 168–169
time to market (TTM), 36, 139
top-down control, 143
Toyota, 164
training sets, 113
transaction platforms, 192, 194–196
trust, role of, 194
T-shaped profiles, 170
two-sided transaction platform, 191

U

Uber platform, 190
unique value proposition (UVP), 65–66, 68, 70–71, 73, 78
unit tests, 167, 168
use cases, 148
user
community, 79
experience design, 73–75
satisfaction, 188, 201
stories, 70–72, 139, 145
user acceptance tests (UATs), 165, 167–168

V

value
creation, 14, 59, 128
proposition for developers, 192
stream mapping, 61
V-cycle/waterfall process, 163
version management system, 151, 164
virality, 182
visualization, 25, 128
visual management, 26, 174, 177–179
voice of the customer (VOC), 140
VUCA environment, 35, 45

W

war games, 47
waste, elimination of, 175
web giants, development of, 97
work in process (WIP), 17, 142

Printed in the United States
by Baker & Taylor Publisher Services